The

WOULD-BE
COMMONER

The

WOULD-BE
COMMONER

*A Tale of Deception, Murder, and
Justice in Seventeenth-Century France*

JEFFREY S. RAVEL

HOUGHTON MIFFLIN COMPANY
BOSTON · NEW YORK
2008

For information about permission to reproduce selections from
this book, write to Permissions, Houghton Mifflin Company,
215 Park Avenue South, New York, New York 10003.

www.houghtonmifflinbooks.com

Library of Congress Cataloging-in-Publication Data

Ravel, Jeffrey S.

The would-be commoner : a tale of deception, murder, and
justice in seventeenth-century France / Jeffrey S. Ravel.

p. cm.

Includes bibliographical references and index.

ISBN 978-0-618-19731-6

1. La Pivardière, Louis de, sieur Du Bouchet, 1661–1702
—Trials, litigation, etc. 2. Chauvelin, Marguerite
Françoise—Trials, litigation, etc. 3. Trials (Murder)—
France—Paris. 1. Title.

KJV130.C464R38 2008   345.44'36102523—dc22

2008003848

Printed in the United States of America

Book design by Victoria Hartman

Maps by Jacques Chazaud

MP 10 9 8 7 6 5 4 3 2 1

Photo credits: page 66, Museum of Fine Arts, Boston, the Elizabeth Day
McCormick Collection, 44.950, photograph © 2008 Museum of Fine Arts,
Boston; pages 68, 88, 89, 128, 136, 151, and 167, Courtesy of Bibliothèque nationale
de France; page 103, Image courtesy of Archives départementales de l'Yonne,
cote 3E 14/418; page 124, © Collections de la Comédie-Française/photo
Patrick Lorette; page 228, Courtesy of Widener Library, Harvard
College Library, 38576.12.46

To the memory of my parents:

FRANCES HELEN RAVEL

(1937–2005)

AND

IRA JULIAN RAVEL

(1933–2007)

Contents

Illustrations and Maps

Illustrations

Maps

Acknowledgments

$\mathscr{I}$t is a pleasure to thank those who have helped along the way. I have received generous support from Philip Khoury and Deborah Fitzgerald, deans of the School of Humanities, Arts, and Social Sciences at MIT. My colleagues in the MIT history faculty, especially Peter Perdue, Harriet Ritvo, and Anne McCants, have wisely known when to ask about my progress, and when to pass over the topic in silence. The staff in the Special Collections Room of the Harvard Law Library cheerfully located and retrieved many obscure seventeenth- and eighteenth-century law tomes. In France, I am particularly grateful to Marc du Pouget, director of the Archives départementales de l'Indre in Châteauroux, to Daniel Guérin and Céline Cros of the Archives départementales de l'Yonne in Auxerre, and to Valérie Caro of the Archives départementales du Loir-et-Cher in Blois. The staffs at the Bibliothèque nationale de France and the Archives nationales have been unfailingly courteous and prompt in their responses to my requests. M. de Menou, the current owner of Narbonne, shared a welcoming fire and an apéritif with me one cool summer morning in 2001.

Professor Christian Biet of the University of Paris — X (Nanterre) has been a source of support and stimulation on both sides of the Atlantic. Closer to home, James Johnson shared his passion for masquerade and imposture over many delightful lunches in Harvard Square. Jeffrey Merrick asked probing questions about an early draft of the manuscript. Nina Gelbart, James Johnson, and Hal Ober read the penultimate version, making invaluable suggestions. Others who have offered advice and inspiration include David A. Bell, Jérôme Brillaud, Gregory Brown, Natalie Zemon Davis, Jonathan Dewald, Sarah Hanley, Julie Hardwick, Lynn Hunt, Margaret Jacob, Colin Jones, Antoine Lilti, Mary Lindemann, Sarah Maza, Lianne McTavish, Nicholas Paige, David Richter, Jessica Riskin, Stéphane van Damme, and Charles Walton. I sorely miss conversations with Barry Russell and David Trott, both recently deceased. Portions of this book were presented at the University of Paris, the University of California, Berkeley, the Clark Library in Los Angeles, Indiana University, and at the annual meetings of the American Historical Association in 2001, the American Society for Eighteenth-Century Studies and the Northeast Society for Eighteenth-Century Studies in 2002, and the Society for French Historical Studies in 2003. Pannill Camp, Sarah Farrar, Tiffany Kanaga, and Morgan Sonderegger provided inspired research assistance.

At Houghton Mifflin, I was fortunate to attract the attention of Eric Chinski, who first saw some merit in the project. He passed me on to Amanda Cook, whose editorial acumen has made this a much better book. Gabriel and Naomi Ravel also improved things, just by being themselves. Bruce Ravel, a scientist who doesn't teach at MIT, encouraged me to tell a good story. Finally, my wife, Cristelle Baskins, never once complained when I brought up the topic of bigamy. She has lived with Louis, Marguerite, and the prior all this time; my thinking about the Pivardière affair has been immeasurably enriched by our conversations.

I dedicate *The Would-Be Commoner* to the memory of my parents, Fran and Ira Ravel, who passed away as I was finishing it.

J.S.R.
Cambridge, Massachusetts

Le monde est un théâtre ou chacun fait son personnage. Les uns jouent des rôles sérieux; les autres comiques. Ceux-ci se masquent; ceux-là soutiennent l'action à visage découvert. Ainsi tous les hommes en se considérant de près se divertissent les uns des autres.

— *La Rivale travestie, ou Les Aventures galantes arrivées au camp de Compiègne, 1699*

The world is a stage where everyone acts his part. Some play serious roles, others comic ones. Some wear masks, while others perform with their faces uncovered. Thus all men, while examining themselves, amuse each other.

— *The Female Rival Disguised, or the Gallant Adventures at the Compiègne War Camp, 1699*

Prologue

THE MYSTERY OF
LOUIS DE LA PIVARDIÈRE

⚜

$\mathcal{L}$ate in August 1698, a resident of Tournus, a small town in Burgundy, received a letter urging him to travel immediately to Paris. This man, known locally as Louis Dubouchet, had been renting a small house in town since spring, which he occupied with his teenage wife, Marie-Elisabeth Pillard, their young daughter, and Pillard's mother. Before moving to Tournus in his late thirties, Dubouchet had been a minor police officer in Auxerre, a center of the Burgundian wine trade to the north. His wife and her mother had run a local inn, but the family had fled Auxerre under mysterious circumstances a little less than a year earlier. In response to the letter, Dubouchet quickly prepared his departure. Marie wanted to travel to the capital with him, but he convinced her to remain behind, promising that he would soon return. In the company of his brother-in-law, he traveled sixty miles north to a small village just outside Auxerre. There they met a messenger from Paris who handed Louis a guarantee of safe-conduct signed by the king.

Bearing this royal pass, Dubouchet made his way the next day to Auxerre, his former residence, where he and his companions boarded a carriage for the trip to Paris. They arrived in the city on August 28 and went immediately to the house of an abbot, who was also a relative. There they dined and met with lawyers, military officers, and others who had been waiting for Dubouchet to come to Paris for much of the summer. After the meal, the visitor went to the residence of a solicitor at the Paris bar named Baudran, where he rested from his trip for the next two days while greeting many other Parisians who wanted to meet him. The abbot, the solicitor, and the dozens of other people who came to their residence to see the newcomer over these three days did not recognize their guest as Louis Dubouchet, provincial commoner. They knew him instead as a gentleman and an officer in the king's army named Louis de la Pivardière. They believed that his wife was not an innkeeper's daughter but Marguerite Chauvelin, mistress of a small estate in the center of France and member of an illustrious judicial family. And, most importantly, they expected that his arrival in the capital would exonerate her of charges that she and her alleged lover, a rural prior named Charost, had murdered him a year earlier.

Speculation in Paris about the fate of Louis de la Pivardière had been rampant since the late spring, when Marguerite and the Prior Charost had gone on trial for murder. Provincial judges had charged them with the cold-blooded murder of Marguerite's husband in mid-August 1697, while he was asleep in their country manor. The wife and the prior, however, argued that the judges had fabricated the allegations because of a long-standing vendetta against the prior's family. Marguerite and the Prior Charost insisted that Pivardière was still alive, but that he would not come to Paris to testify on behalf of his wife because he feared conviction on the capital charge of bigamy. The provincial judges who had initially brought the murder charge argued that Dubouchet was an impostor coached by Marguerite, the prior, and their families to impersonate the murdered country nobleman.

On September 1, three days after his arrival in Paris, the man at the center of the controversy voluntarily incarcerated himself at the Fort l'Evêque prison on the right bank of the Seine, just across the river from Notre Dame Cathedral and the legal buildings that housed the high court. He pledged to remain in prison, and to provide testimony in the case, until he had established his identity as Louis de la Pivardière, and had helped to exonerate Marguerite and the prior. Those who had known Louis before the alleged assassination went with their friends to see if they recognized the man imprisoned in Fort l'Evêque. Visits to the supposed nobleman and his suspect wife, who was incarcerated in a nearby prison, became a kind of recreational pastime for members of Parisian society, part of a circuit of curiosities that entertained the well-to-do residents of the capital. The *Gazette d'Hollande*, a clandestine news-sheet that published twice-weekly reports from the French capital, noted that the man's arrival had "greatly surprised those who had effectively believed he was dead, and who have a great deal of trouble disabusing themselves of the notion. This affair has become the talk of all Paris, and many imagine that it will occupy the town for quite a while."

The Pivardière affair mattered to more than the handful of people directly involved in the Berry and Burgundy in 1698 because it highlighted fundamental questions about class distinctions, marital relations, and the role of the centralizing state in France at the end of the seventeenth century. The first turning point in the case, Louis' 1695 decision to abandon his noble status and his first wife to marry a struggling commoner, seemed inexplicable in a context where nobility granted social prestige, fiscal advantages, and career opportunities from the state. If he could walk away from aristocratic privilege with hardly a second thought, what were the implications for the concept of "nobility," one of the organizing principles of pre-Revolutionary French society? The second turning point, Louis' supposed murder in late

1697 and reappearance five months later, called into question the nature of identity in an era before photo ID cards and DNA testing. Given the vagaries of identification in this period, would it be possible for the man who claimed to be Pivardière to prove his identity in a court of law? Could the king's magistrates establish the irrefutable truth of the matter, and if not, what were the consequences for the authority of the royal judiciary?

As the affair played out, ultimate authority to determine the identity of the mysterious man rested with the royal judges, in particular those who sat in the Parlement in Paris, the final court of appeal in the case. But the issues had such resonance that they were discussed beyond the courtroom — in print, in conversations throughout the capital, and in the theater. Personal judgments were made and just as rapidly overturned as Parisians followed the case; none of these popular verdicts was binding, of course, but the durability of public fascination with the affair suggested that something more than entertainment was at stake. One set of lawyers, following the claims of the provincial magistrates, argued that the man in the Paris prison was a mercenary impostor hired to absolve an adulterous couple of their foul crime. Another set of attorneys, defending Louis' first wife, Marguerite, asserted that personal vendetta had led the judges to acts of calumny. Their published pamphlets containing these competing versions of the story circulated widely among literate Parisians, who constructed their own theories of the case even before the *soi-disant* Pivardière showed up in the capital. In this larger tribunal outside the courthouse, the debate never ended, even after the judges rendered their final verdict in 1699. Such collaborative acts of storytelling were not about determining judicial truth, but about creating usable understandings of aristocratic privilege, the nature of the self, and the role of the monarchy in the lives of its subjects. In this sense, narrative closure outside the court was not only impossible, but undesirable. The Pivardière affair served as material for an ongoing conversation, one not always welcomed by the monarchy, about fundamental questions of authority and identity.

As the *Gazette* predicted, the unusual case intrigued Parisians through the summer of 1699, when the court pronounced its definitive verdict. Since then, dozens of scholars and writers have taken up the story; after World War II, the affair inspired several articles, two French novels, and a 1972 made-for-TV movie. None of these versions, though, has fully exploited the rich archival record left behind by judicial investigations. Most of them simplify the affair by treating it as an illustration of the lost, quaint world of preindustrial France, or an example of the injustices of Old Regime jurisprudence that the Revolution would rectify a century later. In reviving the story of Louis de la Pivardière, I confess that I too have been seduced by its titillating subject matter. The tale of a noble bigamist, who may have been killed by an unfaithful wife, is an irresistible mystery that features provincial corruption, a lecherous cleric, family vendettas, courtroom drama, and a curious interlude on the Paris stage. It appears at first glance to be a window into an alien, premodern world whose theological, political, and economic assumptions are quite different than our own. But it is more than just this. The life of Louis de la Pivardière, it turns out, proved largely incomprehensible to his contemporaries. The reasons why they could not ultimately understand it tell us a great deal about French culture and society at a moment when the hardships of war, famine, and disease had caused many to question the actions of Louis XIV, who had been king for half a century. A generation would go by before a popular author could fashion the raw materials of the Pivardière affair into a version that literate French men and women found compelling. By that point, the case had passed from fact into legend, and none of the readers noticed that the plot now depended on a fundamental falsification of the story, one that every subsequent retelling has uncritically repeated.

We might understand the appeal of this legal case by turning to the playhouse, another arena where seventeenth-century Parisians had the opportunity to respond to well-crafted narratives. There are many reasons why the works of Jean-Baptiste Poquelin, better known as Molière, have continuously held the stage since their debut, but one of them is surely the playwright's ability to tell stories that are not only humorous, but meaningful to a variety of readers and spectators. In the following century, Jean-Jacques Rousseau offered a famous rereading of Molière's masterpiece *The Misanthrope*, which appealed to his age's conceptions of moral virtue. Catholics and their opponents have argued over the meaning of another Molière play, *Tartuffe, or the Hypocrite*, well into the twentieth century, and religious fundamentalists of all stripes may find the play upsetting at the outset of the twenty-first. In another well-known work, his 1670 comedy-ballet *Le Bourgeois Gentilhomme*, or *The Would-Be Gentleman*, Molière played on contemporary anxieties about the definition of the aristocracy, taking up an issue that would consume Pivardière's contemporaries. Monsieur Jourdain, the title character, is a wealthy, middle-aged Parisian merchant who fervently desires to be taken for a member of the court aristocracy. When the comedy begins he has engaged a set of tutors to teach him the latest skills exhibited by his social betters. He revels in summoning his servants so that he can enjoy the spectacle of their prompt obedience; he instructs them to follow two steps behind him whenever they are in town, so passersby will know they are "his men." In the best-known comic scene in the play, a master of philosophy, after ascertaining that his enthusiastic but ignorant pupil is not yet ready for the intricacies of logic, moral philosophy, or the sciences, instructs Monsieur Jourdain in the art of pronouncing the letters of the alphabet. So as not to tax his student during their first lesson, he limits him to the five vowels. As his instruction proceeds, Monsieur Jourdain is taught that all speech which is not verse is prose:

JOURDAIN: What? When I say, "Nicole, bring me my slippers and fetch me my sleeping bonnet," that's prose?
MASTER OF PHILOSOPHY: Yes, monsieur.
JOURDAIN: By my faith! I have been speaking prose for forty years, and had no idea I was doing so! I am deeply indebted to you for having taught me this.

Monsieur Jourdain's naïveté allowed nobles and commoners alike to laugh at one of the most vexing social issues of the day: While noble status was desirable due to its social prestige and financial benefits, the definition of the aristocracy had undergone such fundamental change in the preceding centuries that by 1660 no one, from the king to his simplest subjects, was certain of the qualifications. The issue was so fiercely contested in Molière's day that the royal government established commissions to evaluate the legitimacy of every claimant to aristocratic status throughout the kingdom; these panels evaluated property titles, royal grants, and military service in an effort to establish each family's hereditary nobility. The Crown undertook this task in part to return false nobles claiming exemptions to the tax rolls, and in part to shore up the social prestige of the group. A generation later, as the Pivardière affair played out, the Crown revived the commissions and ordered them to repeat the inquests undertaken in the 1660s, for similar reasons; the repetition suggests just how difficult it had become by Pivardière's day to define what made one noble. Audience laughter at Jourdain's inability to perceive the signs of nobility reinforced the spectators' sense of superiority over the bumbling commoner. No matter how fierce the competition to represent oneself nobly, no matter how much anxiety state-supported social mobility might cause long-standing noble families, aspirants on both sides of the divide could smirk at Monsieur Jourdain, the ludicrous commoner, secure in the knowledge that they had a better grasp of the attributes of nobility.

Yet the tale of Louis de la Pivardière, who had allegedly forsaken his certified aristocratic status, reversed these expectations. Parisians who were intrigued with the case in the fall of 1698 puzzled over Louis' voluntary self-demotion from the nobility and his abdication of an officer's commission in the royal army. It was one thing to laugh at Molière's would-be gentleman when he was incarnated on the stage, as he was several times that fall, but it was quite another to comprehend the behavior of the would-be commoner now incarcerated in one of the capital's prisons.

For these reasons, the tale of Louis de la Pivardière would have sparked general interest among the king's subjects at any point in the two centuries leading up to the Revolution of 1789. But the end of the 1690s, the particular moment when the case entered the awareness of literate Parisians, was a period of intellectual uncertainty and social dislocation that made the affair more intriguing than usual. The first half of Louis XIV's personal reign, from 1661 to 1685, has often been celebrated as the apogee of the Sun King, and the absolute monarchy itself; the generation after his death in 1715 saw the beginnings of the French Enlightenment. But the thirty years between these two periods have never been sufficiently characterized by historians, in part because so many aspects of French thought, culture, and material existence were in transition. The reigning, increasingly dated formulation, put forth in 1933 by the French literary critic Paul Hazard, reflects this uncertainty. One day, Hazard pithily claimed, the French were thinking like the Abbot Bossuet, the cleric who preached at Versailles and provided Louis XIV with a theological basis for divine right monarchy. The next day, Hazard wrote, they thought like Voltaire, still willing to believe in a deity, but increasingly skeptical about clerical infallibility and scornful of religious dogma.

How did this transition occur? Hazard studied high culture and philosophy in an attempt to understand what he called the "crisis of the European consciousness" in this period. He argued that a long-standing struggle in European culture between the forces of tradition and modernity came to a head at the end of the 1600s. He pointed to two specific areas, religion and science. The Protestant and Catholic Reformations of the sixteenth century, he suggested, and the theological disputes they had unleashed, had so corroded religious faith by 1700 that thoughtful observers found it difficult to believe divine will still guided the affairs of humans; they wondered if the Christian deity was still paying attention. The revolution in astronomical thinking, which culminated in Newton's 1687 description of gravity, furthered the idea that it was unnecessary to believe in divine will to explain the workings of the universe. The most radical thinkers, only a fringe element in 1700, even speculated that the god worshipped in the three great monotheistic faiths (Judaism, Christianity, and Islam) had never existed. And if an omnipotent deity was not accountable for the current state of the universe and human society, such a divine figure might not be necessary to explain the nature of the human soul and its relation to the material body either. In the 1630s, Descartes had claimed to prove his own independent existence by demonstrating his ability to think — *cogito, ergo sum*. He also used the fact of his thinking, however imperfect, to argue that an ultimate being, God, had granted him the power of thought. By 1700, however, some of his intellectual descendants had begun to speculate that individual consciousness was not grafted onto a body by an omnipotent being during gestation in the womb. Even the origin and purpose of individual life had been called into question, and with it the nature of each individual's identity.

The case of Louis de la Pivardière, which made its brief mark on the French consciousness in 1698–1699, occurred in the midst of this period of theological and intellectual uncertainty. In addition to the crisis Hazard charted, it is important to note that this cause célèbre took place in the interval between the two major wars that dominated the last thirty years of the reign of Louis XIV: the War of the League of Augsburg (1688–1697) and the War of the Spanish Succession (1701–1713). During these two conflicts the Sun King mobilized upwards of four hundred thousand soldiers out of a population of twenty million. These struggles, in which French armies fought a coalition that included most of the other great powers of Europe, had profound economic, political, and social repercussions throughout the kingdom. The wars also coincided with two famines, in 1693–1694 and 1709–1710, that had devastating short-term demographic consequences for France. By the time the aged king died, his subjects were fewer, his treasury emptier, and his authority less certain than it had been in 1685. These multiple, overlapping crises explain the contemporary fascination with the case of Louis de la Pivardière. It was an accident of history that the Pivardière affair came to the attention of the French during a time of intellectual upheaval, war, and famine. But it was no coincidence that the case of an aristocrat who became a commoner, and then possibly an impostor, intrigued men and women whose assumptions about human society and the natural world had already been shaken.

Things end well on the comic stage, as seventeenth-century French theatergoers knew. But would they end well for the mysterious man in the prison cell, or for the two people accused of murdering him? From the fall of 1698 through the following summer, the city avidly followed the legal drama because it provided the raw material for conversations that specifically addressed the fundamental social, political, and theological questions of the day. Scholars have subsequently derived moral philosophies and metaphysical propositions from texts written by Descartes or seventeenth-century theologians. But the Pivardière affair offers us the chance to see how contemporaries applied these abstract principles to the moral choices they faced in their own lives. Parisians wanted to fashion a narrative of the case that would make it comprehensible for the unsettling times through which they lived. Not surprisingly, Molière's successors at the Comédie-

Française staged a new play, *Le Mari retrouvé*, or *The Husband Re-turned*, based specifically on the puzzling affair. In the courtroom, meanwhile, a young attorney general named Henri-François d'Aguesseau, who would become lord chancellor of France for much of the first half of the eighteenth century, sought to guide the criminal magistrates to a just decision through careful interpretation of the evidence. In their work, this confusing murder case became a cause célèbre that occupied the Parisian stage and the kingdom's highest courtrooms. But the story of the would-be commoner begins in the Berry, a neglected province worlds away from the playhouses, law courts, and other public spaces of the capital, or the royal court at Versailles.

France During the Reign of Louis XIV

miles

0   50

Romorantin

3.   .5
2.   .4
Narbonne• •1
Châtillon-
sur-Indre

•Bourges

•Issoudun

•Châteauroux

The Berry (Généralité de Bourges)

1. Jeu-Malloches   3. Valençay
2. Luçay-le-Mâle   4. Poulaines
         5. St. Christophe

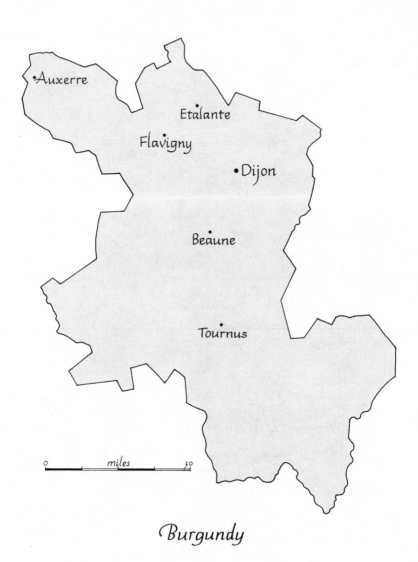

•Auxerre

Etalante

Flavigny

•Dijon

Beaune

Tournus

0   miles   50

Burgundy

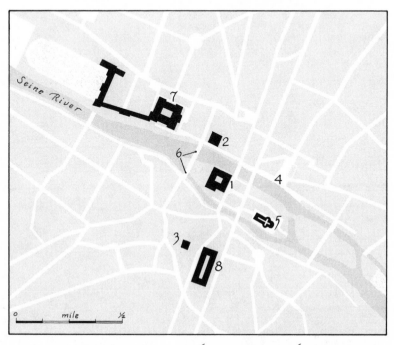

Paris at the End of the Seventeenth Century

1. Palais de Justice
2. Fort l'Evêque Prison
3. Comédie-Française
4. Place de Grève

5. Notre Dame Cathedral
6. Pont Neuf
7. Louvre
8. Sorbonne

The

WOULD-BE
COMMONER

Chapter 1

BECOMING A GENTLEMAN

❧

*L*ouis de la Pivardière was born November 15, 1661, on a small estate in the Berry, a province in economic and demographic decline by the second half of the seventeenth century. He was the last of three sons and two daughters who survived to adulthood, and the only son born to his father's second wife. He and his siblings were acutely aware of the strategies followed by Old Regime families to build wealth and status over time. These included advantageous marriages that allowed for the consolidation of wealth, wise investments in land and annuities, and the purchase of royal offices that conferred various privileges. Contemporary noblemen in more dynamic provinces with extensive social networks and greater wealth had a chance of obtaining access to the upper ranks of the French military and administrative establishment. The young Louis, however, lived in the Berry, a stagnant province that boasted no considerable fortunes. He would find his path to fortune and social advancement blocked at every turn because of his modest origins. As in many other parts of France and Europe, the rule of primogeniture governed inheritance patterns in the Berry, and his father's modest landholdings went to his oldest half brother; shortly before his father's death, he insisted that Louis sign away his right to any remaining inheritance. Although he was one of the 170 or so titular noblemen in his district of the Berry, Louis received neither the training nor the means to live in the high aristocratic style of the end of the seventeenth century. He would have to overcome the handicap of his unexceptional beginnings if he wished to become a "gentleman."

Before the 1500s, Pivardière's native Berry and its capital city, Bourges, had played an important role in the ecclesiastical, political, and economic history of France. The archbishops of Bourges had overseen religious life in much of the southern part of the kingdom, while King Charles VII briefly relocated his court to Bourges in the 1420s, in part due to the presence of the wealthy financier Jacques Cœur. As in many other regions of France, though, the Protestant challenge to Roman Catholicism after 1500 led to theological disputes and civil strife. During the French Wars of Religion (1562–1598), Bourges and its surrounding area remained largely loyalist and Catholic, while pockets of Calvinist resistance took hold throughout the province. The severity of religious conflict, the plunder and pillaging of the countryside by armies fighting on both sides, and the forced emigration of religious dissidents all contributed to the region's material decline by 1600. In the first half of the next century an increasingly heavy tax burden, imposed by the Crown to finance its participation in the Thirty Years War (1618–1648), the final great military conflict between Protestants and Catholics in Europe, further destabilized the province; tax riots broke out frequently in Bourges and other towns through the 1650s. In addition to the demands the war placed on the population, the seventeenth century was a period of famine and disease; plague struck the province particularly hard in 1628–1632, and famine claimed many lives in 1636–1638. During the Fronde (1648–1653), the civil war against the monarchy led by princes of the blood and disaffected royal magistrates, the Berry served as a base of operation for the Prince de Condé, one of the chiefs of the opposition faction. Intense local combat further damaged the area.

By the beginning of the personal reign of Louis XIV in 1661, the year of Louis de la Pivardière's birth, the signs of stagnation were unmistakable. Estimates based on tax rolls show that the total number of households in the Berry dropped from 55,741 in 1565, at the beginning of the Wars of Religion, to 41,865 in 1713, two years before the death of Louis XIV. These figures constituted a decline of one-quarter of the region's population over a century and a half. At the local level, in the parish of Jeu-Malloches, the village closest to Pivardière's estate of Narbonne, the number of hearths declined by half in the same period, from eighty-six to forty-three. This long-term demographic loss was both a cause and a consequence of the region's economic stagnation. Those who remained in the Berrichon countryside had little incentive to produce beyond a subsistence level. Poor roads and mostly impassable rivers hindered transportation of crops or goods to potential buyers; even in 1700, for example, there were no good roads or water routes connecting the northwestern part of the province, where Louis was born, to Bourges. The province as a whole had long been known for its sheepherding, but the scarcity of people and the disruptions of war, disease, and famine by the late 1600s made it difficult to constitute reliable, accessible markets or establish manufacturing enterprises that would consistently purchase raw wool or other material from its residents.

The royal intendants, crown appointees who oversaw the province, wrote reports back to Versailles after 1660 that invariably noted the economic potential of the region, but blamed its backwardness on the inhabitants. "If the people of this province were a little more hard-working," one of them wrote in 1666, "one could easily establish a considerable level of commerce here. . . . but idleness reigns so supreme in this country that I wouldn't dare promise anything from them." Louis-François Dey, seigneur de Séraucourt, the intendant at the time of the Pivardière affair, was more sympathetic to the plight of the inhabitants of the province: "[The residents of the Berry] are little inclined towards work, a nonchalance which stems among the peasantry from the poverty of the soil . . . and among the town-dwellers from a lack of commerce." During his tenure, Dey de Séraucourt frequently requested tax reductions or exemptions for the residents of the region. But the unfortunate consequences of various royal actions overwhelmed his efforts. Peasants often fled their homes, taking their provisions, to avoid billeting soldiers. Clashes between armed troops enforcing the salt tax and bands of brigands who sold contraband salt at lower prices rendered the countryside more dangerous. In 1697, in spite of Dey de Séraucourt's protests, Versailles mandated that the province's inhabitants would have to spend significant amounts of time assisting royal officials in their efforts to clear the countryside of wolves. In short, it may not have been the laziness of the peasants, but the suppression of incentives due to royal policies that made the people of the Berry reluctant to invest labor or their scarce capital in improvement schemes promoted by the Crown.

The Catholic Church, rocked by its struggles with Protestantism and internal doctrinal conflict, succeeded little better than the Crown in meeting the province's needs. A 1691 report to the archbishop of Bourges on the state of a dozen parishes southeast of Châteauroux painted a dismal picture of the priests, the churches, and the faith of the local parishioners. The priest in Bouesse, for example, was so deaf he could no longer confess his parishioners, while his counterpart in Aigurande was "gout-ridden, unable to make himself understood, and hated by his congregants." In three other parishes, the priests were over eighty years old and senile, while the parish seat in Cluis Dessous had been vacant for eighteen years. In Sidiailles, the church was in such a state of disrepair that the clock was about to plummet to the ground, threatening parishioners who had already been injured by stones falling from the edifice. The anonymous church inspector concluded his report by noting that many of the cemeteries associated with the parishes were shut down because tombstones and other masonry had been taken for various purposes. Even more damning, he noted, was the failure of most of the priests to perform the prescribed church rituals, leaving their parishioners' souls in jeopardy. Instead of saying Mass and administering the sacraments, many of the priests simply pocketed the tithes, donations, and other charitable funds they collected, leaving their church buildings, and their congregations, in a sorry state of physical and spiritual disrepair.

By 1700, visitors to the Berry could only marvel at the desolation of a province that had formerly been one of France's wealthiest. Mirabeau the elder, the father of the Revolutionary orator, summed up the situation toward the middle of the eighteenth century when he labeled the Berry the "Siberia of France."

Dey de Séraucourt reported in 1697 that the *élection*, or district, of Châteauroux, where Louis de la Pivardière was born, included 168 gentlemen out of a population of 43,420. Most of them, he noted, lived in rural obscurity, dependent on increasingly unreliable rents in cash or kind from tenant farmers to survive in their crumbling châteaux. The marginal existence of such nobles, so different from the extravagant ceremonial life of Versailles, was common throughout the kingdom by the seventeenth century. The situation of Louis' father, Antoine de la Pivardière, whose noble lineage dated back to the late fifteenth century, typified their plight. Born in 1610 in the Loire Valley north of the Berry, he had received a royal commission to command a hundred infantrymen in 1638, during the Thirty Years War. His first marriage yielded two sons who survived to adulthood as well as the lands of Plessis and Les Fosses in the local parish of Poulaines; Antoine would later expand his landholdings in the parish of Poulaines adjacent to his core estate of Plessis. Once his first wife passed away, he married Marie de Berthoulat, the daughter of a gentleman from the village of St. Christophe, only a few kilometers from Poulaines, in 1654. According to the Poulaines parish register, Marie gave birth to at least five children from 1658 to 1666. Three survived to adulthood: two daughters and a son named Louis, the future would-be commoner.

The priest noted in the parish register that the godfather to Louis de la Pivardière was the "high and powerful" Henri Dominique d'Estampes, marquis and seigneur de Valençay, the wealthiest lord in that region of the Berry and, according to Pivardière's later testimony, a *bon ami* of his father. His godmother was Elizabeth de Gripon, the wife of a military officer who happened to be passing through Poulaines at the time and was pressed into duty at the baptismal font; she would not see her godson again until 1695, when he sought her help in Paris. Upon his birth, Louis' parents immediately turned the infant over to Marie and Pierre Morin, a wet nurse and her husband, who lived in Plessis. This practice was common for much of the Old Regime; and French couples at many levels of society, in both town and country, handed their children off to wet nurses. The resort to wet-nursing had many reasons, including the mother's need to return to work after birth, occasional parental indifference toward infants due to high mortality rates, and the belief that a sexually active mother's milk would be contaminated. It was not until Jean-Jacques Rousseau and other moralists and physicians asserted in the next century that maternal breastfeeding was healthier for the child and promoted bonding between mother and infant that French women began to consider breastfeeding their newborns. Louis appears to have bonded with his wet nurse and her family, perhaps more so than with his own parents, both of whom were dead before he reached twenty. Later, when he married Marguerite Chauvelin, he brought his wet nurse and her husband to Narbonne to live with him.

We know little about the Plessis household in which Louis was raised until his father's death in 1679. By the time he was born, his father had retired from military service and was living off the modest proceeds from his estates; Louis would later recount that the elder Pivardière had sported white hair as far back as he could remember. After Louis' mother died sometime in the late 1660s or early 1670s, his father gave up riding in his horse-drawn carriage, hunted only occasionally with friends, and maintained a household of two female servants named Louise and Margot. Although relatively well-off provincial nobles sent their children to a *collège* or an academy to prepare for service in the military or the royal bureaucracy, Antoine de la Pivardière did not provide such an education to his youngest son. Louis was taught to read and write by schoolmasters while he lived on his father's estate in Plessis. His education continued when he lived with his maternal relatives in the nearby village of St. Christophe after his father's death; there he studied with the sons of the local notary, the innkeeper, and the surgeon.

In these settings he would have learned basic French and Latin and acquired a rudimentary knowledge of arithmetic; many schoolmasters in similar rural contexts also assisted the local priests in their duties and provided religious instruction to their young charges. But he would not have been exposed to the *collège* curriculum, which included more advanced reading and writing instruction in both languages, philosophy, history, geography, and in some cases an introduction to pre-Newtonian physics. Above all, he would have missed training in speaking and in physical comportment; these lessons often culminated in public performances such as theatrical presentations and prepared young French noblemen for social exchange with their peers. At this early stage in his life, therefore, Louis did not receive the preparation that French gentlemen who aspired to positions of responsibility were expected to acquire.

Sometime between puberty and the death of his father when he was eighteen, the young Louis had his first taste of military life. During his adolescence in the 1670s, France fought the Dutch in an effort to expand its northern and eastern frontiers. The Sun King's bellicose policy provided opportunities for adolescent nobles like Louis to embark upon military careers. Warfare in late-seventeenth-century Europe was in a transitional state between the decentralized, feudal practices of the medieval period and the modern state's determination to monopolize military force. The kings of France substantially expanded the size of their armies in the 1600s, but they did so in part at the expense of the nobility, whom they still expected to recruit and outfit their own regiments, much as the vassals of the medieval kings had done centuries earlier. Louis' first military appointment, even before his father's demise, was that of cadet, or apprentice officer, in the regiment maintained by his maternal uncle the Sieur de St. Christophe. While there is no record of Louis' precise responsibilities, he probably served as a page to his uncle or another veteran soldier, learning the rhythms and habits of military life. As a cadet, he would have received an official military appointment and modest pay from the Crown.

Toward the end of the 1670s, as the Dutch War came to an end, the Sieur de St. Christophe disbanded his regiment, and his young nephew returned to Plessis. Shortly before he died in 1679, Antoine de la Pivardière ensured that the lands he had acquired within the parish of Poulaines would pass largely undivided to his eldest son. This gentleman, in his mid-thirties, became the Sieur de Plessis upon his father's demise. His younger brother Germain became the Sieur des Fosses, inheriting the smaller seigneury his father had possessed. Antoine required the three children from his second marriage to sign a document known as an *émancipation*, in which they stated that they would not contest the inheritance of their two half brothers from their father's first marriage. Later, after their father's death, the elder brothers contributed money toward dowries that allowed their two half sisters to enter the Ursuline convent in Valençay founded by the Marquis de Valençay earlier in the century. Their fate was a common one for daughters of the less well-to-do nobility whose families could not offer a dowry large enough to tempt a husband of sufficient wealth or status. Their younger brother, Louis, newly returned from the military, was essentially disinherited by the *émancipation*. When Germain died in 1692, the seigneury des Fosses reverted to the elder brother, further confirming Louis' exclusion from the family inheritance. The under-endowed young aristocrat now suffered from an absence of seigneurial property as well as an education proper to his rank.

Upon his father's death, Louis went to live with a paternal uncle, André de la Pivardière, Sieur de la Touche, the administrator of his father's will. At some point in the early 1680s, as Louis XIV deployed his forces in annual border skirmishes to the north to expand upon his gains from the Dutch War, Louis served again as a cadet, with pay, in the regiment of the Sieur de St. David. He saw action in 1681 at the Battle of Chiny in the Duchy of Luxembourg, part of a series of engagements in the early 1680s designed to solidify Louis XIV's claims on territory he had annexed from the Spanish Netherlands. The following year, the minister of war, François-Michel le Tellier, Marquis de Louvois, founded several cadet companies to offer practical officer training to nobles who aspired to a military career. The cadet curriculum included shooting, fencing, riding, geography, drawing, applied mathematics, money management, and principles of fortification. German language instruction was also available, as was remedial reading and writing for the semiliterate. But it was expensive to attend these training academies, especially on a cadet's standard pocket wages of six sous per day. Cadets needed their own income or material support from their families; by the late 1680s, the government had mandated that the family of each member of the cadet companies had to commit 150 livres per annum to their son's training. While this curriculum might have provided Louis with the preparation and contacts he needed for a successful military career, it is likely that his older half brothers, who were consolidating their father's estate, were unwilling to bankroll his ambitions. His position as the family's cadet son prevented him from obtaining cadet training in the royal army; once again, he had missed an opportunity for advancement.

By the mid-1680s, Louis was casting about the lower Berry, attempting to exploit family connections and seigneurial networks. In 1685, he was party to a lawsuit stemming from the death of his maternal uncle and former military commander, the Sieur de St. Christophe. The affair, adjudicated by a royal magistrate in the town of Issoudun, about twenty miles southeast of Poulaines and St. Christophe, involved a challenge to the intended sale of land owned by his mother and her two brothers. For five months, he rented a room in Issoudun in the home of a local barber-surgeon while he followed the course of the lawsuit; these modest quarters suggest that his noble title did little to distinguish him from small-town commoners in this corner of the Berry. The case was ruled in Louis' favor, and he received four to five thousand livres. At this juncture, Louis must have decided, it was more practical to cash out any property holdings he might acquire rather than eke out a minimal subsistence on the land.

While Louis de la Pivardière, bearer of a noble name without any of its financial or cultural advantages, spent the early and mid-1680s trying to enhance his birthright, his future first wife was experiencing her own difficulties. Marguerite Chauvelin's family was from the countryside near the town of Vendôme, northeast of the Berry. Her forefathers obtained titles of nobility in the late sixteenth century, and their male descendents served with distinction in the king's judicial and administrative bureaucracies until the Revolution. Germain-Louis Chauvelin, the family's leading member in the generation after Marguerite, held cabinet-level positions in the government of Louis XV in the 1720s and 1730s, including the post of minister of foreign affairs. For more than a decade, he was one of the most powerful men in France. Both his father and his brother were attorneys general at the Parlement in Paris, one of the high court's most sought-after positions. Marguerite, however, came from a collateral, less distinguished branch of the family. Her grandfather, initially an abbot, resigned his clerical charge, married, and obtained a position as a councilor in the Parisian courts. Sometime in the 1630s, he purchased Narbonne, an inconsequential estate in the Berry whose origins can be traced to the thirteenth century. Marguerite's uncle, an army captain who never married, later inherited Narbonne. It is unlikely that either man ever spent much time on their rural estate, and by 1652 at the latest, Marguerite's father, Jacques Chauvelin, appears as the seigneur of Narbonne in the local civil registers.

Narbonne today consists of a two-story rectangular building with a tower, a shed, and a small garden. In the second half of the seventeenth century, the current building, which then provided

A photograph of Narbonne as it appears today. This building is the only one that remains of four similar structures, which defined the compound's internal courtyard.

living quarters for the lord and his family, was one of four similarly shaped structures that together enclosed an interior courtyard. The other three structures housed stables for horses, cattle, and sheep, a granary, and a woodworking shop, as well as sleeping quarters for some of the servants. A small building with an oven for baking bread stood in the courtyard directly in front of the main residence; nearby was a chicken coop. Just outside the compound lay a small stand of fruit trees, a vegetable garden, and other cultivated areas, at the end of which stood a chapel containing the remains of previous seigneurs of Narbonne. The enclave boasted several wells and fountains, as well as a set of empty ditches around the exterior, intended for fortification purposes at an earlier time. Narbonne at the end of the seventeenth century, while serviceable, was a far cry from the splendor of Versailles, Fontainebleau, or even the Renaissance and neoclassical châteaux north of the Berry in the Loire Valley.

The seigneur of Narbonne also possessed nearby woods, ponds, and arable lands. By the seventeenth century, however, the estate's owners and their servants no longer utilized these resources themselves; instead, they derived an income by selling the right to farm, fish, and hunt on these lands to local peasants. They depended on this revenue to supplement the produce of the gardens and the estate's livestock. One contemporary estimate placed the annual cash revenue of the seigneurs of Narbonne at approximately eight or nine hundred livres. A day worker in Paris or Lyon at this time could earn about one livre for a day's work, so the owner of Narbonne, given the greater overhead, was not substantially better off than a typical urban manual laborer. The estate was a small affair that, if run properly, would permit the seigneur, his family, and a handful of servants a subsistence existence in a good year. In comparison to the most important aristocratic families in the province, Narbonne's revenues were paltry. In his 1697 memoir, the intendant Dey de Séraucourt listed the largest annual land incomes in the Berry at thirty thousand livres; the land revenues that year of the Marquis de Valençay, son of Louis' godfather and the most important seigneur in the vicinity of Narbonne, were ten thousand livres per annum.

This, then, was the rural estate where Marguerite Chauvelin lived prior to her marriage to Louis in 1687. Although Marguerite's father appears to have been in possession of Narbonne by the early 1650s, Jacques Chauvelin's posts in the Crown's fiscal bureaucracy would have required his frequent presence in Paris and Versailles; the family most likely remained in the capital throughout the 1650s and 1660s. Marguerite had one sibling, an elder brother who would have inherited Narbonne from their father, but he has left no archival trace and may have passed away before reaching maturity. His younger sister was born in 1660, a year before Louis, probably in Paris; there is no record of her birth in the parish registers of Jeu-Malloches, where her baptism would have been noted if the family was living at Narbonne. In Paris, she might have been tutored at home or placed in a boarding school run by nuns; in either case, she would have received some instruction in reading and writing French, as well as a grounding in Christian morals. Had she continued her Parisian education into adolescence, a young girl of her background would have been taught how to run a household of some consequence. She might also have been exposed to the latest in literature and culture, depending on the school or tutor.

The convent might have been Marguerite's fate, as it had been for Louis' two sisters, and for four of Marguerite's paternal aunts, had Narbonne not been available as her dowry. In 1672, however, at the age of twelve, she was married to her first husband and established residence at the estate; Marguerite's mother may also have joined them. Later that year her first child, a daughter, was born. Marriage and pregnancy at such an early age was unusual in seventeenth-century France, where betrothals were often postponed until spouses were in their twenties and secure in their inheritances. Some men and women never married, even if they survived past adolescence. As she reached puberty, her parents must have been determined to seek the best match available in the lower Berry, given the limited revenues of Narbonne. The family of Charles de Menou, Marguerite's first husband, had themselves been seigneurs of Narbonne in the 1400s and no doubt welcomed the estate's return to the family fold. After her daughter's birth in 1672, Marguerite did not give birth again until 1679, at the age of nineteen, when the baptism of her first son, Charles, appears in the parish register of Jeu-Malloches; the couple had five more children in the next six years, all of whom survived to adulthood. The reasons for Marguerite's seven-year hiatus from childbirth are unknown, but her avoidance of pregnancy, even if unintentional, no doubt lowered the chances of mortality for both the subsequent children and their mother.

There is reason to believe that Marguerite's first marriage was not a happy one, in spite of its fecundity. Dissatisfied couples could not divorce in seventeenth-century France, due to ecclesiastical law; marriage was an inviolable sacrament of the Catholic Church. Couples whose marriages faltered, however, did have the option of seeking a separation of persons and goods, a civil procedure that permitted them to live separately and divide their property according to its ownership prior to the marriage; both parties were forbidden to remarry while the other was still alive. In cases where one spouse, usually the wife, feared that the other might dissipate the couple's wealth through poor judgment or reckless actions, it was also possible to file for a separation of goods only. It appears Marguerite took this path against Charles de Menou, according to a 1679 judgment pronounced by a local magistrate. By the terms of the decree, rendered the same year that the couple's second child was born (and perhaps why she once again conceived), Marguerite was granted sole control over Narbonne. The multiple complaints filed by Marguerite, listed in the final judgment, indicate that she took deliberate action after her husband had established a pattern of fiscal irresponsibility. At nineteen, with at least two children under six years of age, she became responsible for running the affairs of her rural estate. Later legal documents from 1685, including judgments rendered in cases between Marguerite and some of her tenant farmers, suggest that she had taken full charge of the estate; her husband, although he continued to father her children, is not named in the papers.

The next mention of Charles de Menou places him in his grave; he was interred in the churchyard at Jeu-Malloches on April 23,

1685. For two and a half years after his death, Marguerite managed the affairs of Narbonne herself. Then, in November 1687, she and Louis were married at the parish church in Jeu-Malloches. Marguerite's second husband was by that point an aristocratic drifter, a third son of little wealth who had been haphazardly trained for a military career but who lacked the resources or connections to field even a modest provincial squadron of infantrymen. His primary occupations, according to those who knew him at the time, were hunting, gambling, and eating and drinking with other gentlemen in the vicinity. He freely admitted that he had little knowledge of, or interest in, the daily management of Narbonne. He seemed to have been ill-prepared to take on the roles of seigneurial lord and head of a household consisting of a spouse, stepchildren, and servants.

Louis would later claim that the couple first met while at a fair held in Luçay, six miles north of Narbonne; they may both have been staying at the house of one of Louis' relatives. Louis also recalled that he (or perhaps his brother) prevailed upon a gentleman residing in the vicinity of Narbonne to ask Marguerite's mother for her hand on Louis' behalf. In 1687, however, twenty-six years old and still casting about for a stable life situation, Louis may have initially had other intentions. While traveling in the Berry in 1687, a lawyer named Jean Antoine Archambault happened to stop at Narbonne one night for dinner and lodging. After the meal, Magdeleine de Menou, Marguerite's fifteen-year-old daughter, pulled Archambault out into the courtyard, where she said she had a secret to confide. The daughter called Archambault's attention to a gentleman standing by the fireplace inside and claimed that the man had asked her mother for the young girl's hand in marriage. According to Magdeleine, however, her mother had other ideas; she herself sought to marry the man, whom Archambault identified as Louis. Archambault told the girl that she should submit to her mother's wishes. Five or six days later, at a fair in Valençay, Archambault saw Marguerite, Magdeleine, and Louis purchasing furniture, and later, while dining at the château of the Marquis de Valençay, heard that marriage arrangements between Louis and Marguerite had been completed. Perhaps in compensation for raising her hopes, Louis gave the young girl a new outfit for the wedding at the same time he provided her mother with two new sets of clothes. Not long after her mother's wedding, Magdeleine was married to Charles Philippe Séguier, Sieur de Plessy. The tale is consistent with the external facts that suggest the unlikelihood of any enduring affection between Marguerite and her second husband. Louis may have initially been attracted to Marguerite's eldest daughter, but he was ultimately persuaded to accept a more practical match with her mother.

Given the discord of her first marriage, and her inclination to manage Narbonne herself, why did Marguerite agree to a second nuptial alliance so soon after the first had ended? In addition to the children she needed to feed, numbering at least six by 1687, it appears that her finances were shaky. This was not a surprising state of affairs for a fief located in the northwest corner of the Berry; indeed, a decade later Dey de Séraucourt proclaimed the district in which Narbonne was situated "one of the most sterile and inhospitable in the kingdom." A list of assets drawn up by Marguerite and Louis a couple of months after their marriage, intended to protect the inheritance of Marguerite's children with Menou, indicates that Marguerite and Menou owed a total of fifteen hundred livres to various creditors, a sum significantly larger than the annual revenues generated by her estate. Marguerite may well have hoped that a marriage with one of the region's noble families would placate the creditors detailed on the list of assets, including a man named Gaulthier, a local blacksmith to whom she owed more than eight hundred livres in principal and interest.

Her new spouse, however, was probably not in a position to

retire her debts immediately. The same list notes that Louis brought to Narbonne several tapestries, some pieces of furniture, and kitchenware, probably purchased on credit from merchants in Valençay, and two horses worth a total of three hundred livres. He also had on hand more than twenty-four hundred livres at the time of their marriage, including cash recently received from his older half brother. He had most likely parted with a large portion of the money he had received from the inheritance case in Issoudun a year or two earlier, with little prospect of a steady revenue to help offset the operating expenses of Narbonne. For him, the primary attraction of the marriage was the opportunity to obtain title to a landed estate, Narbonne, and its income, however modest, just as his half brothers had upon the death of their father. Indeed, contributions at this time from his half brothers were likely intended to facilitate the marriage in order to situate Louis within the local seigneurial networks in their corner of the Berry. For both parties, the decision to marry was driven by status and economics, not romantic interest; neither spouse had the potential to attract a more financially advantageous match.

Marguerite may have looked for male friendship, but not necessarily physical love, outside her second marriage. The head of the nearby priory of Miséray, Sylvain-François Charost, would have been an obvious choice. Miséray, like Narbonne, dated to the high Middle Ages; according to legend, it was originally a chivalric brotherhood established in the twelfth century in the forest of Heugnes near the cells of two hermits, Girard and Godefroy. By the late seventeenth century, it was a small religious community of no more than half a dozen monks, with several servants and fifteen hundred livres in annual income from its lands. It stood a short twenty- to thirty-minute walk from the Narbonne compound. Charost, the prior of Miséray in the late 1680s and the 1690s, thus enjoyed an estate that was comparable in value to Narbonne. Like Louis, the prior was a younger brother in a family of comfortable, but not excessive, income. In terms of family strategies for maintaining and increasing wealth and provincial prestige, Charost's family, not ennobled, was also unable to finance the expensive career ambitions of its male offspring. While his eldest brother followed in their father's footsteps by becoming the chief magistrate in Châtillon-sur-Indre, a town thirteen miles southwest of Narbonne, and another brother entered the military, Sylvain-François and a third brother embarked upon clerical careers. In the mid-1680s, probably around the time Marguerite's first husband passed away, Sylvain-François took up his post at the priory of Miséray; he was about twenty years old, slightly younger than Louis and Marguerite. As the head of the priory, it fell to him to celebrate the Mass in the small chapel outside the walls of Narbonne on a regular basis. Marguerite's family, its servants, nearby peasants, and anyone traveling through the neighborhood might have attended these rites. He may have even married Louis and Marguerite in 1687, although the record is unclear. In the early 1690s, however, neighbors began to claim that the prior and Marguerite had become lovers, a durable rumor that would have potentially fatal consequences.

It is true that Charost's ecclesiastical duties were not his only point of encounter with the masters of Narbonne. The three of them also conducted business affairs, including loans of money and goods and exchanges of land rights. In addition, Louis, Marguerite, and the prior all noted a strong friendship between the two men in the late 1680s and early 1690s that included hunting excursions and other forms of amusement. Eventually, the prior lent Louis money to advance the latter's military career. While some of this mutual dependence may have been exaggerated after the fact, the exchanges described are all perfectly reasonable interactions for a nobleman, his wife, and a local cleric living in close proximity in a sparsely populated rural area. In such circumstances, one can easily imagine how the three came to rely on one another materially and emotionally, perhaps depending on the friendship to reinforce their distinction from the area's village merchants, peasants, and their own servants. Did the interactions between the prior and Marguerite go beyond the bounds of propriety? At a remove of three centuries, lacking any hard archival evidence, it is impossible to determine the precise contours of the relationship between the twice-married mother of six and the theoretically celibate man of the cloth who was four or five years her junior.

Whatever the connection might have been between the prior and his two neighbors, all the evidence suggests that Louis and Marguerite settled into a predictable routine of rural sociability in the first years of their marriage. On feast days and religious holidays, they socialized with other local notables and rural clerics. Occasionally the gatherings were at Narbonne, where religious services in the compound's small chapel, conducted by the prior, would be followed by feasting. Sometime in 1688 Marguerite gave birth to the couple's first child, Marie, now the youngest of her five children still living at Narbonne; two frequent guests at Narbonne, the local notables the Sieur de Preville and the Dame de Jouy, attended the child's baptism in the Jeu-Malloches parish church and served as godparents. Four years later, Louis' second child, a son named Antoine after his deceased father, was born. For Louis and Marguerite, the rounds of rural conviviality and the drama of pregnancy and birth were set within the rhythms of agrarian life. Marguerite managed the daily affairs of the compound, just as she had by the end of her first marriage, but not entirely without Louis' aid. We can catch glimpses of him — between his hunting parties and gambling bouts with neighborhood gentlemen — taking animals to market for sale, signing leases with tenant farmers or selling plots of land outright, appearing in court on behalf of the couple's various legal interests, and fulfilling the seigneur of Narbonne's ceremonial obligations of fealty and homage to the Count of Luçay. While one magistrate would later note that "it appeared there was never a great closeness" between the couple, there was no reason to believe in 1688 or 1689 that their relationship was outside the usual boundaries of a time and place that put minimal emphasis on spouses' emotional compatibility.

In the fall of 1688, as Louis and Marguerite were settling back into life at Narbonne with their newly born daughter, Louis XIV issued a manifesto to the Holy Roman Emperor, the smaller Germanic princes, and William of Orange, stadtholder of the Netherlands and recently crowned king of England. The Sun King called for them to acknowledge French seizures of land along the Rhine during the preceding decade as permanent boundaries. Even before he received a response, however, Louis began to send his troops into the Palatinate, a territory on France's northeastern frontier. By spring of the following year, French soldiers had embarked on a campaign of massive destruction in the region, burning major towns to the ground before the eyes of their residents, who barely had time to flee. Memories of the devastation lived on for several centuries, forming part of the antagonism between Germany and France that culminated in the three catastrophic wars the nations fought between 1870 and 1945. More immediately, however, the brutal French actions led to the outbreak of the Nine Years War, also known as the War of the League of Augsburg, which pitted the French almost single-handedly against the other major powers of western and central Europe. This "great miscalculation," as one historian recently put it, resulted in an exhausting war of attrition between France and its enemies fought around the entire perimeter of the French kingdom. Under the terms of the 1697 Treaty of Ryswick, Louis XIV emerged with somewhat less territory along his northern and eastern frontiers than he had claimed in 1688. The war he inadvertently initiated did not end well for the Sun King.

The Nine Years War marked a new high in French and European military conscription. During the Middle Ages and the Renaissance, European kings and princes had fielded forces that rarely exceeded 70,000 men in wartime and 10,000 in time of peace. By the Nine Years War, however, this figure had shot up to 420,000 troops on paper, the largest force assembled by a king of France before 1789. In order to expand his military quickly, Louis resorted to a number of traditional and new expedients, including expanded tours of duty, social and financial incentives to nobles who equipped their own regiments, aggressive recruiting practices, and a reliance on formerly independent urban and provincial militias. One antiquated form of forced recruitment, employed for the final time in France during the Nine Years War, was the summoning of the king's *ban et arrière-ban*, a method of aristocratic conscription that dated to the Middle Ages. The *ban* referred to the calling of those nobles who owed military service to the king as part of their vassalage; the *arrière-ban* signified the summoning of those lesser knights who owed service to the king's vassals. The practice, helpful to the Crown into the 1500s, had become increasingly comical by the seventeenth century, when it was invoked in 1635, 1674, and 1689. By that point, as royal military strategists found, most of the competent sons of the nobility were already in the king's service, leaving a corps of impoverished, inexperienced provincial nobles for call-up. The terms of service in the 1600s were three months per year within the French kingdom or forty days on foreign soil, but in 1674, Louis XIV called the *ban et arrière-ban* primarily as a means of raising funds from nobles who were willing to pay to escape the drudgery of military duty. In 1689, at the start of the Nine Years War, Louis XIV's Minister of War Louvois thought he might use the *ban* for internal affairs, such as coastal patrols, in addition to fundraising. Unlike the Middle Ages, when the *ban* had been central to the monarchy's ability to field a fighting force, by the late seventeenth century it had become an insignificant portion of a king's military preparations.

When the call for the *ban et arrière-ban* went out in 1689, Louis de la Pivardière, now seigneur of Narbonne and vassal of the Count of Luçay, was obliged to appear. Noblemen from his district of the Berry assembled in the Loire River town of Blois, then proceeded upstream to Orléans where one of the king's lieutenants took charge of their company. Although there are no records of the company's activities that year, or of his reaction to this experience, it is not hard to imagine Louis' mixed emotions upon his return to military life. In the late 1670s and early 1680s, when he had apprenticed in the military, his path up the ranks had been blocked by a lack of financial resources. Now, in his late twenties, he took his place alongside other landed country gentlemen summoned to military duty by the king. The context in which he once again took up arms, however, was one that was clearly anachronistic in the eyes of those who ran the military. Louis' previous military experience must have alerted him to the diminished expectations held by Louis XIV's war strategists for the ragtag group of nobles.

Louis abandoned the ranks of his country peers sometime in the next two years to seek a commissioned post in the army. Apparently his taste of military life with the *ban*, even if tainted by association with rural gentlemen unfit for service, tempted him to renew the career he had begun in the late 1670s as an officer-in-training. Perhaps he had never abandoned his dreams of military glory, or maybe he sought an escape from the drudgery of life at Narbonne with Marguerite. Although the rank of cadet had been appropriate when he was in his late teens and early twenties, by 1690 he was almost thirty, too old to be serving an apprenticeship. It was time for him to move up the ranks. Regiments, the largest units within the armies of the Sun King, were commanded by rich, aristocratic colonels who could afford to purchase their venal offices from the Crown and supplement the wartime allowances provided by the royal treasury. Some regiments also featured a second-in-command sporting the rank of lieutenant-colonel. These regiments, typically composed of four to twelve hundred men, were split into companies of thirty to two hundred men under the direction of captains who also purchased their commands and drew on their own purse strings to equip and train their recruits. Within the companies, below the level of captain, a series of subaltern officers was responsible for the day-to-day drilling and inspection of the troops and the supervision of non-commanding officers in charge of supplies. The highest-ranking officer at the subaltern level was the lieutenant, followed by the sous-lieutenants, whose positions during peacetime tended to disappear. Finally, at the bottom of this pecking order came officers known as ensigns in infantry units, or as cornets in cavalry companies. Although they were technically officers, men in these inferior ranks found themselves in a difficult situation. Those who were ambitious wore fashionable wigs, coats, and headwear to give the impression of wealth. Their supposed affluence served as a recommendation for promotion to the more prestigious, but far more costly venal ranks, where they would be called upon to equip their troops. Their superiors, familiar with their underlings' need to maintain appearances, often extorted funds or contributions from them for the financial upkeep of companies. But even the best-paid lieutenants during the Nine Years War could count on an annual salary of no more than two hundred livres — outside sources of income were essential to support a military career.

No doubt aware of these fiscal requirements, Louis sought an initial appointment at the lowest rank. He turned to the patronage networks within which he was known, in the vicinity of Narbonne and Poulaines, for a commission as a cornet. First he approached the Marquis de Valençay, the son of his deceased godfather, who maintained a dragoon regiment, a squadron of cavalrymen equipped and trained to fight on foot when necessary. Valençay rebuffed his request, but Louis then gained access to François d'Aubusson, Duc de la Feuillade, a relative of his deceased mother and general and governor of the province of Dauphiné, whose son would serve as an officer in the War of the Spanish Succession. Feuillade agreed to fund Louis and successfully solicited a post for him with another dragoon commander, Elie de St. Hermines. Louis remained in the St. Hermines regiment throughout his service during the Nine Years War. Although his initial foothold in the military rankings was modest, he may well have imagined for the first time in his life that he had begun to acquire some of the traditional signs of aristocratic privilege to match his birthright: a landed estate and a position in the army's officer corps.

While Louis XIV's propagandists stressed the "glory" of his military campaigns in countless pamphlets, broadsheets, and the paintings that adorned the Hall of Mirrors at Versailles and other royal venues, the men who fought the battles knew differently. During his years of service, Louis experienced the horrors and the boredom of the siege warfare and battles of attrition that characterized European martial practice at the end of the seventeenth century. Military encounters under the Sun King were protracted affairs whose main strategy consisted of overwhelming opponents with quantitative superiority during extended conflicts. Each season, Louis XIV and his opponents would engage in at most one or two significant, lethal combats. The rest of the time both sides would feign military preparedness in an effort to exhaust the supplies and the will of their opponent. The huge increase in the size of armies meant that issues of supply were often as critical to military success as brilliant tactical strategy, technological innovation, or individual valor on the battlefield. The exhaustion of the countryside by the end of the seventeenth century, in the Berry and elsewhere, also meant that kings and princes were at times forced to provision their armies themselves. Advances in military fortifications and siege warfare, spearheaded on the French side by Sébastien le Prestre, Sieur de Vauban, Louis XIV's great military engineer, further predisposed kings and commanders to adopt siege tactics that led to lengthy, often indecisive engagements. The military historian John Lynn has characterized this form of warfare as a "battle culture of forbearance," where the key to victory lay in a stoic ability to absorb the opponent's most forceful blow and remain standing. The abrupt, devastating triumphs of the Napoleonic battlefield, or the blitzkrieg tactics of the Germans in World War II, were far in the future. In spite of the Sun King's propaganda, his greatest military advantages were France's territorial size and demographic superiority, which allowed him to hold off coalitions composed of most of the rest of Europe for more than a quarter of a century.

Louis' first season of battle with the St. Hermines regiment, in 1690, took him to the Rhineland theater of war. But the main conflicts on France's northern borders that summer were in Flanders, not Germany, and it is doubtful that Louis' regiment saw battle. The next year, however, the St. Hermines regiment was assigned to Flanders and participated in the bombardment of Liège, a Flemish town that had proclaimed neutrality but agreed to garrison a regiment of allied troops. Here Louis experienced firsthand the deafening sound of mortar fire and its dramatic consequences upon impact. Two years later, by his own account, he was at the siege of Charleroi, a Flemish fortress from which allied troops often ravaged the nearby French-controlled countryside, tying up as many as 15,000 troops in a defensive capacity. This methodical engagement lasted from September 12 to October 10, 1693, when the allied garrison capitulated under threat of French mines that would have blown huge breaches in the fort; less than a third of the allied garrison troops survived the siege. The following year,

Louis' final in the service of the king, the St. Hermines regiment once again drew an assignment to the army of Flanders, but in the summer and fall of 1694 the Flemish front was quiet, and it is unlikely that Louis saw significant action.

In 1692 Louis was promoted to the rank of lieutenant in the St. Hermines regiment, suggesting that his military career was finally on track. One historian has calculated that the average cornet in the dragoons during the Nine Years War held his post for approximately two years, which would place Louis well within the average time frame for promotion. But in order to survive at the front, Louis was forced to sell his horse and its outfit, as well as some of his own clothes. He became reliant on his wife to advance him the funds he needed to continue his military activities, and he borrowed money from his neighbors at Narbonne, including the Prior Charost, when he returned in the winter after each year's campaign. In 1691 Louis had incurred a debt of fifty-two livres, never repaid, for food and lodging provided by an employee in the king's fiscal bureaucracy named Chauveton. A Berrichon merchant named Fleury claimed that Louis never made good on a debt of fifty-five livres he owed for the purchase of fabrics, perhaps for his company's uniforms or other needs, in 1692 or 1693. He obtained funding from the archbishop of Metz, the brother of his patron the Duc de la Feuillade. Doubtless there were other creditors hounding the financially strapped lieutenant by the end of the war. These fiscal difficulties imply that he was unable to afford the next jump in the ranks, from lieutenant to captain, which required a major capital investment in venal office and troop provisions.

In the latter years of the war, when Louis made his way home from the Flemish front at the end of each season's campaign, he may have wondered how he would present his situation to his financially shrewd wife and other local creditors. He may also have wondered how much longer the war would last. Famine and disease in 1693–1694 diminished the combatants' ability to meet the demands for manpower and material support necessitated by late-seventeenth-century terms of engagement. In France, these unfortunate developments contributed to the deaths of almost three million men, women, and children, a mortality rate roughly double that experienced by Louis XIV's subjects in any two-year period in the 1680s. This increased frequency of death, combined with a birth rate that fell by half in the same period, meant a sharp demographic decline; in twenty-four months the kingdom's population fell by 6.8 percent. Although the French would overcome this population setback during the first decades of the eighteenth century, in the short term it meant fewer people to work in the fields and towns, fewer tax revenues for the Crown, and greater material and emotional hardship throughout the kingdom.

This landscape, devastated by famine and disease and disrupted by massive military mobilizations, was the one through which Louis traveled on his way back to Narbonne by the mid-1690s. Not only would his military adventures have given him time to meditate on his own increasingly frustrated career ambitions, they would have also provided him firsthand experience of the discontent throughout the kingdom. Nor was it likely that his annual return to Narbonne provided him much cheer. We do not know what sort of reception Louis received in these later years from Marguerite, the wife whom he had seen sporadically since the beginning of the war, or from his two children, to whom he must have been a stranger. When he asked Marguerite for more money to fund his military ambitions, she undoubtedly harangued him about the difficulties of making ends meet on their modest estate in difficult times. Departures at the start of each new campaigning season must have been a relief for Louis; Narbonne carried too many reminders of past failures, current debts, and the likelihood of future stagnation.

As early as 1695, rumors were spreading that both Louis XIV and his enemies were more interested in negotiated settlements than continued belligerence on the battlefield, a point that Louis' quiet experiences on the Flemish front in 1694 would have reinforced. And once the war ended, as he knew, the king's armies would shed subaltern officers and payroll rapidly. With his prospects for further engagement in battle and promotion diminished, the struggling lieutenant might well have contemplated a return to his prewar existence with dismay. Marguerite had terminated her first husband's access to the revenues generated by Narbonne; would she do the same with Louis if his military adventure failed to yield high office and the attendant social prestige and financial opportunities? By war's end in 1697, the trappings of nobility — his landed estate and his military office — seemed hollow. Having finally made good on his birthright, Louis de la Pivardière had become a country gentleman. It was an unenviable fate in late-seventeenth-century France.

Chapter 2

THE MURDER NARRATIVE

⚜

$\mathcal{S}$ometime in early August 1697, Marguerite received a troubling letter from a local solicitor who had handled legal affairs at Narbonne since her first marriage. The lawyer wrote that he had been approached by a woman who sought the address of Louis de la Pivardière; this woman claimed that Louis had taken a second wife in Auxerre. There is no record of Marguerite's immediate response to this news, but one can imagine her reaction. Her husband's lengthy absences may well have led her to suspect him of infidelity, but now she had strong reason to believe that his letters from the front, which had arrived regularly during the war, were part of a long-standing charade. Perhaps she discussed this news with her servants or local confidantes, but she and her household were also involved in preparations for the mid-August feast of Our Lady, a traditional summer gathering for prayer and festivity. On August 15, she was expecting a group of local notables to join her at Narbonne for a Mass at the estate's chapel, celebrated by the neighboring Prior Charost, after which the company would retire to the château for a meal, conversation, and gaming.

That day, as her guests joined Marguerite at her Berrichon

residence, Louis unexpectedly returned to Narbonne. The former military officer had fallen from the admittedly low rung to which he had climbed as a lieutenant in the St. Hermines dragoon regiment. He arrived at the compound dressed in a nondescript brown coat that covered a red vest with leather buttons and a dark gray shirt and pants. He wore neither a wig nor boots and traveled alone, unattended by a valet. He walked the final miles to Narbonne, leading a lame mare by the reins. As he entered the compound, he passed a group of servants and local peasants carousing at the front gate, then stabled his broken-down horse himself. Louis, now bereft of any retinue and leading a decrepit animal on foot, presented a pathetic figure as he returned to the estate he had left seven years earlier in pursuit of military glory. A critic of the Crown might well have interpreted this exhausted homecoming as a symbol of the futile wars waged by Louis XIV from 1688 to 1713.

From the stable, Louis proceeded to the main house, where he came upon his wife and her guests in the midst of their meal. Marguerite and company may have heard earlier in the afternoon that his arrival was imminent, thanks to an "officious peasant" who had seen Louis en route. He was received warmly by the diners, all of whom had long been his acquaintances. Louis and the prior greeted each other with enthusiasm, sitting side by side at the table and clinking glasses in a toast to his return. One neighbor, Charles François, Sieur de Préville, godfather to Louis' eldest child, invited the returnee to join him for a hunt the next day. On the surface, at least, his neighbors continued their relationship with him exactly as it had been years earlier. Marguerite's response to the arrival of her husband was more ambivalent; she diplomatically stated that "his return did not give me the same pleasure as it had at other times before I knew of his conduct [in Auxerre]." Some of the guests lightly reproached the lady of the house for the cool reception she offered her wayward spouse; a few of them later reported, perhaps apocryphally, that Louis tartly excused his wife by explaining that "I am her husband, but not her companion," implying that he suspected his wife of infidelity.

In spite of the façade of good cheer erected by the lord of the manor and his guests, the underlying tension between the estranged spouses quickly broke up the party. The long, midsummer day was drawing to an end, and the guests excused themselves by saying they wanted to begin their journeys home while it was still light outside. The prior left first with the Sieur Dupin; Louis and Marguerite together escorted their other guests to the entrance to Narbonne. The couple returned to the estate's main lodging as the shadows lengthened and inevitably fell into a strained conversation. Alone on the second floor in the room where the banquet had taken place, Louis approached his wife for an embrace, but she rejected his advance, chastising him instead for having taken a second wife. She told him she was willing to help extricate him from the Auxerre imbroglio if he would "conduct himself in a more orderly manner in the future." He asked where she had learned of his bigamous marriage, without admitting that the report was true. She did not divulge her source, and Louis refused to acknowledge his misadventure. He began to fear that she would have him arrested during the night or the following day for his alleged violation of their marriage. A witness to the encounter, Marguerite's maidservant Catherine Lemoyne, added that the accusations between the spouses had flown both ways. According to her, Louis had initially accused his wife of infidelity, charging that she had slept with Prior Charost. His wife then responded that if she had two men, he had two women, and launched into her accusation of bigamy.

The couple was unable to resolve their differences that evening. Louis, weary from his journey and wary of his wife, retreated to their bedroom, a large space on the first floor of the home between the kitchen and a smaller room near the staircase where their two children normally slept. The room was furnished with a tapestry, a mirror, a table, and a bed, all purchased in Valençay a decade earlier at the time of their wedding. Above the chimney was a large picture "representing the creation of the world and the animals," an image perhaps intended in happier days to encourage the couple to reproduce. Marguerite, clearly upset, withdrew to a room on the second floor, above the kitchen, and had their children, now nine and four years old, brought to sleep with her. While it was the middle of summer, she ordered her maidservant to light a fire in the room, claiming she was cold and feeling ill. Marguerite and her children then lay down to sleep; they may have been joined by two of her servants, although the evidence regarding the maids' sleeping arrangements that evening is contradictory. Marguerite Mercier, another maidservant and goddaughter to Marguerite Chauvelin, slipped out briefly to bar the front gate, although she did not lock it. The residents of Narbonne then settled in for the night.

In the two years that followed, a battery of magistrates and investigators from the Berry to Paris spent countless hours attempting to determine what transpired next. Not surprisingly, there was little about that dark, quiet, late summer night that went uncontested. Louis claimed that he got up at one point during the evening only to find his wife blocking the way out of the house, but Marguerite asserted that she never left her second-floor chamber once she and her children had lain down to sleep. Their daughter remembered that from behind the locked door where she lay in bed she heard a man pleading for his life. A neighbor reported that gunshots fired from the estate shattered the early morning calm. The only unanimous point of agreement was that the next morning, when the servants rose to milk the cows, the front gate was open and Louis had disappeared. The lame mare that had accompanied his return was still in the stable, along with some pistols and a coat he had left there the night before. No one knew the whereabouts of the master of the house.

Life went on. The servants attended to their morning chores. Around ten A.M. Nicholas Mercier, father of the maidservant and goddaughter Marguerite, stopped by the estate while collecting tithes for the parish priest in Jeu-Malloches. There he found Marguerite Chauvelin calmly eating lunch; the two had a brief, pleasant exchange, after which Mercier declined the lady's invitation to dine in the kitchen with his daughter. But over the course of the next several days, word began to circulate of the lord of Narbonne's mysterious disappearance. His friend Préville, for instance, inquired after his health when Louis failed to show up for the hunt they had discussed the previous day. The maidservants may have begun to speculate out loud; several days after the feast, Nicholas Mercier claimed to have seen numerous bloodstains on the floor of the room where Louis had slept the night of his return. Some said that the lady of Narbonne had been seen at the well washing out bloody rags several days after the feast. Soon a local rumor arose that a corpse, naked and covered with bayonet wounds, had been found in a ditch near the estate. Others claimed that Louis' severed head had been tossed into the woods not far from Narbonne. Less than three weeks after the night of August 15, people from Luçay to Châtillon were convinced that the Sieur de Narbonne had met an untimely end, most likely at the hands of his wife.

It is not difficult to understand the spread of such grisly tales. The northwestern corner of the Berry, geographically and economically isolated from surrounding regions, was a closed community where news and gossip traveled fast. Stories about local notables who controlled important rights to farmland, firewood, fishing, and hunting held a special interest for peasants and administrators throughout the area. Furthermore, Marguerite

Chauvelin had been the topic of wagging tongues for two decades. Born and raised in Paris, she was an outsider who had inherited a position of local importance. She had separated from her first husband before his death in 1685. A decade later, in the continued absence of her second husband, her relationship with the Prior Charost had been the subject of salacious speculation throughout the area. If the rumors were true, the prior would have been in violation of his vows of chastity, making the tale of adultery even more intriguing. Nor was this the first time such tales had circulated; the previous winter, when Louis had failed to make his usual appearance at Narbonne after the fall military campaigns, gossipmongers insinuated that the lusty couple had plotted and carried out his assassination. These theories had been silenced when Louis briefly returned to Narbonne in May 1697, but his sudden disappearance the following August renewed the old suspicions. Creditors in Jeu, Luçay, and Valençay, and peasants who leased land and other seigneurial rights from Narbonne, may have been only too content to repeat these scurrilous charges while sitting around their nighttime hearths.

Whispered rumors soon became *bruit public*, or public noise. Marguerite swore before the Luçay judge that sometime between August 16 and September 5, a secretary and minor legal official named Louis Breton had asserted in public in Luçay that she had killed Louis and disposed of the body. Other "calumniators" as yet unknown to her were also spreading similarly vicious lies, she alleged. Who were they? Breton worked in the *siège présidial*, or royal judicial office, of the town of Châtillon-sur-Indre, located about thirteen miles southwest of Narbonne. Marguerite suspected that his rumor-mongering in Luçay had been at the behest of his superiors at Châtillon who had a long-standing rivalry with the family of the Prior Charost. One of those feuding officers, François Morin, Sieur de la Tremblaye, was present at a summer fair in Châtillon on September 5, where he heard many people speculating about the rumored demise of Marguerite's husband. The crowd was crying for vengeance, he claimed, and in a matter of such importance it was incumbent upon him to request a judicial investigation into the assassination of Louis de la Pivardière.

It was not immediately evident why the royal judges of Châtillon would investigate a criminal matter at Narbonne. Precedent and convenience suggested that any criminal affair on the estate should be handled by the nearby seigneurial court of the Count of Luçay, to whom Louis had sworn fealty soon after his marriage to Marguerite a decade earlier. Although royal ordinances enacted by Louis XIV fortified the jurisdictional claims of the king's regional magistrates in Châtillon and elsewhere over those of the ancient, more local, seigneurial judges, Narbonne was situated at a significant distance from the two closest royal judicial seats in Châtillon and in Romorantin. The king's magistrates in those two towns had been content during the 1680s and 1690s to allow the seigneurial judge of Luçay to preside over legal matters that had arisen at remote Narbonne. The de facto jurisdiction of the Luçay official may explain why Breton, the Châtillon secretary, appeared in Luçay to make public accusations against Marguerite; the Châtillon judges may have been trying to push the seigneurial judge into an investigation of the murder.

Morin, thirty-two years old, was the *substitut du procureur générale du Roi*, or the officer assigned to represent the interests of the king and the public in the jurisdiction of Châtillon. He was obligated by royal law to request an investigation into an alleged homicide. But he also had a personal motive that stemmed from decades of dynastic rivalry among the officers of the Châtillon court. A generation earlier in 1662, his father had sought the highest judicial post in the Châtillon *présidial*. He lost his bid, however, to the father of the prior of Miséray after a protracted court battle in which the presiding magistrates ordered Morin's father to pay two hundred livres in damages and legal expenses to the prior's father. The bad blood between the two clans flared again twenty years later when the senior Charost died, leaving the post vacant. Although Morin sought the job his father had failed to obtain, the position was eventually awarded to another Charost, Jean-Baptiste André, the older brother of the prior of Miséray. By 1697, the conflict had cooled somewhat. Lesser Châtillon officials sought patronage from both clans without overt fear of retribution; Breton, for example, was a second nephew of the Prior Charost. Furthermore, Morin was a friend of the Sieur de Séguier, who had married Marguerite's eldest daughter by her first marriage in the late 1680s; at one level this friendship made it less likely he would pursue a case that might harm his friend's in-laws. But the old wounds, festering just below the surface, had never completely healed. The news of an assassination at Narbonne that allegedly involved a member of the Charost clan inevitably drew Morin's interest.

After hearing the rumors circulating at the fair on September 5, Morin, acting on behalf of the Crown and the public interest, filed a request to investigate the disappearance of Pivardière with seventy-four-year-old Jean Bonnet, Sieur de Bigorne, a junior magistrate in the Châtillon court. Bonnet, who had spent his judicial career in Châtillon under the elder Charost and his oldest son, also had reason to pursue a vendetta against the prior's family. He had tangled with Charost père and fils in a number of lawsuits over four decades, and may have also unsuccessfully sought the post of *lieutenant général,* or senior magistrate at Châtillon in 1662 and again twenty years later. Morin and Bonnet thus found themselves united in their long-standing hostility toward the Charost clan; it was not surprising that Morin selected Bonnet over the other judges in the Châtillon court to pursue the case. Over the next two years, however, as events in the Pivardière affair unfolded, both

Morin and Bonnet would claim that they had undertaken the investigation purely out of professional obligation. They repeatedly denied that the vicious family feuds over the benefits of royal office in the Châtillon *présidial* had prompted them to take a lead role in an affair they would normally have left to the local seigneurial judge.

In spite of their assertions, the nature of Old Regime criminal procedure cast doubt on their claims of impartiality. Louis XIV had introduced a policing bureau in Paris and other major cities of the realm at the start of his reign, but the Crown lacked the resources and the manpower to police the majority of French men and women who lived outside the main towns. Without a force to collect evidence and eyewitness testimony about a crime, the Crown relied on an inquisitorial approach in which the magistrates themselves gathered evidence before passing judgment. Furthermore, judges were not required to notify suspects of the charges against them, nor were they obliged to disclose other testimony or evidence to witnesses under examination. Questioning took place in secret, and witnesses and accused individuals were not permitted to have attorneys present during examination. In some circumstances, magistrates could authorize the use of torture to obtain relevant information. No transcripts were made during official court sessions, and judges did not have to publish a legal rationale for their verdicts. When one remembers that Old Regime judges obtained their positions by purchasing them from the Crown, regardless of their legal education or experience at the bar, the entire procedure appears corrupt by today's standards.

In our system, of course, any individual is innocent until proven guilty, and the burden falls on the state to prove the guilt of the accused. By contrast, in seventeenth-century France, religion, custom, and theory largely supported the notion that the monarchy's primary obligation was to maintain order throughout the realm, rather than respect what we call human rights. Memories of the murderous religious wars of the sixteenth century, and the bloody tax riots and troubling vagabondage of the seventeenth, reinforced the idea among elites that individual rights were less important than a commitment to public order. It would be wrong to think that the Crown was blind to questions of judicial abuse; kings and ministers during the sixteenth and seventeenth centuries enacted reforms with the aim of providing fair, uniform rulings across the kingdom. The ordinances issued throughout this period directed royal judges to presume neither guilt nor innocence; they were to undertake their investigations in an impartial effort to discover the truth of each affair. The state insisted, at least on paper, that holders of judicial office have appropriate legal training. The criminal ordinance of August 1670, which remained the fundamental criminal law code in France until the Revolution, contained provisions that prevented magistrates from using the law to pursue private objectives.

In spite of these efforts, many of the king's subjects at the end of the seventeenth century were cynical about the motives of the king's magistrates. In 1670, one legal scholar asked to participate in that year's rewriting of the criminal code noted that "the magistrates were constituted to serve and protect the people, but at present it seems that the people serve them, as sources of income to be exploited." A decade or two later, a leading Burgundian magistrate, after the adoption of the criminal ordinance, offered a similarly candid assessment of the legal establishment's failings: "Few judges truly make an effort to carry out their duties in a commendable fashion. Some neglect them absolutely and completely lack any of the qualities they should display. Among those who make an effort to demonstrate their competence and their knowledge, the majority do so mostly out of self-interest or ambition. . . . They harvest nothing but a false honor that fades as quickly as a blossom, or dissipates like the wind or a puff of smoke."

As if to reinforce these critiques, a notorious case unfolded at the same time as the Pivardière affair. In late 1698, near the town of Mantes, halfway between Paris and Rouen, the son of a local nobleman who had been banished from the region for loose morals and theft returned illegally to his family's estate. The local magistrates seized him and hanged him on a tree outside his father's estate, then pursued his eighty-two-year-old father in part to satisfy the son's debts and in part on a dubious, ten-year-old theft charge. The old man's daughter appealed her father's case to the Parlement in Paris, but before the high court could halt the local investigation, the father was tried, convicted, and hanged in the town square of Mantes. After his execution, it came to light that the judges had long coveted his land, located adjacent to their own property, and had attempted to seize it once they had executed him. In this instance Parlement corrected the wrong, sentencing the corrupt judges of Mantes to restore the family property and pay heavy penalties for their actions. But this decision could not bring the elderly gentleman back to life, and the calculating self-interest with which the provincial judges had acted did little to inspire confidence in the kingdom's judiciary.

This understandable mistrust of the royal magistrature was a backdrop to the Châtillon investigation into the murder of Louis de la Pivardière in the fall of 1697. The complaint Morin gave to Bonnet on September 5 contained two major allegations, both of them leveled against Marguerite. Bonnet and Morin could not name the Prior Charost as a suspect; as a man of the cloth, he was subject to ecclesiastical law, rather than the king's criminal ordinance.

The investigating magistrates alleged that Marguerite's supposed infidelities, her *mauvaise conduite*, literally her "bad conduct," had driven her husband away from Narbonne many years before. Second, she had arranged for the murder of her husband on the night of August 15, 1697; this latter charge, if proven, could result in her execution. Bonnet also authorized the publication of a *monitoire*, a controversial procedure that called for local parish priests to announce the criminal investigation during three consecutive Sunday services, each time stating that it was the Christian obligation of parishioners with knowledge of the affair to make it known to the priest. The cleric, in turn, would pass the information on to the investigating magistrate. Bonnet's decision to publicize the criminal allegations from local pulpits added to the notoriety of the case.

On September 6, three weeks after the supposed crime, Bonnet and several Châtillon *huissiers* (low-level court employees who provided manual labor and other menial services) traveled to Jeu-Malloches, where they heard testimony of the bizarre events at Narbonne the night of the alleged assassination. Bonnet interviewed commoners who lived in the village of Jeu, but he did not venture into the countryside to speak with any of the local notables who had attended the feast at Narbonne the day of the alleged murder. Some informants insisted that the prior and his valets had murdered Louis in his sleep while Marguerite looked on. None of the fifteen individuals whom Bonnet interviewed, however, had actually witnessed the murder, nor did any of them know the location of the corpse. Nevertheless, Jean Bonnet issued a decree calling for the arrest and detention of Marguerite, her children by Louis, and the maidservants. He and his men then returned to Châtillon without traveling the extra half mile from Jeu to Narbonne to inspect the alleged crime scene, as the 1670 criminal ordinance prescribed. Bonnet later claimed that they avoided Narbonne because they did not have enough manpower to arrest Marguerite and her children and servants.

Nine days later, on September 16, a full month after the alleged murder, Bonnet sent approximately eight huissiers back to Narbonne in search of Marguerite. When the squadron arrived at the estate, neither she nor her children were there. In her absence, she had left the two maidservants to tend the animals and maintain the gardens. Only one of the adolescent maidservants, Catherine Lemoyne, remained within the walls of the estate. The huissiers took her into custody. In addition, the men confiscated the live-stock not taken out to pasture, all the furniture within the main residence, and all other movable items of value on the premises, including grain stores and other foodstuffs. They hauled the trea-sure back to Châtillon, allegedly to prevent the estate from being pillaged while it was abandoned. Marguerite's supporters, how-ever, argued that this justification was a flimsy excuse for an act of outright theft. Either way, the squadron from Châtillon once again left Narbonne without having undertaken a formal investi-gation of the crime scene.

It was not until September 28 that Bonnet actually traveled to Narbonne with a recording secretary to inspect the physical evi-dence related to the supposed assassination. This time, when the Châtillon judge and his men passed through the gates of the estate that just six weeks earlier had hosted an exuberant late summer gathering, they found a compound empty of humans, animals, and the amenities of everyday life. The doors and even the hardware that had attached them to the house had been stripped from the main residence. They filed through the open door frame into the nearly empty first-floor bedroom where Louis had slept the night of August 15. Curiously, they were escorted by Nicholas Mercier, the local peasant who had chatted amiably with Mar-guerite Chauvelin the morning after the supposed murder. At Marguerite's request, he had often rendered "various services" on the estate. It is therefore initially puzzling that he would aid the Châtillon magistrates in their investigation. Perhaps paternal con-cern trumped his loyalty to the mistress of Narbonne. It is also possible that he aided the judges as part of a plan to help his daughter; if he could divert their attention long enough, she could escape.

Whatever Nicholas Mercier's true sentiments toward Marguerite Chauvelin, when he led Bonnet and his underlings into the deserted château he was at great pains to provide evidence that would incriminate her. During a visit to Narbonne several days after the alleged murder, he remembered noticing bloodstains on the floor of the room where Louis had slept. Now, six weeks later, he showed the magistrates several sizable stains on the floor at the foot of the bed, one of which was supposedly still blood-colored; others appeared to have been scrubbed. The bed itself was a wooden frame that supported a quantity of straw "still newly beaten, and still filled with much grain." Upon closer inspection, Bonnet and his men claimed to observe a number of dried bloodstains in the straw. Mercier then led them down to the cellar of the main residence, where they saw an empty pit rumored to have harbored the body of Louis after his murder. Such subterranean ditches, however, were also common storage spaces for salt, a vital component of any larder at the time. Bonnet and his troop then signed the written account of these investigations prepared by his secretary, and the men impounded the supposedly bloodstained bed of straw, which they transported back to Châtillon to be maintained as evidence in the case. Bonnet appears not to have considered that the bloodstains might have been planted in the bedchamber at some point between the night of August 15 and six weeks later, when he actually investigated the crime scene.

Although Bonnet and Morin now had one maidservant and a handful of transcripts in their custody, they needed more "evidence" to prove their case against Marguerite. One missing link was Nicolas Mercier's daughter Marguerite, who had been obtaining provisions from the miller when the huissiers had seized Catherine Lemoyne in mid-September. When the young Mercier returned to Narbonne later that day, she found the gates sealed by magisterial decree; she learned from neighbors, and perhaps her father, that her fellow maidservant, along with most of the estate's goods, had been dragged off to Châtillon. Realizing that the

Châtillon judges would look for her next, she fled northward to the town of Romorantin, where she found shelter with an uncle who was a vintner. Her refuge did not last long, however; within two weeks, her presence became known to the Dame de la Fosse, a Romorantin resident who was Louis' stepsister. In early October, La Fosse sent word of Mercier's whereabouts to the Châtillon judges; her actions suggested that she hoped the maidservant's testimony would contradict the rumors that Louis had perished at the hands of his wife and thereby end the dishonor threatening the Pivardière family. Upon their arrival in Romorantin, Bonnet and his agents met the Dame de la Fosse, who led them to the fugitive maidservant. In the presence of Bonnet, La Fosse pointedly said to Marguerite Mercier, "Tell me the truth. As far as you know, has your master been killed?" The maidservant responded that he had not. Despite this denial, Bonnet arrested Mercier and carted her back to the Châtillon prison, where she joined Lemoyne.

In early October 1697, a month after they had begun their investigations and almost two months after the alleged assassination, the Châtillon judges or their representatives had traveled three times to Narbonne and its surroundings, and at least once to Romorantin. They had spoken with a few dozen individuals who had no firsthand knowledge of the murder. They had carted away much of what was not bolted down at the estate back to Châtillon in the name of their investigation. The prime suspect, Marguerite Chauvelin, had gone missing, and outside of a dubious pile of stained straw they had no direct evidence of any wrong-doing. There was no trace of a corpse. Morin and Bonnet would need more evidence, ideally a confession or testimony from eyewitnesses to the murder, in order to make the charge stick. Under the criminal ordinance, a sentence of death handed down in a subaltern court like that of Châtillon was automatically appealed to the Parlement in Paris. In the high court, if more than two out of a panel of ten judges dissented from the death verdict, a less punitive sentence would be registered. The suit might even be dismissed and disciplinary action taken against the lower court magistrates who had mishandled the affair. Faced with a case that was, for the moment, less than compelling, they turned their attention to the two adolescent girls languishing in the Châtillon prison.

By the late summer of 1697, Marguerite Mercier, the goddaughter of Marguerite Chauvelin, was several months into her second period of service at Narbonne. The first one had begun in the early 1690s when her father placed her on the estate, perhaps when Mercier was less than ten years old, and ended in 1695 when she went to work for another local notable. She therefore knew Marguerite, Louis, and the long-standing local suspicions harbored by others in the area about the masters of Narbonne. Catherine Lemoyne, on the other hand, had been in the service of Marguerite Chauvelin for only a few months. She had never seen Louis in person prior to his return to Narbonne on August 15. Neither girl could read nor write, and it is unlikely that they had traveled much beyond their corner of the Berry. Their life experiences had hardly prepared them for the highly contested role they were about to play in the murder investigation.

In early October 1697 they found themselves in the Châtillon jailhouse. Old Regime prisons attached to legal courts were intended to house suspects and witnesses while their cases were being adjudicated. They were not sites of incarceration for convicted criminals, and in principle detainees were treated humanely, although funds and facilities were often lacking. In Châtillon, the courthouse jail was located in an old castle that housed many other municipal and royal functions. The prison consisted of two main rooms on the ground floor of the building, the larger of which was occupied by the jailer and his wife. The maidservants were held, unchained, in this room, while male prisoners were kept in the adjoining chamber. A smaller, harsher confinement cell, illuminated by a small opening the size of a fist, was located in the castle ramparts. The jailor and his spouse, who had been appointed to their position by the elder brother of the Prior Charost in 1691, provided them with rudimentary meals, as the king's ordinance required. While they were imprisoned, the maidservants sold their hair to wigmakers, then used the money to purchase more food as well as sandals, leggings, and mittens as the weather grew colder. In addition to the jailer and his spouse, they had contact with the huissiers who had brought them to Châtillon, and who were responsible for overseeing the well-being of the young women while they were being held.

The key figures in their lives, however, were Bonnet and Morin, the Châtillon judges who had tracked them down and now relentlessly interrogated them about their missing master and his wife. While transcripts of these interrogations have not survived, extensive summaries of their contents in contemporaneous accounts allow us to piece together the servants' encounters with the magistrates. Between them, the two adolescents underwent ten interrogations in the Châtillon prison between late September 1697 and early January of the following year. Each interrogation was a confrontation between one of the young women — imprisoned, illiterate, and uncertain of her fate — and the robed Bonnet, accompanied by one or more huissiers and a secretary who recorded the exchanges. Following the royal ordinance regulating these matters, Bonnet and his secretary sat behind a raised table, while Lemoyne or Mercier, surrounded by armed guards, sat on a small stool facing the authoritative magistrate. The secretary recorded the questions asked of the servants, as well as their answers.

Even before the servants were arrested, rumors swirled about their testimony. Many neighbors told Bonnet on September 6 that the servants had claimed to be eyewitnesses to Louis' murder. Upon her arrest in Romorantin, however, Marguerite Mercier insisted that her master was still alive. During her first interrogation on September 17, the day after she was taken into custody, Catherine Lemoyne repeated the same story: She had neither seen nor heard anything after going to bed the night of August 15. She knew nothing about any murder, and her mistress was innocent. But Lemoyne underwent a second interrogation on September 27, after spending ten days in the Châtillon prison, and, at that point, her story began to change. She had not seen her master dead, but she had heard a rifle shot during the evening. She had found bloody linens in the cellar the next day and had seen her mistress washing them by hand several days later. In addition, on August 17 or thereabouts, she had overheard the prior say to Marguerite, "We must get out of here; if we're caught, we'll be sunk." And during her third interrogation on October 4, she painted a bloody picture of the crime scene, claiming to have seen her master's body, draped in bloody linen, lying lifeless on his bed; the bedchamber, in the words of the interrogation transcript, was "inundated" with his blood.

Marguerite Mercier underwent her first interrogation by Jean Bonnet on October 9, after her fellow servant Lemoyne had already been questioned three times. Mercier also told a different story during examination by the Châtillon judges. Under Bonnet's questioning, she claimed to have been an eyewitness to the murder. Her godmother had entered the bedroom where Louis was sleeping with two valets in the service of the prior. One of the two men fired a shot into the sleeping man's body, while the other ran him through several times with a saber. Awakened by the assault, Louis pleaded with his wife for mercy, offering to give her gold and silver in exchange for his life. (Given Louis' chronic need for funds, and his wife's knowledge of his financial straits, this was unlikely.) Not only did Mercier's mistress not grant him a reprieve, according to the maidservant, but she administered the final blow, grabbing the sword out of the hands of his assailants and running him through herself. By mid-October, the Châtillon judges claimed to have both an eyewitness to the murder and to the immediate aftermath of the deadly assault.

What might account for the changes in the maidservants' story? One theory at the time, not surprisingly advanced by the judges themselves, was that under oath the servants were forced to tell the truth about the events at Narbonne on the evening of August 15. In the judges' view, the plot that Marguerite had ordered her servants not to reveal was inevitably brought to light when subjected to investigative scrutiny. A counter-theory, however, held that once in their control, Bonnet and Morin browbeat the defenseless girls into concocting an eyewitness account of a murder that had never transpired. Catherine Lemoyne, for example, when asked later why she had testified to having seen Louis' bloodied corpse lying in his bed in Narbonne, responded that she had never made such a statement. Her actual testimony to Bonnet was irrelevant, however, because she claimed he had the secretary write down anything he wished. Furthermore, it was alleged that Louis Breton, the secretary who recorded the interrogations, and who had spread rumors in Luçay in the days following August 15, was suspect. The year before he had been condemned by the prior's brother to pay a substantial fine "for irreverences he [Breton] had committed," a judgment that would have predisposed him to assist in building a case against the prior. The maidservant Lemoyne, unable to read the transcript of the interrogation, had no means to prevent the collaboration between the allegedly corrupt judges and the compromised secretary that resulted in the falsification of her testimony.

Through the end of October 1697, one consistent aspect of both servants' accounts was the absence of the prior from the murder scene. Although the servants allegedly testified that the prior's valets had participated in Louis' murder, Bonnet and Morin had as yet no solid evidence that implicated the prior, scion of their enemies, in the alleged murder. They did, however, possess testimony from those who lived near Narbonne that Marguerite and the prior had long been engaged in an illicit love affair in violation of his clerical vows. Meanwhile, the prior, like Louis and his wife, had vanished from the Berry and was therefore unable to defend himself against any accusations.

Sometime in early November, the Châtillon magistrates contacted the archbishopric of Bourges, the ecclesiastical seat charged with administrative oversight of the priory of Miséray. Bourges, like many other important French religious centers, maintained its own *officialité*, or judicial unit, whose charge was to enforce canon law and investigate potential violations by Catholic clerics. On November 20, Maître François Jacquemet, a *vicegérent*, or church magistrate, arrived in Châtillon-sur-Indre. That day, Bonnet and Morin summarized their findings in the murder investigation and showed Jacquemet the Lemoyne and Mercier interrogation transcripts. The next day, Jacquemet issued a decree in the name of the archbishop of Bourges calling for the arrest and interrogation of the prior on charges of illicit sexual activity and participation in the murder of Pivardière. The following day, November 22, in the presence of Bonnet, Jacquemet conducted his own interrogation of the maidservants.

The transcripts of these sessions, and of several more conducted in December and January, rewrote the murder scene yet again. Lemoyne now claimed that the prior had been present in Louis' bedchamber when she had glimpsed her master's dead body. Mercier, who had already testified to being an eyewitness to the murder, alleged that it was the prior, and not her mistress, who had yanked the sword from the hands of the valets and dealt the mortal blow to Louis. In these new interrogations, Lemoyne and Mercier claimed that promises of bribes from the prior and threats from their mistress had prevented them from fully describing the prior's role in their initial interrogations. In addition, Mercier told the ecclesiastical judge that she had recently become very sick. Lying on her deathbed, preparing to face the "ultimate tribunal" in the afterlife, she was informed by her confessor that there would be no hope of eternal grace unless she revealed everything she knew about the events at Narbonne the night of August 15. She had authorized her confessor in the event of her death to divulge the full story to the ecclesiastical officials, thereby ensuring a clear conscience. Miraculously, or so the interrogation transcript implied, she had survived to provide this new, revised version that directly implicated the prior of Miséray in the murder of her master.

Thus, by the beginning of 1698, Bonnet and Morin, with the help of the Bourges ecclesiastical magistrate, had provided a full-blown account of the murder of a provincial gentleman. Based primarily on their investigations in and around Narbonne and on the testimony of the two maidservants in their custody, the Châtillon judges alleged that Marguerite and the prior had become lovers during Louis' lengthy wartime absences. When they learned of his impending return to Narbonne in mid-August 1697, they concocted a plan to murder him, which they set into motion after the guests had left Narbonne the evening of August 15. Marguerite put her children to bed that night in an upstairs room where she could lock them in, away from where they usually slept. Once the children fell asleep, around eleven in the evening, Marguerite and her servant and goddaughter descended the staircase and passed silently into the courtyard, taking care not to wake the sleeping Louis. Marguerite had previously sent Catherine Lemoyne, whom she had known only a few months and did not trust, off to a neighboring estate, asking her to fetch eggs for the morning meal, even though it was almost midnight. Outside, Marguerite and Mercier met up with the prior and two of his valets, who were armed with a rifle and a saber. The murder party then entered the kitchen, lit a candle, and quietly opened the door that led from the kitchen to the room where the master of the house lay sleeping. One of the valets pulled aside the bed curtain and, noting that Louis lay sleeping in an awkward position for him to fire, dragged a bureau up to the bed and clambered on top of it to shoot a bullet into the sleeping man's head. The shot bloodied Louis' face but did not kill him, so the other valet began to run him through with the sword. Louis, struggling to resist the assault, repeatedly cried for mercy, spurting blood onto the bedding and the floor. Finally the prior, tiring of the struggle, grabbed the sword from his servant and administered the final blow himself. Marguerite Mercier cried out in horror at the attack, but threats from her godmother and the prior that she would meet the same fate silenced her.

Soon after Louis died, Catherine Lemoyne, who had heard shots and screams from the château as she returned with the eggs, burst into the room. Under pain of immediate death, she was sworn to secrecy, and she stood silently by while the prior's man-servants carried off the bloodied corpse. The body removed, Marguerite fetched a bucket of ashes with which to scrub the blood-stained floor. She told her servants to remove the crimsoned linen and straw to the cellar, and she had clean bedding and new sheets arranged on the wooden bed frame. In their haste, however, the maidservants failed to remove all the blood-stained straw or erase all the traces of the murder from the wooden floor, thus leaving the telltale remnants that Bonnet and his men supposedly discovered six weeks later. About two hours after they had left with the dead body, the prior's valets returned to Narbonne, where Marguerite herself prepared a meal of scrambled eggs for them. The mistress of the manor joined them for the meal, purportedly laughing and regaling the prior's men with stories. The meal over, the valets went back to the priory and Marguerite Chauvelin and her maidservants went off to bed for a few hours until daybreak, when they would be called upon to explain the absence of the allegedly murdered nobleman.

This grisly tale of premeditated murder held sway in the province until early January, when the Châtillon judges suddenly confronted a substantial challenge: a seemingly resurrected Louis de la Pivardière. Sometime around the tenth of the month, a man claiming to be the missing Berrichon nobleman surprisingly turned up at Narbonne. He found the compound in ruins, further deteriorated since the late September raid ordered by the Châtillon judges. On January 13 he made his way to Romorantin, the seat of another provincial magistrate who ranked slightly higher than Bonnet in the royal judiciary. In response to a plea filed by Marguerite with the high court in Paris the previous September, this judge, Jean LeComte, had been instructed to conduct an inquiry into the "life and existence" of Louis. Until the latter appeared on his doorstep in January, however, the magistrate had done little to fulfill his mandate. Now he began to question his mysterious visitor about his background, his marriage, and the evening of August 15 and its aftermath. After this recitation, the judge took the man into protective custody and set out from Romorantin at the head of a party of armed men whose task it was to usher the missing nobleman around the region. The mounted guard included a Châtillon notary sympathetic to the Charost clan named Pierre Sousmain, both of the prior of Miséray's younger brothers, and a secretary and attorney from the Romorantin court. Sousmain paid for their lodging and meals with funds he had received from the Charost clan. This group of armed horsemen made a considerable impact as it rode around the countryside in search of witnesses who had known the absent lord of Narbonne; the resources devoted to this expedition reinforced the importance of the affair and buttressed the argument that the man at the center of the entourage was the missing Berrichon aristocrat.

In the four or five days following Louis' arrival in Romorantin, the group ushered the newcomer, now decked out in appropriate finery, to several familiar locations. His half brother's widow, the Dame de la Fosse (who had led Bonnet to Marguerite Mercier's hiding place the previous September), identified him as her brother-in-law, as did several other notables in the town. In Luçay-le-Mâle, north of Narbonne, the Sieur Bailly, the seigneurial judge who normally held jurisdiction over criminal investigations at Narbonne, recognized the man as Louis. He was joined by his secretary, other local gentlemen, the town priest, who had previously been the *curé* in Jeu-Malloches, often administering the sacraments to Louis, and several merchants, all of whom signed statements of recognition. In Valençay, the Romorantin magistrate led his retinue to the local Ursuline convent, where Louis' two sisters identified him as their missing brother; other nuns who had seen him over the years also identified him as the missing nobleman. Several Valençay merchants with whom Louis had done business for years before his disappearance, as well as two surgeons, swore to the judge that the man he had in tow had long been known to them as Louis de la Pivardière.

Finally, on Saturday, January 18, the Romorantin judge's procession arrived in Jeu-Malloches, the little town a kilometer away from Narbonne where residents had known Louis as a local seigneur before his disappearance. The magistrate and Sousmain took the man to the town's tavern. As locals emerged from the village church after Vespers, they stopped by the inn, where many of them recognized their supposedly deceased neighbor. The Pivardière entourage also enlisted some villagers to tell nearby residents not in town for church services about Louis' return. Nicolas Mercier, for example, was sent to alert the Sieur de Préville, Louis' longtime hunting companion, of his return. Préville, incredulous, hurried to town with two other acquaintances of Louis, all of whom identified the man as their absent friend and neighbor. Other dinner guests present at Narbonne the night of August 15 also confirmed Louis' existence in Jeu that day. A valet in the service of Louis' elder half brother brought Marie de la Pivardière, his eldest daughter, to the Jeu tavern to identify her father. Although the girl had previously claimed she had heard her father's death cries the night of August 15, she now recognized the man in the Romorantin magistrate's custody as her parent. By the end of the day, approximately sixty people had signed statements identifying the man in the cabaret as the missing lord of Narbonne.

The Romorantin judge's retinue was not the only party in Jeu on January 18, though; by then, word of the identification procession led by LeComte had reached Châtillon. Gathering several of the huissiers who had raided Narbonne four months earlier, Jean Bonnet hurried to Jeu-Malloches to challenge the proceedings. He also sent word to the ecclesiastical judge François Jacquemet in Bourges, who met him there. While the man who claimed to be Pivardière was presented to townspeople in the cabaret, these two judges and their men gathered in the nearby presbytery. The two parallel investigations, one convinced that Louis was very much alive, the other determined to prove he was dead, proceeded warily. As the Romorantin judge finished taking testimony, Bonnet and Jacquemet interrogated some of his witnesses about their sworn statements, even threatening some of those who had identified the man in custody as Louis with arrest on charges of perjury. They may have even sent some of their men to spy on the Romorantin magistrate's activities. For his part, it is possible that LeComte pressured witnesses into overly hasty affidavits in which they identified the man in his custody as the missing Pivardière.

The best surviving indication of the confusion that day in Jeu-Malloches is an encounter between the ecclesiastical judge Jacquemet and the Jeu parish priest, a man named Pournain who had previously been a monk under the Prior Charost at Miséray. After Vespers, Pournain reported to his superior, Jacquemet, that he had been served with a summons by the Romorantin judge to identify the man claiming to be Louis. Pournain had frequently had disagreements with Marguerite; furthermore, once the Bourges magistrate had indicted the Prior Charost the previous November, Pournain had staked a claim to the benefices accruing from Charost's priory of Miséray. He therefore had every incentive to deny that the man in custody was the missing husband of Marguerite. Nevertheless, when confronted with the individual in the cabaret, Pournain signed a statement saying that he recognized him as Louis. When he returned to the presbytery, however, he expressed his doubts to Jacquemet, indicating that the light in the cabaret had been dim and that he had seen the man only from behind. The ecclesiastical judge berated him for signing a statement in the face of so much uncertainty and subsequently attempted to discount his testimony that day. Had the parish priest been intimidated into recognizing Louis against his will? Did the Bourges judge subsequently doctor his account of this encounter to support his own version of the notorious case? By the end of the day the level of chaos had only increased, in spite of the carefully prepared efforts of Sousmain and LeComte.

The next morning, January 19, the Romorantin judge LeComte, the alleged Louis, and their entourage rode from Jeu to Châtillon-sur-Indre, the headquarters of the judicial investigation. Emboldened by their efforts in Jeu and elsewhere, they intended to confront Marguerite Mercier and Catherine Lemoyne with the man in their custody, in the hope that the girls would identify him as their missing master and effectively end the Châtillon investigation. LeComte, Sousmain, and their group were aware that gaining access to the girls would not be easy and might be illegal; as long as the murder investigation continued, the two servants were the legitimate prisoners of the Châtillon magistrates, held in a guarded prison within the town's main stronghold. To increase their chance of forcing their way into the prison, LeComte and Sousmain sought extra manpower. Outside the town gates they met with the Châtillon *prévôt*, a judicial official below Charost and Bonnet within the town's legal structure. This man, Claude de Laître, supported the Charost clan in the bitter struggle for judicial supremacy in Châtillon. He agreed to order all the huissiers in his charge to help LeComte gain access. Together, this force of more than a dozen armed escorts, with the supposed Louis in their midst, advanced on the jailhouse.

When they reached the main entrance to the castle housing the prison, they found their way blocked by Bonnet and Morin, who had gathered a number of locals to witness the confrontation. Mounted on his horse, the man who was allegedly Louis claimed to recognize Morin, offered him some tobacco, and jauntily asked if Morin remembered him. The Châtillon magistrate responded testily that it was not up to him to make the identification. The Châtillon magistrates then asked their Romorantin counterpart to state who had authorized him to perform judicial functions in their town. LeComte replied that he bore orders from the high court in Paris, which he would show them once admitted to the prison. After further verbal sparring, the Romorantin group, augmented by the Châtillon policing squadron, gained entrance to the castle, perhaps by force; the elderly Bonnet, in his seventies, appears to have been shoved out of the way when he tried to defend the entrance of the prison too vigorously. Inside the castle, in the presence of thirty to forty witnesses, the Romorantin judge interrogated each of the girls separately. To the surprise of the group escorting the missing nobleman, both of them repeated the eyewitness accounts that they had recounted in previous testimony to the Châtillon and Bourges judges. Even more astoundingly, when confronted with the man whom hundreds of other Berrichon residents over the previous week had recognized as the missing lord of Narbonne, Marguerite Mercier and Catherine Lemoyne denied that he was Louis de la Pivardière.

The confrontation at the Châtillon jailhouse is perhaps the most puzzling event in the Pivardière affair save for the alleged murder itself. Until this moment, it had seemed quite likely that the teenage girls had been the victims of coercion on the part of the Châtillon judges, who had held them in prison for several months. Their evolving tale of the murder, which had grown suspiciously more detailed with each retelling, appeared unduly influenced by their captors. The presence of the Romorantin judge, unsympathetic to the murder charge and accompanied by a significant armed force, would seem to have offered a prime opportunity to deny the story they had told under pressure from Bonnet and Morin. Yet they insisted that they had witnessed an assassination, and Marguerite Mercier actually voiced her suspicion that the man presented as Louis de la Pivardière was an impostor. The girls may have stuck to their story out of fear of reprisals from the Châtillon judges once LeComte and his men departed. And Catherine Lemoyne, who had been working at Narbonne for only a short time before Louis' one-day return in August 1697, had almost no memory of the master she met for the first time that day. Her inability to identify him may have been misconstrued as a reaffirmation of the murder. But observers at the Châtillon jailhouse that day, and interested Berrichons following the case, drew another conclusion: They began to suspect that the man who had suddenly reappeared in the Berry in January 1698 was an impostor put up to the task by the desperate Marguerite and her lover, the prior.

The day before in Jeu-Malloches, and elsewhere in the Berry, doubts were whispered. "The light had not been strong in the tavern when I met him," some folks claimed, "and his back had been turned in such a way that I never got a good view of his face." In

Châtillon, an Augustinian monk who had met Louis before the alleged murder testified that the man he saw in January 1698 suspiciously averted his eyes and refused to speak to him. Others asserted that the person they had been asked to identify had worn several outer garments, and even so had seemed smaller and thinner than the local lord and military officer whom they remembered. Some witnesses, when confronted by the powerful Romorantin judge and Louis' armed escort, may have decided it was in their best interest to voice the truths they imagined the judge wished to hear. Others claimed that they had all been the victims of an elaborate hoax staged by Marguerite and the prior's family to raise the murdered Sieur de Narbonne from his grave.

In the Châtillon prison, after the maidservants denied that the man they confronted was their missing master, Morin made an astute demand. He requested that the Romorantin judge release his charge into the custody of the Châtillon judges, so that they could investigate his true identity. If this really was the supposedly murdered nobleman, they wanted to confirm it themselves before dropping their investigation. But LeComte, abetted by the Charost brothers and the Châtillon notary Sousmain, who had stage-managed the procession throughout the Berry, refused this request. LeComte stayed in Romorantin one more day, then headed out of town with his entourage in search of more sworn testimony identifying the missing nobleman. By January 23, perhaps convinced they had enough evidence, or perhaps out of funds to continue housing and displaying his charge, LeComte and Sousmain released the man who claimed to be Louis de la Pivardière on condition that he return to the Berry when summoned. The supposed Pivardière quickly fled the province, while LeComte headed back to Romorantin to finish his paperwork. Bonnet and Morin began their counteroffensive. On January 27, they filed a request with the high court in Paris in which they alleged that LeComte should be relieved of his responsibilities in the case due to procedural violations and jurisdictional transgressions. A few days later, the court agreed to look into their motion and temporarily suspended the Romorantin magistrate from his duties in the affair. LeComte, in turn, filed charges against Bonnet and Morin alleging that they had been conducting a calumnious investigation since the previous September. The initiative of Marguerite and the Charost clan that had looked so promising when Louis returned to the province in mid-January had now lapsed into uncertainty.

⚜

There was more confusion to come. The Prior Charost had been in Paris in late November 1697 on business related to the priory of Miséray when Jacquemet, the ecclesiastical judge from Bourges, had issued a warrant for his arrest. When the January return of the supposed Louis fizzled out in the Berry, failing to exonerate him, the prior laid low, seeking refuge in the ecclesiastical networks of the capital. On February 1, however, with the Châtillon magistrates still vigorously pursuing their murder investigation in the wake of Louis' second disappearance, the Bourges ecclesiastical court rendered a verdict in absentia against the prior, convicting him of violating his vows of chastity with Marguerite and conspiring to murder Louis. On the strength of this sentence, he was pursued in Paris, where he was arrested in mid-February wearing a black habit. His captors hauled him back to Châtillon, where on February 24 Bonnet and Morin imprisoned him in the same facility where they held Marguerite Mercier and Catherine Lemoyne. To complete the humiliation of the prior and his family, Bonnet and Morin mandated that, while incarcerated, he be guarded at all times by a team of three huissiers, and that he wear heavy, abrasive leg irons, like a common criminal.

Having carefully set the stage, the Châtillon magistrates and the Bourges ecclesiastical officials now prepared to bring the imprisoned son of their long-standing enemies before Marguerite's two maidservants, whose responses a month earlier had derailed Louis' triumphant return to the Berry. Both girls had sworn under oath that the prior had participated in the planning and execution of the Pivardière assassination; under French law, they were now required to confront him. When the maidservants saw the prior, their former cleric at Narbonne, however, they did not respond as the Châtillon judges expected. Instead of confirming his part in the murder of their master, they suddenly retracted the entire murder plot that they had affirmed only six weeks earlier. In a tumultuous session, they turned on the Châtillon magistrates, alleging that the judges had bullied them into providing false testimony. Marguerite Mercier, when asked by Bonnet if anyone had threatened her, said, "No, but the fear brought on by being in prison made me say many things [that were untrue]." Catherine Lemoyne, when asked by Bonnet if someone had counseled her how to testify, replied, "It was you who threatened us." Later in the session, when faced with a perjury charge, Lemoyne responded:

> I ask nothing else of the Good Lord, except that he does with me as he wishes. [She heaved a huge sigh, then said she would not sigh anymore.] I laugh at what you're writing, because I know that the Sieur de la Pivardière was here, and that I would have recognized him if I hadn't been threatened, and that because I'm not clever you get me to say whatever you wish.

Only fragments of the transcripts have survived, but one contemporary judge who read them in their entirety said that he had never heard of a "more troubled, or more agitated" confrontation in a criminal case. The maidservants, he noted, when not defiant, turned to despair at their plight; Mercier at one point lamented, "[H]ave pity on me, my Lord, for I am a girl who knows nothing about the world, and if I said anything I did so only out of fear."

The prior, in spite of his ill treatment at the hands of the judges and jail keeper, was alert to the girls' anger and trepidation, as well as the influence he exercised over them as a member of the clergy. He shrewdly drew out the inconsistencies in the girls' account of the supposed murder and its aftermath, helping them make the case that their testimony had been distorted by the abusive magistrates. Bonnet menaced the girls with threats of perjury charges even as his secretary faithfully recorded the answers that undermined the case he had been constructing for almost half a year. Unqualified religious faith, exacting judicial practice, and human inconsistency were all on view in these transactions. The contradictory, complex encounters between the wily prior, the stern magistrate, and the mercurial peasant women underscored the difficulty of determining the truth in this perplexing case.

Bonnet, Morin, and the ecclesiastical judge, huddling after the disastrous session, quickly settled on a course of action. They clapped the prior back in his leg irons and placed each of the maidservants in solitary confinement. Both servants were told that their perjury trials would begin immediately; it is possible they were also threatened with torture, a tactic authorized by the criminal ordinance. Within a week, Mercier and Lemoyne both sent for the magistrate; when Bonnet appeared, they threw themselves at his feet, asking for forgiveness. Then, in front of Bonnet and his secretary, they retracted the retraction they had sworn a week earlier, returning almost word-for-word to the initial tale of adultery, conspiracy, and murder. The Châtillon judges had salvaged the eyewitness testimony to the murder of Louis de la Pivardière, but at what price to their case? By this point, the work of the three main sets of judges investigating the affair, the civil authorities in Châtillon and Romorantin, and the church officials in Bourges, had yielded a maze of contradictory testimony, a good deal of it invalid due to procedural violations. Even worse, the various parties had filed a bewildering number of lawsuits and charges against one another as the investigations had proceeded. Charges of impropriety and bias against the Romorantin judge by his Châtillon counterparts, and charges of incompetence and impropriety by the prior against the Bourges ecclesiastical officials, were added to Marguerite Chauvelin's initial objection that Bonnet and Morin were biased and incompetent.

The maidservants' initial retraction and subsequent about-face took place in the second week of March 1698; the next two months did little to clarify matters. Lemoyne, Mercier, and the prior languished in the Châtillon prison, the latter still bound in heavy chains. The provincial judges continued to file suits against one another disputing issues of jurisdiction and legal procedure. In late May, meanwhile, Marguerite Chauvelin voluntarily incarcerated herself in a Parisian prison that housed individuals awaiting trial in the Parlement. She did so at the suggestion of her powerful relatives in the Parisian legal establishment, who would be able to advocate on her behalf more effectively once she had placed herself in the custody of the high court. Furthermore, the change of venue might put the Châtillon judges back on the defensive.

Hanging over all these machinations was the question of the existence of Louis de la Pivardière. The murder narrative constructed by Bonnet and Morin still stood, even though the Châtillon judges had never found his body, and the eyewitness testimony of the maidservants had been called into question. The doubts about the identity of the man who had appeared in the Berry had only grown after his unsatisfactory reappearance in January. If he was the missing gentleman, why had he fled the province so abruptly and refused to return, when his presence would have immediately exonerated his wife and their friend, the Prior Charost? Were they afraid that further exposure to scrutiny would reveal him as an impostor? In March, the Parlement received a mysterious request from a man somewhere in the provinces who claimed to be the same person who had appeared in the Berry in January. He offered to come to Paris to testify in the affair if the court would grant him safe-conduct; he feared that he would be seized on charges of bigamy while in transit. The court, suspicious of the motives of the man who had hastily fled the Berry when the maidservants had challenged his identity, refused to accede to his wishes. Nevertheless, by the end of spring the tangle of conflicting accusations and lawsuits had grown so great that the high court had no choice but to shift the legal venue to Paris. There the case would be transformed from a confusing provincial conflict to a cause célèbre that would capture the attention of a kingdom obsessed with social status, marital relations, and judicial corruption.

Chapter 3

PRELIMINARY JUDGMENT

*T*he Parlement of Paris was a venerable, multifaceted institution by the end of the seventeenth century. It was the eldest of the twelve parlements, or supreme law courts, in France. By the time of the Pivardière murder trial, the Parisian high court was handling more cases than it would in any other period before the Revolution. When in full session, approximately two hundred seventy magistrates permanently staffed eight chambers and rotated among three others. In addition to its judicial responsibilities, the Paris Parlement and the other high courts in the kingdom played a political role. Although no representative body met in France for almost two centuries before 1789, law and custom required the kings of France to register all new laws with their parlements. If the magistrates determined that a royal decree contradicted previously registered law, any parlement might issue a remonstrance against the new edict. On occasion, during the seventeenth and eighteenth centuries, the judges used this right of remonstrance for thinly veiled political purposes. At the time of the Pivardière affair, a position on one of the Parisian court's benches cost around 100,000 livres, plus yearly fees to the Crown to maintain the post;

only the wealthiest members of the administrative nobility could afford to buy themselves a place on the bench. The potential for corruption was correspondingly higher than in the provinces, but so was the sense of duty to serve God and king; the heightened level of scrutiny focused on the magistrates also acted as a deterrent to judicial abuse.

The courtrooms in which these powerful judges heard cases, and the offices that supported them, were housed in a sprawling complex known as the Palais de Justice, so named because it was the royal residence where the king had personally governed justice to his subjects until the second half of the fourteenth century. Located on the Ile de la Cité, only steps away from Notre Dame Cathedral, the Palais housed the Sainte Chapelle, a glorious example of High Gothic church architecture and stained glasswork, constructed by King Louis IX in the thirteenth century to serve as his private chapel. It would be a mistake, however, to think of the Palais at the end of the seventeenth century as a solemn, monastic environment cordoned off from the chaos of everyday life in continental Europe's largest city. The concentration of judicial, financial, and administrative functions within its walls drew people from all over Paris and beyond. Men and women involved in lawsuits found themselves in noisy consultation with lawyers or scribes who set up shop within the court's chambers, or in open spaces and hallways just outside the courtrooms. These wealthy judges, lawyers, and litigants in turn attracted hawkers, street traders, and other merchants to the Palais; one can find evidence that they had been granted specific places within the complex to set up shop by the early 1400s.

By the 1600s, the primary sites of commerce within the Palais were a long, covered east-west corridor known as the *galerie* and the *cour du Palais*, the compound's primary open area situated at its eastern end. Here one could purchase ribbons, hats, mirrors, dolls, toys, jewelry, clocks, and many other items. Legal advice and

Abraham Bosse, *La Galerie du Palais*, engraved in the 1630s. This print, itself no doubt for sale within the Palais, portrays the world of commerce, rumor, and chance encounter that existed within the walls of the high court at the time of the Pivardière affair. Note the bookseller's stall on the left. Museum of Fine Arts, Boston. The Elizabeth Day McCormick Collection. Photograph © Museum of Fine Arts, Boston.

financial transactions were available for a price, as were some of the women who worked in the stalls or mingled among the crowds. One late-sixteenth-century observer, reflecting on the diversity and intensity of activity within the Palais' walls, commented that "[I]t was not a palace, but rather a city within Paris itself." A Venetian ambassador estimated its daily population at roughly forty thousand people, while others noted that a mixture of the wealthy and great alongside the poor and destitute made it a striking amalgam of Parisian and French society as a whole.

Given this mixture of people and purposes, it is not surprising that the Palais was also a hotbed of news, rumor, and gossip. When the high court decided notorious legal cases, or the magistrates were engaged in politicized clashes with the monarchy, the courtyards and hallways of the Palais were filled with whispers and speculation. We have seen how rural communications networks functioned in the Berry: Word of the alleged assassination of Louis spread quickly among peasants and rural notables, then was amplified by the reading of *monitoires* in church parishes to the point where an unsubstantiated death became a reality for Louis' and Marguerite's neighbors and acquaintances. In Paris, a larger world of print and gossip helped to spread news and rumors, allowing thousands who had no personal knowledge of the people involved in legal cases to speculate on these affairs.

The Palais itself, home to a number of printing presses and booksellers, was one of the most important outposts of the printed word in seventeenth-century Paris. Printers rushed to typeset notable verdicts and proclamations by the magistrates. Once printed, they took their place in booksellers' stalls in the *galerie* alongside pamphlets, almanacs, legal briefs, and the latest works of theology, medicine, natural philosophy, poetry, and fiction, in both French and Latin. Bookshop browsers in the Palais might in turn report the news they found on unbound sheets of print to others milling around the premises, perpetuating the cycle of news, gossip, and entertainment. The comings and goings of people and print connected the Palais to the Parisian world outside its walls. Litigants, merchants, and beggars circulated between the Palais and other public spaces such as the Pont neuf (the broad, new bridge at the western end of the Ile de la Cité that connected the two banks of the Seine), the markets of les Halles and the docks along the river, and the town's many taverns and coffee shops that served a populace thirsty for drink, and information.

Unlike Amsterdam or London, where the first regular periodicals appeared in the first half of the 1600s, seventeenth-century Paris lacked a daily newspaper, mostly because of the government's increasingly tight control on the circulation of political

information in print. But the 1630s saw the birth of a particularly Parisian nexus of printed and spoken information, the *bureau d'adresse*, created by an enterprising doctor and do-gooder named Théophraste Renaudot. This space, located on an island in the Seine not far from the Palais, was a clearinghouse for information about employment, the sale of lands, public offices and businesses, and medical services for the poor and sick. In addition, Renaudot succeeded in founding a monthly periodical, *La Gazette de France*, that carried news and information vetted by the Crown's censors. Although Renaudot was forced to close the *bureau d'adresse* in the early 1640s after the death of his patron, the Cardinal Richelieu, the *Gazette* continued to appear, and subsequent *bureaux* appeared episodically until the 1690s. By then, a publication titled *Le Livre commode des addresses de Paris* (*The Convenient Book of Paris Addresses*) made available the information formerly gathered by Renaudot and his followers and dispensed orally at specific sites.

The world of the Palais de Justice circa 1700, then, while driven by the grave judicial rites of the Parlement, was also intimately connected via print and the spoken word to public spaces throughout the capital. The king's high court was part of a larger communications network created in the physical spaces of Paris and nurtured by the circulation of many kinds of print and manuscript sources. The focus of these information networks was at

---

Opposite page: Bureau d'adresse pour l'an 1696. The engraving that adorns this almanac, published the year before the Parlement of Paris began to hear the Pivardière case, presents an allegory of the circulation of news in the *bureaux d'adresse* and other public spaces of seventeenth-century Paris. Within the idealized confines of this *bureau*, men and women of various stations meet to read and discuss reports from Versailles and abroad from the year just passed; they also exchange information and gossip. An elegantly impassive "muse" of information, quill and inkpot in hand, presides over the scene from the upper right-hand corner.

once larger and more diffuse than the one inside the Palais, where judges were expected to administer the king's justice precisely and impartially. Outside the courthouse walls, Parisians turned to printed news and oral exchange of information for entertainment of course, but also as a means to debate and ponder matters of social and cultural importance. By the summer of 1698, the Pivardière case had become a prime example of the sort of *fait divers*, or current event, that a literate French public loved to debate. Was the man who had returned to the Berry the previous January an impostor? Did he have two wives? Parisians had no personal stake in these questions, because the people involved were largely unknown in the capital. But issues of social hierarchy and the instability of identity had general relevance for anyone enmeshed in the Old Regime, and the ensuing conversations, in print and in person, helped Parisians examine their society, and their places within it, critically.

The criminal appeals chamber of the Parlement, known as the Tournelle, met in a round tower on the north side of the Palais complex; it connected directly to the Conciergerie, the prison where Marguerite Chauvelin had committed herself in May 1698. As one Old Regime commentator noted, "It is called the Tournelle because judges from other chambers serve there only by turns, so that the practice of convicting people and sentencing them to death does not ruin the natural gentleness of judges and make them inhumane." Sixty-six magistrates staffed the Tournelle every year, but only twenty-six were on call at any given time. A panel of ten judges was selected from the pool for each case. The judges would hear pleadings from lawyers representing the parties to a case and might question the parties themselves if they were present. At the end of these pleadings, the attorney general, representing the interests of the king, and therefore his subjects, or the "public," would read his recommendation to the panel. Finally, another one of the chamber's magistrates on duty, known as the reporter, would evaluate the procedures undertaken at the lower court level and offer his opinion, after which the panel of judges would vote. A majority of at least two votes was necessary to convict a defendant on appeal.

The Tournelle held its first hearing in the Pivardière case on May 10, 1698, even before Marguerite Chauvelin voluntarily incarcerated herself. The second hearing did not take place until the last day of May, followed by five hearings during June and four in July. Courtroom proceedings during the Old Regime were not transcribed as they are today, but some, including those held in the Pivardière case, were open to the public. By the beginning of July, the affair had begun to attract attention beyond the Palais, particularly in the pages of the clandestine French-language news-sheets that were printed abroad by Huguenots and circulated widely in the capital. The July 17 edition of the twice-weekly *Gazette d'Amsterdam*, for example, provided an initial account of the case, dated July 11, 1698:

> There is a trial in the Parlement that has already been heard for several sessions in criminal court, against the Prior of an Abbey in the Berry who is a prisoner in the Conciergerie in Paris. He is accused of having assassinated a gentleman from the region last month, in conjunction with the man's wife. This lady has also placed herself in prison, and alleges that her husband is alive; she has letters from him, and witnesses who confirm his existence. They say that this gentleman has a special reason that keeps him from presenting himself before the court. The two servants of the lady, who swore to having witnessed the attack upon and death of the gentleman, subsequently retracted their testimony, then reaffirmed it in later proceedings.

This note provides an interesting glimpse of the extent to which knowledge of the case was spreading by mid-July. In its broad outline, the report is correct; it identifies Louis, Marguerite, and the prior as the principals in the case and mentions the inconsistent testimony of Marguerite's maidservants. But the author is vague on Louis' whereabouts and reasons for hiding, incorrectly identifies the prior's location (he was still imprisoned in Châtillon-sur-Indre at this point), and confuses the date of the alleged assassination (nine months earlier, not one). In short, one can imagine that the Dutch journal's correspondent either fashioned his summary from secondhand reports or sat through the actual court proceedings but did not pay close attention to the details. It was the spicy nature of the charges, and the mysterious figure of the missing husband who refused to appear in court, that caught the attention of the journalist, his readers, and the many individuals who were following the case. A dispatch in the same newsletter ten days later noted that "curiosity attracts a large crowd to the hearings whenever this case is on the docket, because it appears to be the most tangled affair that has appeared before the court in over a century."

While we do not know exactly what was said in court during the eleven sessions devoted to the case from May through July, four legal briefs, or *factums*, published by attorneys in the case repeat some of the arguments advanced in the courtroom. These briefs were not purely technical documents. While they argued points of law and summarized oral pleadings made in court, they also constructed narratives of the Pivardière affair intended to sway the magistrates as well as the reading public. Under the Old Regime, these printed briefs were one of the few categories of state-approved, printed texts that enjoyed almost complete freedom from royal censorship. Authors, publishers, censors, and readers of these texts all abided by the fiction that they were intended solely for use within the courtroom; regulations required only that the name of the brief's author and its publisher appear within its pages. By the 1770s and 1780s, barristers used these documents to attack the Bourbon monarchy; in earlier periods, while their political intent was often less evident, their authors were still aware that the *factum* provided an opportunity to address a reading public beyond the walls of the courthouse. The briefs were on sale in the public spaces of the Palais, of course, but interested readers could find them elsewhere in the city. One letter writer in the summer of 1698, remarking on the general interest in unusual legal cases and the ubiquity of the briefs they generated, noted that "all one hears in the streets [of Paris] are hawkers crying out '*Factums!*'"

The four briefs penned on behalf of participants in the case all went on sale in Paris in July, after the majority of the hearings had been held and word of the unusual affair had begun to spread. They presented the two different views of the affair being aired in the court. One was the murder narrative pieced together by Bonnet and Morin over the preceding ten months. Their brief consolidated the evidence drawn from their material investigations, the testimony of the two maidservants, and the many rumors of Marguerite's infidelity and consequent plot to kill her husband that had circulated in the Berry; it provided the Tournelle judges and Parisian readers with a racy narrative of premeditated murder and imposture. The attorney who authored the pleading established its general tone in a breathless summary of events at the start of the text:

> A priest-prior and a married woman are accused of being the principal actors in this bloody and cruel scene, which it appears they began by committing adultery and sacrilege, and then finished with a planned murder. Now they try to hide the evidence of their actions in an almost impenetrable chaos of impostures and chicaneries that are the usual artifices of criminals . . . in their efforts to mislead the wisdom of judges and the public.

The attorney writing on behalf of the Châtillon magistrates provided psychologically simplified, yet undeniably salacious, portraits of the principals in the affair. Marguerite's anxieties over her estate and children, the prior's very real friendship with his two rural neighbors, and Louis' military adventures were all collapsed into a sordid drama driven by carnal desire deep in the Berry. The exigencies of courtroom pleadings and the public appetite for scandal led the lawyers to simplify the case for rapid consumption by inattentive magistrates and curious Parisian news seekers.

In response, attorneys working on behalf of Marguerite, the prior, and the missing Louis articulated an alternative version of the absent nobleman's story. Until their courtroom pleadings and printed *factums* appeared in mid-July, the case against the Châtillon magistrate's version of the affair had never been stated so clearly. To begin, the attorneys underlined that the testimony of the two maidservants was suspect. They then reiterated that the body of Louis had never been found, in spite of the grisly rumors that had circulated around Narbonne about severed heads and lacerated bodies. These two shortcomings hinted at the implausibility of the narrative constructed by the provincial magistrates. The lawyer who penned Louis' brief also related two vignettes that mocked the superstitions of the rural world. During Louis' January 1698 return to the Berry, the lawyer claimed, the missing nobleman entered the church in Jeu-Malloches while the priest celebrated Vespers on the feast day of the parish's patron saint, Anthony. When Louis crossed the threshold of the church,

> there suddenly arose such a great commotion that Vespers was interrupted. Everyone ran up to the newcomer to see if they were mistaken. A specter, a phantom, could not have caused more alarm, more surprise, or more astonishment. Even though the parishioners had been told of his death, their certainty of his demise dissipated in an instant. No one present paused even a moment before recognizing the Sieur de la

Pivardière, and after Vespers more than two hundred of them
swore before the Lieutenant General of Romorantin that they
recognized the newcomer as the missing lord of Narbonne.

This passage, with references to specters and phantoms, flat-
tered literate Parisians wishing to distinguish themselves from
backward provincials awestruck by Louis' reappearance.

The same brief further emphasized the intellectual distance
between the provinces and Paris in an account of a confrontation
between Louis and Bonnet, which also took place in January, be-
side a pond at Narbonne. Louis, informed that Bonnet and a crew
of huissiers were dredging the pond in search of his body, allegedly rode out to speak with the magistrate. According to the brief,
upon Louis' arrival he tauntingly told the Châtillon judge that he
could spare himself the pain of searching the pond for that which
now appeared to him on its bank. Bonnet, supposedly frightened
by the "spectral" appearance, fled the scene on horseback, without
response. Later Bonnet supposedly excused his behavior by saying
that he believed he had seen the "shadow" of Pivardière. The author of the brief, however, in an effective rhetorical turn, wondered why Bonnet had run from the shadow, sarcastically suggesting that the frightened magistrate should have held his ground
and interrogated the ghost; after all, "the shadow of the Sieur de la
Pivardière found along the bank of a pond would have been an ex-
tremely convincing proof of his death." These two scenarios, un-
corroborated in any surviving evidence from the various trial investigations, may well have been fabrications on the part of Louis'
lawyer; the brief for Bonnet and Morin, for example, dismissed
the scene alongside the Narbonne pond as an "effort to embellish
the novel of Pivardière." But the vignettes served to cast doubt on
the provincial magistrates and the witnesses they relied on by
characterizing them as dupes, unable to distinguish between reality and imagination.

The strategy of discrediting the provincials was not sufficient on its own, however, to counteract the tale of the lecherous prior and the unfaithful wife narrated in the courtroom and in
the Châtillon magistrates' *factum*. The courthouse arguments and
printed pleadings on behalf of Marguerite, the prior, and Louis
also had to convince the criminal judges and the curious public
that the nobleman was still alive. Under ordinary circumstances, it
would have sufficed to produce the person who claimed to be
Louis for examination by the criminal judges. But the man who
had traveled to the Berry in January refused to journey to Paris in
July to exonerate his alleged wife and clerical friend. The attorneys for the Châtillon magistrates claimed that his refusal confirmed the outrageous act of imposture orchestrated by Marguerite and the prior; were their accomplice to dare an appearance
before the high court, the probing magistrates would swiftly verify
the deception that had first been exposed in the Châtillon prison
six months earlier. Louis' and Marguerite's lawyers, however, had
a different explanation for his reluctance to come forward, one
that accounted for the whereabouts of Louis between the fateful
night of August 15 and his reappearance in the Berry five months
later. Their tale startled everyone.

Two years earlier, on April 30, 1695, the attorneys asserted,
Louis de la Pivardière had married Marie-Elisabeth Pillard, the
undistinguished daughter of a deceased innkeeper in Auxerre, a
regional center in northern Burgundy. He told his new wife, her
family, and their circle of Auxerrois friends that he was the son of
a Parisian merchant named Antoine Dubouchet, and that his own
name was Louis Dubouchet. He kept his nobility, his first marriage, and his military commission hidden from Marie. At the
same time, through a series of letters and occasional visits to Narbonne, he deluded Marguerite into thinking he was still serving at
the front as an officer in the king's army. This double deception,
the attorneys claimed, lasted for more than two years, until the

fateful encounter between Louis and Marguerite at Narbonne the night of August 15, 1697. While arguing with his first wife, he realized that she knew of his bigamous marriage, and began to fear that she would turn him over to the royal authorities. Men convicted of bigamy faced one of two penalties in late-seventeenth-century France: a lengthy sentence as an oarsman on the king's galleys — a sentence that few survived — or public execution.

The lawyers argued that Louis, faced with those possibilities, had deemed it imprudent to stay at Narbonne. Before sunrise on August 16 he gathered a few belongings, clambered out the window, let himself out the front gate, and began the trek back to his second wife in Auxerre. As word of the scandalous events at Narbonne circulated locally, innkeepers in Châteauroux and Issoudun, two Berrichon towns on the route to northern Burgundy, sent Marguerite sworn statements saying that Louis had stayed at their lodgings in the days after the August 15 confrontation; one innkeeper even claimed he had bowled with the fugitive husband and nobleman on the town green, as if to emphasize Louis' lack of cunning in the matter.

For the next several months, the attorneys argued, Marguerite, the prior, and his family went to great lengths to find Louis and persuade him to return to the Berry to counter the murder accusations. When Marguerite learned of the investigation initiated by Bonnet and Morin, she traveled to Paris to seek aid from her family, whom she hoped would help her preempt the Châtillon investigation by seeking redress from the Parlement. Wasting no time, she filed papers on September 18 asking that she be permitted to question Bonnet's "competence," in part for jurisdictional reasons and in part because his huissiers had seized her property without reasonable suspicion of guilt. The high court, refusing to grant a direct request to investigate her charges of calumny against the royal judges of Châtillon, instructed LeComte, the Romorantin judge, to look into her accusations. In addition, according to their attorneys, Marguerite and the prior sent an emissary, Charost's younger sibling Joseph, also a prior, to find Louis in Auxerre. Arriving in the north Burgundian town in early October, the younger Charost quickly found his way to Marie, whom he questioned while Louis was away. Later that day, upon learning of Marie's visitor, Louis confessed his double life to his young wife and her family. He then fled Auxerre with Marie and her mother; Louis' fear of arrest on bigamy charges supposedly trumped all other concerns, just as it allegedly had the night of August 15, when he learned that Marguerite knew of his second marriage.

The younger Charost returned to the Berry empty-handed. Not long thereafter, the defense attorneys claimed, Marguerite and the Charost family sent another emissary to the missing husband. This time they selected Pierre Sousmain, the notary from Châtillon-sur-Indre who had worked alongside LeComte in the Berry the previous January, to prove Louis' existence. His administrative and legal background made him more likely than the younger Charost to return with convincing proof that Louis was not dead. Taking no chances, Marguerite and the Charost clan sent him off with a fully drafted affirmation of Louis' existence, to be executed in the presence of an official witness. Sousmain, both more resourceful and more cautious than the young Charost, traced Louis to the village of Etalante, fifty miles east of Auxerre. Perhaps wary of frightening him off yet again, Sousmain did not personally travel to Etalante. But he did arrange a meeting with him in the town of Flavigny, twelve miles southwest of Etalante. Louis and Marie traveled there on October 22; that afternoon, the lawyers alleged, while Marie remained at the inn, Louis and Sousmain appeared before two local notaries who transcribed the statement Sousmain had brought with him and witnessed Louis' signature. This text, described as a "declaration, ratification and authorization by the Sieur Louis de la Pivardière," affirmed that the man who appeared that day in Flavigny was "*Louis de la*

Pivardière, écuyer, sieur du Bouchet, de la seigneurie de Narbonne." It denounced the murder investigation undertaken by the Châtillon judges, stating that "*quelques affaires particulières*" had until then prevented Louis from returning to the Berry to exonerate his wife, and expressed his desire that this document end any doubts about his existence. The act avoided any mention of his life in Burgundy with his second wife.

The encounter over, Louis and Marie returned to their hide-away in Etalante, while Sousmain traveled back to the Berry. He had in his possession four notarized copies of Louis' declaration, along with cover letters from the missing nobleman. By distribut-ing these declarations as widely as possible throughout the region, Marguerite and the Charost faction hoped to offer a rejoinder to the judges. By late November, however, when the maidservants had testified to the murder of Louis and the ecclesiastical magis-trate from Bourges had indicted the prior, it was clear that the documents had failed to quash the murder investigation. A notar-ial act would not do; the suspects needed Louis de la Pivardière, in the flesh, to return to the Berry. Sometime in late November or early December, accordingly, Sousmain, the prior, another of his brothers, and two of the prior's valets gathered in Dijon in re-newed pursuit of Louis. The task was a delicate one. They sought to persuade Louis to return with them to the Berry, ideally with-out resorting to physical force; at the same time, they had to make sure he did not flee.

Entering Etalante, they were told by several locals that "Louis Dubouchet" was away for the day. Satisfied with this intelligence, they found lodgings for the evening and went to sleep. The next morning as they awoke, in the words of the prior, they "saw the Sieur de la Pivardière from the window of our sleeping quarters, going off to hunt with a rifle on his shoulder." One can only imag-ine the group's consternation upon seeing Louis blithely saunter-ing by the window on his way to hunt game. Regaining their composure, they sent Sousmain to speak with Marie and her mother, whom he had met six weeks earlier in Flavigny. The two women told him that Louis was prepared to return to the Berry to prove that he was still alive; they claimed that Louis had told them he would return to the Berry if requested to do so by his first wife. Eventually the prior and his company prevailed: Louis agreed to travel to the Berry, present himself before the Romorantin judge, and be paraded around the province.

This chronology, the attorneys for Marguerite and the prior argued, accounted for the actions of the missing husband between his alleged murder in August 1697 and his reappearance in the Berry the following January. His failure to appear before the high court in the summer of 1698 was in keeping with his actions ever since the evening of August 15. Unless the Parlement was willing to grant him a safe-conduct to come tell his story in Paris, he could not risk leaving his country hideout and being arrested on a bigamy charge. Nevertheless, the lawyers claimed, it was obvious that Marguerite Chauvelin's husband was still alive, and that the accusations of murder were groundless.

How plausible was the tale of bigamy that emerged in the courtroom and on the pages of the printed legal pleadings in the summer of 1698? Even today in the West, in an age of more efficient communication, effective administrative oversight over broad territories, and relatively easy divorce, cases of bigamy occasionally come to light. In 2003, for example, it emerged that a recently deceased Tampa, Florida, millionaire named Douglas Cone had married and fathered children with two women who lived twenty miles from each other. He had been married to his first wife for fifty-one years, and his second for almost thirty. Given this improbable story, it is not difficult to imagine that bigamous alliances occurred with greater frequency before 1800, at a time of lesser bureaucratic control, poorer communication, and difficult and costly transportation that made it easier to escape a marriage gone sour. In fact, bigamy in this period should be understood as one of a series of responses to the problems posed by clandestine marriages and the difficulty of obtaining legal divorces.

Legal and theological understandings of marriage in the pre-modern period were first theorized by medieval canon lawyers who determined that the exchange of free consent between the two parties was the primary and sufficient criterion for marriage. Once a couple had verbally consented to a union, these jurists understood the marriage to be contracted irrevocably, independent of parental or community approval or ecclesiastical confirmation. This doctrine, however, led to the problem of clandestine marriage: If a man and a woman secretly married, how could their union be independently verified if challenged by family members, the community, or one of the spouses themselves at a later date? Both the Church and civil authorities developed practices that in theory remedied the problem of clandestine marriage in the Middle Ages, including the publication of marriage banns, parental consent, witnesses to the exchange of consent between the spouses, and a preference that marriage ceremonies occur on church property with a priestly benediction.

By the time of the sixteenth-century reformations, however, clandestine marriages had become a significant embarrassment to the Catholic Church and a nightmare for civil authorities. Protestant denominations, citing the laxity of Catholic practice, all required specific rituals performed by ministers to legitimate a marriage. The Catholic Church followed suit at the Council of Trent in 1563 by ordering that a legitimate marriage be performed by the priest in the parish where the couple resided, entered in the parish registry, and witnessed by two individuals known to the priest and the couple. In spite of these reforms, the increasing mobility of sixteenth- and seventeenth-century Europeans and uneven adherence to the new regulations meant that clandestine marriage persisted. Only two years after Pivardière's second marriage, for example, Louis XIV issued one of many royal decrees threatening clergy with the loss of their benefices and banishment if they ignored the numerous safeguards intended to prevent clandestine marriages.

Furthermore, in Catholic countries like France or Spain, where marriage was one of seven sacraments exclusively administered by the Church, it was impossible to obtain a divorce if a marriage proved unsatisfactory. Even in Protestant England, where divorce was legal, it had to be validated by a private act of Parliament, a costly and cumbersome procedure that undoubtedly kept intact many problematic marriages. The difficulty of divorce led discontented spouses to bigamy, as well as a number of other escape strategies. These alternatives included informal separation, where both parties agreed to live separately, sometimes remaining in the same community, and desertion, a solution often available only to men in occupations that called for them to travel widely. In France, aggrieved spouses might seek a *lettre de cachet* or secret arrest warrant issued by the king that permitted one spouse to have the other incarcerated for an indeterminate period. The English developed the unusual custom of "wife sale," whereby a husband who had tired of his spouse led her to market with a rope around her neck, as though she were a beast or a commodity, and sold her to another man, often in an arrangement agreed upon ahead of time. At the extreme end of the spectrum, a distraught spouse might resort to murder or suicide.

The nature of the "crime" of bigamy makes it impossible to determine with any certainty its frequency in France or anywhere else in this period. Some bigamists certainly went undetected, while civil and ecclesiastical authorities and local communities may have chosen not to prosecute unions that resulted in financial or emotional benefits to one or both parties. Statistics in England

and Spain suggest that bigamy occurred with some frequency in those countries. The situation in France, although less well-documented, may have been similar. One eighteenth-century French legal commentator noted that "while bigamy is a very great crime according to the laws of Church and State, it is rare to see examples made; ordinarily one only punishes the guilty if one of the husbands or wives complains." After 1600, while some bigamists were still put to death, it was more common for those convicted of the crime to be placed in public stockades while wearing signs that identified their crime. Once they had been publicly shamed, male bigamists would be branded and condemned to the king's galleys; François Morgue Delorme, for example, an unemployed scribe, was convicted of bigamy in Paris in 1727, forced to stand in front of the law courts for three days while wearing a sign that said *BIGAME*, branded with the letters *G-A-L* (for galleys, or *galères* in French), and sentenced to nine years of forced maritime labor. Convicted female bigamists would be exiled from their communities.

The story of Jean Capé, a Frenchman who was married to two women in the final decades of the seventeenth century, provides an interesting comparison to the bigamous actions of Louis de la Pivardière. In 1687 Capé, a native of Béarn, moved to the town of Salins in the Franche-Comté east of Burgundy to take a position in the *gabelle*, the royal salt tax administration. There he met Marguerite Doros, a minor, who soon became pregnant. She gave birth to a son named Alexandre, an event that prompted the couple to get married in Besançon, the capital of the Franche-Comté north of Salins, in 1688. The curé in Salins gave his permission to move the marriage to the larger city, while the archbishop of Besançon gave them dispensation to publish marriage banns only once, rather than the required three times. Business affairs required Capé to travel with some regularity, but for a while he diligently supported his wife and son, sending letters to his spouse affirming his affection; the mayor and aldermen of Salins later signed testimony stating that the town residents considered Doros to be the legitimate spouse of Capé at this time.

After several years, however, Capé grew tired of the marriage; the onset of the Nine Years War may have spurred him, as it did Louis, to pursue opportunities elsewhere in the kingdom. In 1692, Capé summoned Doros to meet him in Chambéry, a town in the foothills of the French Alps. There he insisted that she sign a document attesting that they were not legally married, and that consequently he had no responsibility to support her or their son. In exchange, he offered her six thousand livres. The details of the negotiations are hazy; later Doros would claim that she did not go to Chambéry, and that an impostor signed the document. Another version of events that emerged during the trial indicated that Doros did meet Capé in Chambéry, but balked at the signing. Capé, who then had to leave on business, deputized an acquaintance to conclude the deal. A signed document, produced during the later trial, supposedly related that Doros had given birth to two other children, fathered by an anonymous military officer, after marrying Capé. Acknowledging her guilt, she purportedly signed a revised agreement absolving Capé of all marital responsibility and accepting only six hundred livres. The narrator of the case pointed out that Capé had accused Doros of adultery with a military officer because "everyone knows that most of these gentlemen seek out *amours de passage*, without much concern for long-term fidelity."

After the purported signing of the document in 1692, Doros and her child retired to Salins, while Capé settled in Chambéry, where he became a *commissaire des guerres*, a venal position charged with inspecting the troops, their supplies, and their quarters; he most likely was involved with the administration of the Italian army. He soon fell in love with Antoinette Dorset, whom he married in 1696 in her parish in Chambéry. The parish register indicates that the marriage banns were published only twice. The groom is listed as Jean Capé, Sieur Dulacq, while no mention is made of his home parish. The similarities to Louis, who also altered his name and obscured his origins, are striking. Five months later, Dorset gave birth to a child who "more diligent than ordinary children, rushed out to see the light of day." Capé lived in harmony with his second wife, fathered another child with her, and then passed away in 1704. Upon his death, however, the shady circumstances of his separation from Marguerite Doros, who appears to have known of his activities after 1692, returned to haunt Antoinette Dorset. After he died, both women attempted to sell his administrative post. A lawsuit ensued, pitting the two duped women against each other in the courtroom. The court carefully studied the circumstances under which each marriage took place to determine which one was legitimate. In the end, the magistrates held that the Chambéry document purportedly signed by Doros to excuse Capé from his marital responsibilities was illegal, because their marriage had been legitimately contracted and concluded in the eyes of the state and the Church. The impossibility of dissolving a properly contracted marital union while both parties were still alive made Capé's second marriage to Dorset an illicit union. Doros was declared Capé's legal widow, and her son Alexandre his legal heir, while Dorset and her children were denied any rights to Capé's estate and enjoined not to "trouble" the first wife and her son. In this instance, the consequences of Capé's bigamy fell most heavily on his disinherited second wife and their two children.

The incident parallels the Pivardière affair in many ways. The chronology of the two cases is almost identical; Capé's first marriage took place a year after Louis' marriage to Marguerite, and his second wedding transpired the year after Louis married the Auxerre innkeeper's daughter. One is struck by the casual attitude of the clerical officials charged with certifying the appropriateness

of Capé's unions. In spite of repeated directives by the government to publish the banns three times and verify the identity of
the spouses with clerics in their home parish, the regulations
governing marriage were largely ignored. Perhaps this haphazard-
ness was a consequence of the dislocations suffered by the French
population in time of war. Once the Nine Years War was well under way, both Capé and Louis left their homes to pursue opportunities for wealth and advancement that arose during the conflict;
their wanderings also brought them into contact with their second
wives, even though their first spouses were still alive. Capé, who
obtained a relatively profitable war commission, was more successful in parlaying involvement in the king's military engagements of the 1690s into a lucrative military position.

The two cases differ, however, in one key respect. Long before
he met Antoinette Dorset, Jean Capé determined to leave his marriage with Marguerite Doros, taking deliberate steps in Chambéry
in 1692 to do so. It is possible that in the midst of war and the social tensions of the early 1690s, Capé thought himself legitimately
rid of his first wife once the agreement was signed and the money
exchanged. He apparently had no fear of being accused of bigamy
when he married Dorset four years later. In contrast, the defense
attorneys insisted that Louis never explicitly broke with his first
wife. In fact, even though married to Marie, he continued to write
to Marguerite at Narbonne, maintaining the pretense that he was
a lieutenant in the St. Hermines dragoon regiment on the Flemish
front. Most bigamists, in France and indeed elsewhere in western
Europe and its colonies in this period, did not want to maintain
two separate marriages; they wished instead to leave their first
spouse, but were afforded no way out of problematic marriages by
the civil or ecclesiastical laws. But Louis de la Pivardière was not a
typical seventeenth-century bigamist; according to his attorneys,
he actively sought to maintain marriages in two French provinces
at the same time, and temporarily got away with this deception

due to the social dislocations occasioned by war, plague, and famine. The criminal judges of the Tournelle were being asked to validate this unusual version of the relatively common practice of bigamy, among the many other irregularities presented by the defense's account of the affair.

The courtroom pleadings for each defendant, therefore, and the briefs penned on their behalf, featured both technical evaluations of the legal procedures undertaken by the various provincial magistrates and simplified, popularized narratives of the highly complex affair. The magistrates alone considered the legal formalities, but everyone interested in the case that summer puzzled over the logical and psychological inconsistencies in the two versions of the affair. Courtroom attendees most likely saw Marguerite on display at each session; in addition, between hearings she entertained acquaintances and other visitors who wished to discuss the case in her prison cell. Her missing husband, however, was at the center of these speculations. As the hearings reached their conclusion, more than one observer must have yearned for a courtroom appearance by the man in hiding. In the absence of the shadowy figure, though, Parisians could once again turn to the published briefs, two of which featured unusual frontispieces: engraved portraits of Marguerite and her missing husband.

Marguerite's portrait reinforced the unblemished reputation that her lawyers claimed she enjoyed. The text of the brief emphasized that she was "of noble extraction, related to and allied with people of quality and dignity, and had always lived with honor, beyond all reproach." Neither of her two husbands had ever had cause to suspect her conduct, as the letters she received from Louis during his military service, "full of tenderness, esteem, and friendship for her," demonstrated. The frontispiece reinforced this message. The engraver has given her the fashionable headdress of

Marguerite Chauvelin
femme de Louis de la Pivardiere

Engraved portrait of Marguerite Chauvelin, summer 1698, from her legal brief. The portrait bears the legend "wife of Louis de la Pivardiere." In spite of her previous marriage and her relatives' well-known careers at the Parisian bar, her unique attribute for the purposes of the case is her relation to her husband.

---

the day and a simple, yet elegant dress that emphasizes her cultivated status, similar to that of the Parisian women in the 1696 *Bureau d'adresse* almanac.* Her shoulders and most of her chest are covered, suggesting her prudence and chastity, particularly when compared to portraits of many significant court women during the reign of Louis XIV. Her dress, along with her rather plain visage, marked by a mole on her left cheek, suggests a woman who is

*See the illustration on page 68.

LOUIS DE LA PIVARDIER, Écuïer
Sr. du Bouchet. Cy devant Lieutenant de Dragons
au Regiment de Ste Hermine ; Designé sur le Naturel.

Portrait of Louis de la Pivardière, summer 1698, from his legal brief. The legend at the bottom of the portrait emphasizes that Louis' officer rank is a critical component of his identity, even though he is not represented in military garb.

past the first bloom of her youth — and therefore not an obvious choice for the younger prior. The image reinforced the brief's claim that this woman had little motivation to plan and execute the assassination of her husband in order to devote herself to a lover from the local priory.

In a similarly utilitarian manner, the engraving that graced the front of Pivardière's brief, a pendant to that of Marguerite Chauvelin, was intended to persuade those following the case that, despite his strange behavior, Louis was very much alive. The image shows a youthful man with large eyes, a hooked nose, and sensual lips. He is dressed in simple, yet stylish, gentleman's clothing, with a flowing wig fashionable for the period. The caption at the bottom provides an elaborate title, including Louis' military rank during the Nine Years War and the name he had taken in Auxerre, *écuier Sr. du Bouchet*. This label is followed, in smaller type, by the claim "*designé sur le Naturel*" (drawn from life), presumably indicating that the anonymous artist based his portrait on a live session with his subject. More importantly, this phrase suggests that the engraving is a stand-in for the missing man who would presumably appear soon in a Paris courtroom.

Yet it is almost impossible to imagine that Louis could have posed for the portrait before the publication of the brief and frontispiece. From his January 1698 appearance in the Berry through the summer of 1698, the "*soi-disant*" Pivardière, as the opposition legal briefs called him, was in hiding in Burgundy. It is doubtful that any Parisian artist or engraver would have traveled to his provincial hideout to sketch the fugitive; Louis, if alive, would not have willingly disclosed his location and risked arrest for this purpose. An impostor would certainly have avoided efforts to record his physical appearance. It is altogether likely, therefore, that this image of a young rake bore little resemblance to the grizzled, thirty-seven-year-old war veteran on the lam. These impressions are strengthened by later trial testimony that Louis had bad teeth, a mark on his right cheek, and leg wounds from the wars. In other words, this middle-aged man was most likely as broken down as the horse he had led back to Narbonne in August 1697.

If the engraving is not based on an artist's interpretation of the missing man's physical appearance, why did the lawyer who wrote the brief and oversaw its publication believe that the image would help to prove Louis' existence, or exonerate Marguerite and the prior? This question, while intriguing, is rooted in modern sensibilities. In an age prior to photography, neither the engraver nor his viewers understood this image to be a forensic document.

Rather, seventeenth-century French portraiture attempted to represent men and women by embellishing upon the originals, whom most viewers would not know by sight. These images invoked unknown, or unknowable, subjects in terms that would call to mind social types meaningful to seventeenth-century viewers, who expected stock character portrayals rather than true representations. The reader of Louis' brief expected a visual image to complement the *factum*'s textual portrait of the obscure provincial nobleman at the heart of the mystery. The frontispiece fulfilled these expectations by representing Louis as an aristocrat and a military officer who was also an impetuous playboy not above taking a second wife if attracted to her physically. In contrast to the propriety evoked by Marguerite's portrait, Louis' image suggests a hint of immorality that viewers would recognize, and maybe forgive, in a dashing military officer. By modern standards, the engraving that fronted his brief bore false testimony. But at the time, the image was part of a carefully packaged pleading.

A perplexing dilemma, then, faced the magistrates of the Parlement of Paris in late July 1698. The most compelling narrative, that of the unfaithful wife and her ecclesiastical lover who had murdered a jealous husband, was not supported by the facts of the case. But the interpretation of events that seemed most likely to be true — that of the continued existence of the bigamous husband — was called into question by Louis' failure to appear in court during the trial. Known facts did not square with plausible motivations, just as the image on the brief bore little resemblance to the man. After reading these briefs and listening to oral pleadings in court, what would the Tournelle decide?

The criminal court rendered its verdict on July 23. In their conclusions, published just prior to this decision, lawyers for Marguerite and the prior had asked that the court order Bonnet and Morin to absolve their clients of any wrong-doing and to pay them twenty-five thousand livres in damages. The decision, printed in fourteen closely set pages, dashed their hopes. It did nullify a number of the Châtillon magistrates' more questionable findings. But it also stipulated that the prior and the maidservants, detained in the Châtillon prison, be transferred to the custody of judicial officials in Chartres, a day's ride south of Paris, along with all the significant documentary evidence. The Chartres magistrates would conduct the new inquiry. Furthermore, the Parisian judges ordered the seizure and imprisonment of the man claiming to be Louis; in Chartres, he would be ordered "to respond to the charges made against him." The verdict stopped short of declaring this man an impostor, and refrained from definitively condemning Marguerite and the prior of adultery and conspiracy to murder. But the judges insisted that the compromised provincial investigations be repeated by impartial judges at Chartres. Their unwillingness to dismiss the case and award damages based on the alleged, but unproven, assertion that Louis was still alive indicated that they expected to find Marguerite and the prior guilty once the missing man had been properly interrogated.

Chapter 4

NOBLEMAN, COMMONER,
OR IMPOSTOR?

✣

*T*wo days after the court rendered its verdict, the *Gazette d'Amsterdam* reported that the man claiming to be the missing husband would soon turn himself in, once his second wife, still in Burgundy, had been paid a tidy sum to confirm their marriage had not happened. But others, the writer noted, doubted that the "pretend husband" would ever present himself to the authorities. These observers, convinced that Louis had been assassinated at Narbonne, were convinced that the impostor who had appeared in the Berry in January would not risk incarceration in the more discerning capital. Another observer, writing in the clandestine *Lettres historiques*, found it implausible that Marguerite and the prior would resort to an impostor at all, given the difficulty of maintaining the deception in such a high-profile affair. This journalist urged that the man in hiding be given an immediate amnesty, so that he might come to Paris to explain the details of his bigamous second marriage. The entire affair was "mysterious," and possibly even scandalous; if the Tournelle magistrates truly thought Louis had been murdered, why did they also nullify the provincial judges' investigations that had produced proof of the crime? "Believe me, this decision was not made by judges in a state of ignorance. Passion, partisan interest, and larger concerns are involved," the writer warned darkly. The Parlement's verdict, it appeared, had done little to resolve the uncertainties and suspicions of those following the affair.

As these rumors swirled about the capital, Marguerite's lawyers regrouped. They were led by her relative Louis Chauvelin (1656–1719), a barrister, a former provincial intendant, and a powerful councilor of state who had contacts throughout the Palais and at Versailles. A key component of the family's strategy in the summer of 1698, well before the writer of the *Lettres historiques* suggested it, had been to ask the Parlement to issue a safe-conduct for the alleged Louis so that he could travel to Paris without worrying that he might be imprisoned along the way on charges of bigamy. During the trial, however, the judges had turned down this request, and they refused it again in the July 23 verdict. In the aftermath of the decision, Louis Chauvelin solicited a safe-conduct from the king, even though the royal dispensation he sought would violate the court's demand that Louis surrender to the Chartres magistrates. The monarch, perhaps wishing to tweak his erstwhile political rivals, the high court magistrates, granted the request sometime in August. The document issued to the man in hiding, copies of which were printed and sold to curious readers in Paris, specified the need to protect the missing aristocrat against arrest on charges of bigamy. Within a month after the Parlement verdict, plans were made to bring Louis to Paris, rather than to Chartres. The Chauvelin strategists figured they could make their case more effectively if Louis appeared in the metropolis, where word that he had finally surfaced would spread more quickly to the magistrates and influential courtiers at Versailles.

Once the king issued the safe-conduct, Louis agreed to leave his hiding place around August 25. He arrived in Paris three days later, going directly to the home of the Abbot Chauvelin, another

relative of his first wife; the abbot, other members of the clan, and
a solicitor named Baudran and his children offered him a meal and
a warm welcome. After dining there, he was invited to return to
the Baudran household, where he spent the next three days "meeting with many people." Some of them were acquaintances from
the Berry who came out of curiosity and left prepared to testify
that the newcomer was Louis de la Pivardière. The Berrichon notary Vigan, for example, the man who had first alerted Marguerite
to Louis' second marriage, happened to be in Paris at this time.
Informed that Louis had surfaced, he went to Baudran's residence
to see if the man there was the same person he had known in the
Berry. After he was ushered in to see the missing nobleman, Vigan
and the newcomer settled into a conversation about Berrichon
matters that convinced Vigan he was speaking to the same person
he had first met at Narbonne more than a decade earlier. Similar
conversations with other Berrichon natives transpired over those
three days. In addition to these supporters and curiosity-seekers,
the man heard from his first wife and the Charost clan. Marguerite
sent him a letter from her cell in the Conciergerie in which she
"marked her joy" to learn of his arrival in the capital, while the
prior's sister-in-law expressed her delight at his return during a
visit to the Baudran household.

The provincial newcomer's first three days back in the capital,
it appears, were part of a well-coordinated strategy. While they
spread the word of his return throughout Parisian social networks,
the Chauvelin clan also scoured the city for former acquaintances
who would verify his identity. Meanwhile, Louis Chauvelin and
the family's other legal experts prepared the newcomer for the
inevitable courtroom confrontations that lay ahead. On September 1 their guest voluntarily incarcerated himself at Fort l'Evêque
prison, a facility on the right bank of the Seine that faced the
Palais complex where Marguerite was being held. The prison's
name, "the Bishop's Fortress," derived from its medieval origins as

the judicial seat and jail of the bishop of Paris. In 1674, however, the Crown had taken possession of the building as part of the extensive penal, judicial, and administrative reforms of the capital in the early years of the Sun King's reign. Although the criminal ordinance of 1670 called for the humane treatment of prisoners, the limited resources of the monarchy and the inertia of the ancient institution prohibited any significant amelioration of conditions in the jail. This cramped, ancient four-story building, only nine meters wide along the river and thirty-five meters deep, housed around two hundred fifty prisoners daily in its less-than-sanitary confines. While the lowest rung of Old Regime criminals — the thieves, prostitutes, assassins, and others — did not reside within its walls, it nevertheless had a reputation as one of the two unhealthiest prisons in Paris; many of its cells were vermin-infested holes shut off from daylight and adequate ventilation, and the subterranean chambers were particularly foul.

Better treatment was available, however, for those with the means to afford it, and it is likely that Marguerite's relatives provided well for him. The upper floors of the prison contained individual, relatively spacious cells, and the warden and his subordinates provided reasonably robust meals for extra fees; prisoners could also receive food, clothing, and even furnishings from guests to ease their travails. Inmates were required to attend two daily Masses in the prison chapel, but unless subject to special forms of incarceration, they were free to enjoy the prison's central courtyard and its other common areas throughout the day. The better-off prisoners could lead fairly pleasant existences within Fort l'Evêque in the company of family, friends, and even domestics, who might live with them. One report from January 1724 recounts a gambling party of sixteen people in one of the top-floor chambers, replete with a banker, suggesting that gaming was well-established within the prison. A counterfeiter named Chevallier, who had sold false lottery tickets, carried on his commerce within the prison by smuggling in his printing press and plates.

As the legal challenge to the Tournelle's July 23 ruling moved forward, much abetted by the sudden appearance of the man who claimed to be Marguerite's dead husband, word spread that Louis was now a resident at Fort l'Evêque. Louise Marguerite du Pont, Dame de la Villeneuve, a native of the Berry who had often visited Narbonne a decade earlier to dine with Louis and Marguerite, learned "only two or three days" after his imprisonment that he was at Fort l'Evêque and immediately went to see him. Charles Carré, another Berrichon gentleman who had wined and dined at Narbonne, heard rumors that the man in prison "was not the real Pivardière." Out of curiosity, he went to see if the prisoner was his old friend. Louis Coquard de la Mothe, a lieutenant colonel in Louis' dragoon regiment, gathered together several other regimental officers to visit their former comrade. Louis' godmother, Dame Elisabeth de Gripon, was prompted to see her godson in prison because "she heard so much discussion of his case in society." Even people who had not previously known Louis were curious; a provincial noblewoman named Dame Marguerite Angélique de Cevant headed to see the prisoner because she had heard about his case "from a very large number of people of quality and merit."

Perhaps the most interesting evidence of Parisians' passion for the affair was that provided by Jean Antoine Archambault, the lawyer in whom Marguerite's eldest daughter had confided her desire to marry Louis a decade earlier. One day in the fall of 1698, intrigued by the infamous case, Archambault and two female friends called upon Marguerite at the Conciergerie. Louis' first wife remembered Archambault from their earlier encounter, a fact that no doubt made an impression on his two companions. Leaving the Conciergerie, the lawyer proposed that they cross over to the Right Bank to visit the man who claimed to be her husband. The actions of Archambault and his female friends indicate the ease with which Parisians moved in and out of the capital's prisons; visiting criminal celebrities like Marguerite and Louis was an entertainment akin to seeking news and gossip in the public spaces of the city.

Archambault's party of three was readily admitted to Fort l'Evêque, where they made their way to a room in which the prisoner was meeting with three other men. Archambault peered surreptitiously into the room through several holes and a small window in the door, but was uncertain whether the man he saw was the same person he had met in the Berry eleven years earlier. Afraid that he and his party might be unwelcome, and no doubt not wishing to embarrass himself in front of his female companions, Archambault proposed that they leave. At that moment, however, the prisoner left his chamber to escort his guests to the exit. As he passed by Archambault and his friends, the lawyer got a much better glimpse of the man; he turned to tell his companions that he was now certain the man was Louis de la Pivardière. As the prisoner returned from seeing his guests to the street, Archambault accosted him: "Monsieur, I believe I have the honor of being known to you." The prisoner immediately responded, "Yes, your name is Monsieur Archambault," and recalled the circumstances under which they had met with great precision. The prisoner then invited Archambault and his two guests into the room, where he recounted other specific details of their previous encounter.

Each visitor to Fort l'Evêque carried impressions of the prisoner back to their own circle of family and acquaintances; these reports undoubtedly led to more speculation on the man's identity and the outcome of the puzzling case. By September 8, a week after the man from the provinces had voluntarily confined himself, the *Gazette d'Amsterdam* reported that "his arrival has greatly surprised those who had thought him dead, and who are having difficulty disabusing themselves of the notion. This affair is the topic of conversation all over town; people imagine that the case is far from over." A week later, the *Histoire journalière* noted that the prisoner "had already been recognized as the true husband [of Marguerite] by more than a hundred people, including the Colonel and many other officers with whom he served in the Army." Bowing to this popular interest in the case, and perhaps also wishing to further chastise the magistrates of the high court, the King's Council invalidated the magistrates' instructions that the case be adjudicated in Chartres. If Louis was in Paris, where he had access to the capital's lawyers, printers, and publicists, the prior and the other witnesses and documents could not remain there, nor could that town's magistrates effectively pursue the investigation envisioned by the high court. The king's advisors ordered the Parlement to assume direct responsibility for investigating the case. Clearly they expected that the Parisian magistrates would determine the truth of the matter. For these men of law, and for Parisians avidly following the case, the portrait that graced the front of Louis' brief had come to life.

If the incarcerated man really was Louis, both judges and onlookers reasoned that they might finally learn why he had entered into a second marital union with the adolescent daughter of a provincial innkeeper. The tale that emerged when the *soi-disant* Louis began to recount his story to judicial officials and other visitors to his jail cell took listeners back three years, to his trip from Narbonne to the Rhine frontier in March 1695. Early that month he arrived in the town of Auxerre, a center of trade and transport on the Yonne River numbering ten to twelve thousand people. The town was approximately the same size as Bourges, the capital of Louis' native Berry. Geographically it was almost as close to Paris as it was to Dijon, the largest city and administrative capital of Burgundy. Commercially it was much closer to the French metropolis, because it took as little as four days for a standard transport ship to travel down the Yonne to the point where it met the Seine, then continue on to Paris. The Auxerrois had taken advantage of the cheap river transport to ship firewood and especially locally produced wine to the city on the banks of the Seine since at least the thirteenth century. By the end of the seventeenth century, a complex network of Parisian brokers and merchants bought wine from local growers for resale in Paris, Normandy, Flanders, and beyond. A third of Auxerre's residents toiled in the vineyards that covered the hills for dozens of kilometers outside the town walls, and many of those who did not directly tend the vines owned small vineyards that provided handsome incomes in most years. Most of the wine grown in the region was thus destined for export, not local consumption; unlike the quasi-subsistence agriculture of much of the Berry, Auxerre's economy received constant stimulus from the dynamic national and international market for wine. The town, also situated along a major north-south land route, saw soldiers, merchants, and administrators pass through its gates throughout the year, so Louis' arrival with horses and military equipment would not have drawn much attention.

According to the prisoner, in March 1695 he was on his way to Metz, a major town in Lorraine, when he stopped in Auxerre to rest his horses. He had planned to visit the archbishop of Metz, the Duc de la Feuillade's brother, perhaps to borrow money again. Then he had intended to join his dragoon regiment at its winter quarters near Charlemont in Flanders. In Auxerre he found lodgings at an inn called the Stag Beetle (*Cerf-Volant*), which was run by Marie Caillant, the widow of a recently deceased huissier named François Pillard. Caillant had five children who were still alive in 1695, four of whom were daughters. The only son, like his father, was a huissier. Three of the girls were married, while the fourth, a teenager named Marie, was still single. The prisoner noted that

> having arrived in Auxerre I found lodging with the Widow Pillard, proprietor of an inn, with whom I stayed for some time to rest my horses. During this time I unfortunately became involved with one of Pillard's daughters. I did not tell her I was married. The passion I felt for her, and the talent she had for serving me, led me to take the unfortunate step of marrying her . . . and staying in Auxerre, rather than continuing on my way to rejoin the regiment as I had planned.

This terse statement provides initial insight into the encounter between the discontented career officer and the provincial adolescent in the spring of 1695. After eight years of a marriage that had been one of convenience for both parties, and after many requests for funds that had left him indebted financially and morally to his first wife, it is not difficult to imagine why Louis found Marie appealing. In the fall of 1687 he had wanted to marry Marguerite's teenage daughter, but had settled for her mother. Now the opportunity for an alliance with a young girl who had no children, little property, and no prior marital history presented itself again. This time, in the wake of earlier marital disappointments and frustrated career ambitions, the match proved irresistible. Because there is no contemporary testimony from Marie or her mother, we do not know if Louis had already decided to shed his former identity when he arrived at the Stag Beetle in search of lodging. But it is unlikely that Marie and her mother would have agreed to the eventual marriage if they had thought they were aiding an impoverished aristocrat and military officer to escape his disappointing army career and unsatisfying first marriage. In the France of the mid-1690s, buffeted so fiercely by the dislocations of war, famine, and disease, and in a town such as Auxerre, where anonymous travelers were a constant presence, Louis was able to reinvent himself.

The marriage contract, signed the day before the April 30, 1695, wedding, and the parish register entry, written by a priest named Courcier the next day, provide information as to how Louis fashioned this new identity. The notary who drafted the contract identifies him as "Louis Dubouchet," the son of a supposedly deceased Parisian merchant named Antoine Dubouchet and his wife, Marguerite Mercier. Louis must have taken the name Dubouchet from his father, who had occasionally adopted the title "*écuyer*, Sieur du Bouchet" to distinguish himself from his brothers. The name of his imagined mother, Marguerite Mercier, did not correspond to that of his real mother, Marie de Berthoulat. He may have borrowed it from his first wife's godchild, the hapless maidservant relentlessly interrogated by the Châtillon magistrates. In addition, the marriage contract states that Dubouchet was born in the St. Sulpice parish in Paris. Louis had stayed in that neighborhood the first time he visited Paris as a youth, which may have prompted him to claim it as his false birthplace. The parish register entry notes that the normal Catholic custom of announcing the pending marriage for three consecutive weeks in the home parish of each spouse had been waived for Dubouchet because he had reportedly served fourteen consecutive years in the king's armies. The priest Courcier presumably accepted the argument that Dubouchet had been absent from the St. Sulpice parish so long that there was no possibility he might have already been married. While these documents reveal some of the details of Louis' deception, they do not fully explain his motives.

By 1695 Louis had learned from experience that birth into the noble estate did not guarantee wealth, social prestige, or even material comfort. The actions of the royal government during the reign of Louis XIV further undermined the aura of the aristoc-

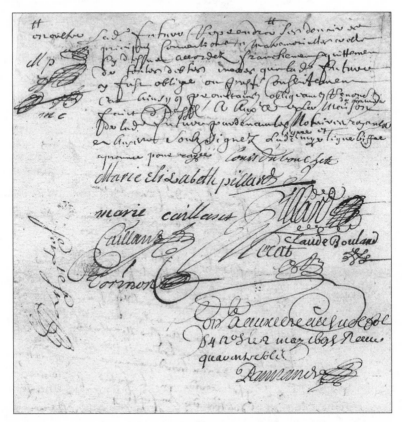

Signature page of the marriage contract between Louis Dubouchet and Marie-Elisabeth Pillard, April 29, 1695. Note the signature *Louis Dubouchet* immediately following the text of the contract, succeeded by those of his wife and his mother-in-law, Marie Caillant.

racy. The Sun King continued the royal practice of selling important positions in the judicial and administrative branches of government to wealthy commoners who had the means to purchase them, then granting these officeholders and their offspring perpetual nobility in exchange for annual "upkeep" payments. The kings of France instituted venal office-holding to create a nationwide bureaucracy beholden to the monarchy, and also to allow the state access to the wealth of nobles who were otherwise exempt from direct taxation. At the same time, in the 1660s, and again in the 1690s during the Pivardière affair, the Crown undertook inquests into the legitimacy of every family that claimed nobility throughout the kingdom. Both practices, the sale of offices and the royal inquests, proclaimed that the state, not local custom, family tradition, or individual merit, determined membership in the ranks of the nobility. At the same time, these royal policies also compromised the standing of the aristocracy in the eyes of all French subjects by demonstrating that membership in its ranks was not an immutable quality bestowed upon individuals by virtue of their birth.

In January 1695, just months before Louis' arrival in Auxerre, the government took another step that further eroded aristocratic privilege. It proclaimed a new direct tax, the capitation, which would be leveled upon all of the king's subjects except the clergy; even the dauphin, the heir to the throne, was subject to it. Furthermore, it ranked all of French society into twenty-two classes for purposes of assigning tax liability. Those in the first rank, which included the dauphin, the princes of the blood, and the state's highest ministers and administrators, owed two thousand livres a year. Those in the eleventh class, which included mid-level royal court appointees and tax collectors as well as officials in small municipalities, owed one hundred livres. And those on the twenty-second and final rung, which included soldiers, day laborers, and artisanal apprentices, paid only one livre. The rankings, produced by anonymous bureaucrats in the Finance Ministry, indicate that, for tax purposes at least, noble status did not necessarily separate one from commoners. Noble categories were scattered throughout the rankings alongside commoner occupations; the lowest noble rank, with an annual tax rate of six livres, was level nineteen, where one could find aristocrats who owned neither fiefs nor castles.

However, neither the capitation, with its refusal to exempt nobles from taxation and its stark equation of nobles and commoners
across ranks, nor the sale of offices and the inquests negated the
importance of nobility in French society. It was not until the Revolution a century later that the French collectively rebelled against
the principle of hereditary privilege, and even then it was resurrected by some of the country's nineteenth-century regimes. But
the cumulative effect of these seventeenth-century government
policies, along with the poverty into which the poorest members
of the aristocracy had sunk by 1700, did prompt some aristocrats
to temporarily deny their noble status. Some rural Norman nobles
in 1670, for example, offended that the Crown would presume to
question their status, disguised themselves as common townsfolk
to avoid interrogation, then returned to their estates after the officials had left the region. Other nobles abandoned aristocratic
pretensions altogether; a Breton nobleman from one of the province's oldest families sold his lands, which only brought in 120
livres a year, to become a wig maker in Rennes. Near Soissons,
many rural gentlemen accepted minor posts as collectors of the
taille, the direct tax from which they were exempt. Other needy
aristocrats throughout the kingdom, defying regulations that prohibited them from engaging in commerce, became merchants,
selling wine or tobacco. Some sought charity from neighbors or
the church. One historian claims that within Louis' native Berry it
was not uncommon for many of the province's nobles to pass as
commoners to avoid higher capitation rates. Another records the
example of a Monsieur du Chatellier from Poulaines, the parish
where Louis was born, who was reduced to becoming a game-
keeper to avoid destitution.

Nowhere in the surviving documentation did Louis indicate an
awareness of these local precedents of social derogation; his decision to become a commoner was made outside the province, for
reasons not entirely triggered by his fiscal shortfalls. Nor did he or

any of his contemporaries connect his transformation to the impact of the Crown's legal and fiscal policies regarding the nobility. But his own experience, and his exposure to the successes and failures of other nobles in his province, in the military, and in Paris and other cities he visited, attuned him to the shifting status of the nobility. The capitation rolls for the Berry in the late 1690s have been lost, so we do not know how the royal tax officials ranked Louis. But if we look at the kingdom-wide table of rankings for the capitation of 1695, it is reasonable to think that his marriage to Marguerite had improved his standing somewhat. Gentlemen possessing both fiefs and castles were ranked at level fifteen, owing forty livres per year rather than six. Before his 1687 marriage to Marguerite, Louis would likely have been classed at level nineteen, with the lowliest aristocrats who possessed neither fiefs nor castles. After he became the seigneur of Narbonne, which endowed him with a small manor house and a fief, he would have probably ranked somewhere between the fifteenth and the nineteenth rungs. The position he reluctantly inherited in Auxerre, as we shall see, that of *huissier d'un présidial*, would have placed him in the twentieth rank, taxed at a rate of three livres. In terms of both the implicit social hierarchy encoded in the capitation rankings, and the tax liability the ranking incurred, there was little to differentiate Louis' situation before he met his second wife in Auxerre from the one he adopted after marrying her. It is quite possible that Louis was aware of these equivalencies as he evaluated his options in Auxerre.

Money and status, though, were not the sole factors influencing Louis' actions in the spring of 1695. Physical attraction to Marie initially prompted him to stay in Auxerre longer than he intended. It is impossible to know when they first consummated their relationship, or whether their initial encounter was consensual. Their first child, a daughter named Marie, was baptized on January 15, 1696, according to the St. Eusèbe parish register. A birth on or near the date of her baptism would imply that she was conceived around the middle of April 1695, about a fortnight before Louis and Marie were married. But given the nutritional limitations of the French diet in the difficult years of the 1690s, and the poor state of neonatal care in preindustrial Europe, it is equally possible that the child was born prematurely. Marie's second child by Louis was baptized almost nine months after the baptism of the first child, which suggests that her second pregnancy lasted significantly less than nine months. This child died a week after the 1696 baptism, and their third and final child died the day of his baptism in 1699. Marie's natal history, therefore, points toward premature, unhealthy pregnancies. More importantly, it suggests that she might have conceived their first child in the days and weeks after the marriage. Did she maintain her honor until after the wedding, thereby forcing Louis to the altar in order to consummate their relationship?

The marriage contract hints that nonlibidinous factors also influenced Louis' decision to become a commoner. Under the contract, Louis and Marie agreed to joint ownership of all goods brought by both parties to the marriage. Louis Dubouchet contributed one thousand silver livres to their communal property, ostensibly from his Parisian merchant father and from his "savings." These funds probably derived from the money he had raised in Narbonne from his wife and neighbors prior to his departure for the front that January. He may also have sold one or more of his horses and some of his military equipment in Auxerre once it became apparent that he would not continue on to the front. Marie's contribution to the couple's endowment was more complicated. The contract specified that her mother would sign over a twenty-five livre annuity to the newlyweds; it also stipulated that she would grant them a one-time gift of two hundred livres. The bride also received rings and jewels worth forty livres, along with a wedding dress and other accessories. On the surface, it ap-

peared to be a union between a family with a foothold in municipal administration and a newcomer engaged in commerce.

These terms indicate that the marriage was not a decision undertaken by Louis and the teenage Marie alone. Marie Caillant,
whose signature on the contract appears immediately after that
of the two spouses, was crucial to the arrangement. Caillant's cen-
trality to the nuptial agreement was further underscored in the
months after the marriage, when she granted her new son-in-law
her deceased husband's nonvenal charge as a local huissier. Taken
with the monetary arrangements outlined in the marriage contract, this grant suggests that once the marriage had been proposed, Louis, his future mother-in-law, and other members of his
bride's immediate family were involved in deliberate negotiations
in the weeks leading up to the wedding. Caillant's only son was
also a huissier, as was one of her sons-in-law; these two may have
smoothed Louis' entry into the ranks of the local squadron. In
short, the marriage did not only unite Louis and Marie as legitimate spouses in the eyes of the church; it also tied Louis' financial
fortunes to that of Marie Caillant and her offspring in the wake of
the paterfamilias' death a year and a half earlier. This was not a
shotgun wedding, and in any event there was little that Marie
Caillant and her daughter could have done to prevent a military
officer from skipping town if he had been so inclined. Instead, it
appears that the marriage served the monetary and social strategies of all parties involved.

In 1695, therefore, the promise of a fresh marriage and new
career options as a merchant or a police officer enticed Louis
de la Pivardière enough to conceal his past. Once married, "Dubouchet," his wife, and his mother-in-law moved swiftly to secure
his entry into the ranks of the town's huissiers. By the summer
of 1695, Louis had assumed his new responsibilities; the officer
whom the king might have called upon in any campaign to risk his
life and that of his subordinates in the pursuit of French glory was

now serving summonses and seizing furniture and livestock from commoners in satisfaction of civil suits. Lacunae in the Auxerre archives prevent us from following the new huissier's activities from 1695 through the spring of 1697; one surviving document from the summer of 1696 shows Dubouchet being called to task for improperly seizing the movable property of a laborer living in a village outside the Auxerre town walls. Although it is impossible to know how scrupulously Louis fulfilled his professional responsibilities, a witness during the Paris trial asserted that he had never mastered the legal formulae necessary to fill out the reports required of all sergeants. Instead, he relied on lawyers and merchants, in particular an attorney named Billeton, who was "a friend of the widow Pillard," to do his paperwork, and he had arrangements with several controllers who accepted these ghostwritten reports.

At some point after their marriage, although perhaps not until the birth of their first child, the couple moved out of the Stag Beetle to several rooms they rented in the house of a wig maker, a connection they may have made through Marie's brother-in-law. It is likely, though, that they stayed within the St. Eusèbe parish. Around the time of the birth and almost immediate death of the couple's second child in the fall of 1696, financial problems began to emerge. On December 16, 1696, Louis and Marie borrowed 742 livres from a royal grain official in Auxerre named Edme de Curne; the following February they borrowed 262 livres more from the same source. The loan documents do not describe why Dubouchet and his young wife had fallen into debt, but their financial woes and Dubouchet's indifference toward his responsibilities as a huissier must have created tension between the spouses, and between the couple and Marie Caillant. Louis de la Pivardière might have escaped to the woods and forests of the Berry to go hunting with his friends and forget his troubles, but Louis Dubouchet would have found it more difficult to round up a coterie of sympathetic companions in a town where he was less well known than his wife and her mother.

Furthermore, in the spring of 1697, negotiators began to gather at Ryswick in the Netherlands; word spread widely throughout France and Europe that Louis XIV and his enemies had tired of conflict and would terminate armed hostilities by year's end. Louis, already saddled with a mounting debt, knew he would soon have to find another cover for his life in Auxerre, or else somehow extricate himself from his second marriage. In April or early May 1697, before Curne could have him thrown in debtor's prison in Auxerre, he left for Narbonne, where he probably suspected he would have to answer his first wife's questions about his plans once the war was over. As we have seen, Louis failed to resolve the bigamous dilemma he had created before Marguerite found out about his double life. Not long after that disclosure, his second wife also discovered Louis' treachery, and the affair was out of his control. Sometime in late summer 1698, after the first Paris verdict, Marie and her mother negotiated an agreement in Paris with the Chauvelin family. The two Auxerrois women received twelve hundred livres in exchange for undoing Louis' second marriage. Marie and her mother also agreed to facilitate Louis' imminent departure for Paris to testify on behalf of Marguerite. Working together, outside official state institutions, the Chauvelin and Pillard clans finally straightened out the marital mess created three years earlier by Louis' deceptions.

Nevertheless, the re-emergence of the noble bigamist had to be verified if Marguerite and the prior were to escape accusations of murder. The Châtillon judges, however, and those who found their murder charge persuasive, did not view the case as one that turned on the plausibility of Louis' metamorphosis from nobleman to commoner. Even if Louis' second marriage had been discretely terminated by the Chauvelin family, the murder charge against Marguerite and the prior remained. The Parlement, they asserted, needed to determine if the man in Fort l'Evêque was an impostor recounting a well-scripted but fictional version of a bigamous second marriage that had never occurred.

By the end of the seventeenth century, the practice of imposture had a storied history, one known to both legal experts and laymen. Since the late Middle Ages, French kings had denounced imposture as a capital offense. Old Regime jurists placed the crime in the category of that which was faux, or falsified. For the most part, these transgressions consisted of forged signatures, counterfeit money, faked contracts, false testimony, and other means of deceit. The 1670 criminal ordinance contained seventeen clauses defining acts of forgery. But imposture as a legal category was also understood to be a subset of falsehood, as the *Dictionary* issued in 1694 by the French Royal Academy made clear. The *Encyclopedia* of Diderot and d'Alembert, published in the mid-eighteenth century, was even more specific: The article by the jurist Antoine Gaspard Boucher d'Argis on the legal meanings of faux stated that "those who take the name and the arms of another, the titles, and other marks of distinction which do not at all belong to them, commit a falsehood." French law since the 1530s had not taken lightly to such crimes of falsification; Francis I had specified death as their penalty, a punishment endorsed with minor nuances by Louis XIV in 1680. The accusations in the fall of 1698 against the so-called Pivardière awaiting his moment in court, therefore, like the murder charges against Marguerite and the prior, were deadly serious.

In addition to these statutes, the Tournelle magistrates had several precedents to guide their deliberations as they reconsidered the affair. The best known of these trials, both in Louis de la Pivardière's time and today, was the mid-sixteenth-century case of Martin Guerre. In this remarkable affair, the son of a wealthy peasant living in Artigat, a village near the Spanish border, married Bertrande de Rols when both were teenagers; he then abandoned his wife and their young son in his early twenties. After an absence of more than ten years, during which time Guerre's father died and the family property transferred to his uncle, a man claiming to be Martin Guerre suddenly returned to the village to reclaim his inheritance and resume conjugal life with Bertrande. After several years, however, the man's uncle, the displaced guardian of the dead father's estate, began to question the identity of his alleged nephew; his suspicions were fed by rumors suggesting that the man who claimed to be Martin Guerre was an impostor named Arnaud du Tilh, and by reports that the real Martin Guerre had lost a leg while in the service of the Spanish king. At the uncle's instigation, the man who claimed to be Martin Guerre was arrested and tried in a provincial court similar to the one in Châtillon-sur-Indre a century and a half later. He was found guilty but immediately appealed his case to the Parlement of Toulouse, a sister institution to the Parlement of Paris. There the criminal court was on the verge of overturning the lower court's ruling when a one-legged man claiming to be the true Martin Guerre dramatically arrived just prior to the announcement of the verdict. The newcomer confronted the man who claimed to be Martin Guerre, family members and villagers compared the two pretenders, and the magistrates examined both peasants. Guerre's sisters and his wife, Bertrande, recognized the one-legged newcomer as the authentic Martin Guerre, an identification that proved decisive in the eyes of the judges. Arnaud du Tilh, who stubbornly stuck to his deception until the final verdict, was executed by the Crown in Artigat in front of the villagers whom he had deceived for several years. Contemporaries and subsequent commentators marveled at his skill in creating his illusion, and questioned Bertrande de Rols' motives in allowing an impostor into her marriage bed.

For the lawyers and magistrates attempting to adjudicate the Pivardière affair, the Martin Guerre precedent had conflicting implications. In his July 1698 brief, the attorney for Morin and Bonnet, the Châtillon magistrates, invoked the case as an example of how the "people" can easily be duped or mistaken. Arnaud du Tilh, the lawyer wrote, had fooled an entire village, including the wife and relatives of the missing man, for three years; the residents of the Berry had similarly been fooled by the impostor who claimed to be Louis de la Pivardière in January 1698. Furthermore, the false Martin Guerre had willingly appeared before the Parlement of Toulouse to plead his case; the false Louis, having learned from Arnaud du Tilh's mistakes, remained in hiding, afraid to expose himself to examination by the Parlement of Paris. The lawyer who penned the brief on behalf of Louis, however, argued that the Martin Guerre case implied that it was unlikely the man from Auxerre was an impostor. The success of Arnaud du Tilh, he pointed out, was because of the ten-year absence of the real Martin Guerre. Memories had dimmed of the man's appearance, and he was certain to have changed physically. In contrast, it had been only five months between Louis' alleged assassination and his reappearance in the Berry, which was hardly enough time for the locals to forget his appearance, or for his physique to have changed appreciably. The hundreds of people who verified Louis' identity in January 1698 could not have been mistaken.

If one accepted the proposition that the man on display in the Berry at the beginning of 1698 was Louis, then the case appeared to be an example of Martin Guerre *à l'invers* (in reverse). The true Martin Guerre, a peasant presumed lost or dead, ultimately reclaimed his wife, son, and property. The real Louis de la Pivardière, an aristocrat presumed murdered by his spouse and her lover, had not yet reassumed his former identity. But was the man in Fort l'Evêque prison the same person who had married Marguerite Chauvelin in 1687? A second case, in this instance

from the mid-1600s, offered another example of an individual
who had successfully defrauded an entire family into believing he
was a long-lost son. In 1638, Claude de Veré, the fourteen-year-
old eldest son of a minor noble family in the Loire Valley town of
Saumur, had joined the French army as a commissioned officer
during the Thirty Years War. After a number of years his father
died, and his mother and younger brother, Jacques, hearing nothing from Claude, feared the worst. They left town, retreating to
the mother's estate outside Saumur. Twelve years after Claude's
departure, in 1650, during the Fronde, a regiment laid siege to a
castle in the area. One of the regimental officers, taking advantage
of an interlude in the hostilities to tour the countryside, encountered Jacques de Veré. The latter immediately believed he recognized his long-lost brother, in part because of a scar on his forehead caused by a childhood burn. He brought the officer home to
his grieving mother, who identified him as her son. But the officer
balked, refusing to acknowledge the woman's assertion; instead, he
asked for time to gather his thoughts. The next day, in response to
the Dame de Chauvigny's anxious query, he admitted he was her
long-missing son. He claimed that he had not initially wished to
admit his identity due to his guilt over the grief his long absence
had caused her.

The mother and her younger son wasted no time in organizing
a feast to honor the officer's return. Neighbors and friends who attended, no doubt prompted by the joy and relief of Madame de
Chauvigny, testified that while her son Claude had changed since
his departure twelve years earlier, such physical and emotional al-
teration was to be expected of a man who had lost his innocence
amid the hardships of war. The only dissenting voice to this happy
turn of events was that of the Sieur de Piedfelon, the brother
of Madame de Chauvigny, who refused to recognize the military officer as his nephew. (His opposition recalls that of Pierre
Guerre, Martin's uncle; the Sieur de Piedfelon may also have had

an economic stake in exposing a man he suspected of imposture.) Family and friends, however, dismissed Piedfelon as a crotchety old man who took pleasure in ruining the joy of others. After several months of family harmony, the officer's regiment was ordered to march to Normandy. "Claude" left with his younger brother in tow.

While in Normandy, now openly identified as the heir to the Veré estate, the officer managed an advantageous marriage to Magdeleine Dauplé, the daughter of a wealthy local gentleman. Although he should have sought the permission of his mother back in Saumur, he convinced Jacques to substantiate his claim that neither of their parents were living. When his troop received orders to proceed to the Flemish front, he left behind his new wife, but not the dowry he had received. With the coming of winter, he and his brother decided to return to their patrimony near Saumur, again without Magdeleine. There they passed the time with their overjoyed mother, but Claude also occasionally escaped the family estate in Chauvigny in favor of the entertainments found in Saumur. He became acquainted with Anne Allard, daughter of another local noble family roughly equivalent in wealth and prestige to the Veré clan. When Allard became pregnant, Claude arranged for the news to spread that his Norman wife had suddenly taken ill and passed away. (Like Louis, the perils of bigamy appear not to have deterred him.) He apologized to his mother for not having sought permission for his Norman nuptials and obtained her consent to this new union. The marriage took place in March 1653, after which Claude quit the military to settle down in Saumur with his wife and extended family.

Anne Allard gave birth to two healthy children over the next three years. The Dame de Chauvigny, thrilled that her eldest son had married and settled down to raise his children, turned over her fortune and estate to Claude, who expanded the family's holdings and refurbished their castle. His younger brother, Jacques, who readily agreed to this disposition of the family goods, enjoyed the pleasurable company of his sister-in-law and nephews. One day in 1656, however, a ragged foot soldier appeared at Chauvigny claiming he was Claude de Veré. The man explained that after he had left the family fold in 1638, his lust for women and dissipation had blocked his attempts at advancement within the military, ultimately forcing him to abandon his commission, probably due to a lack of money, and to enlist as a simple soldier in the French Guards. He had been taken prisoner during the siege of Valenciennes in Flanders in 1656; once released, he had determined to return home to face the reproaches he knew he deserved from the family he had long abandoned. Both the mother and the brother, however, refused to acknowledge the newcomer as their own. The Dame de Chauvigny reportedly told the foot soldier, "I have had but two children in my life, and I am sure that the two living alongside me now are the ones I brought into this world. Therefore you must be an impostor!"

Unable to make any headway at Chauvigny, the stubborn soldier sought out the lieutenant criminal of Saumur, a provincial magistrate who wielded an authority comparable to that of Morin and Bonnet in Châtillon-sur-Indre, or LeComte in Romorantin. This official, realizing the delicacy of the affair and the local standing of the families involved, conducted his own investigation before filing any charges. On the surface, the claims of the bedraggled soldier seemed unlikely. The Dame de Chauvigny had publicly proclaimed the return of her son six years earlier to the enthusiastic reception of almost everyone who had known the boy before he left for war. His younger brother, who stood to inherit the family fortune upon Claude's disappearance, had eagerly relinquished his claims upon the return of his brother. Over the preceding three years, the man who claimed to be Claude de Veré had conducted himself in an exemplary fashion; he had financed his children's education and administered the family's estate in a selfless, efficient fashion. There was little to indicate that he was an adventurer who sought to profit from the confusion and desire of a heartbroken mother and brother. In contrast, the man who now claimed the title of the elder de Veré sibling was a soldier of fortune who by his own admission had lost his officer rank due to his womanizing and dissolute ways.

In an effort to clear up the mystery, the local magistrate resorted to a face-to-face confrontation between the *soi-disant* missing son and the Dame de Chauvigny. Surprisingly, the results were inconclusive. The family matriarch recalled the joy with which she had greeted the man she assumed was her son six years previously, and the tenderness, love, and sense of family responsibility he had displayed since. She also admitted, however, that her inordinate desire to see her missing son after twelve years might have led her to mistake an impostor for her own, and that his subsequent benevolent conduct may well have served to confirm her in this error. At the end of the session, completely confused, the poor woman confessed she did not know the truth of the matter and pledged to abide by the results of the magistrate's investigation. The magistrate then summoned the Sieur de Piedfelon, the cantankerous uncle who had never acknowledged the return of his nephew, to confront the soldier. The two had not yet seen each other. Immediately upon his entry into the room, the soldier threw himself crying into the welcoming arms of the old man. Once the magistrate pried them apart, he recorded their encounter, in which the soldier recounted obscure details that matched testimony provided by both the Sieur de Piedfelon and the Dame de Chauvigny.

The confrontation between the soldier and the uncle proved to be the case's turning point. Soon thereafter, most of the extended family, having had a chance to visit with the newcomer, proclaimed him to be the true Claude de Veré. The magistrate issued a warrant for the arrest of the man who had married Anne

Allard, and began to interview officers and soldiers from the regiments of the two men. Those from the Harcourt Regiment, the one that had passed through Saumur in 1650 during the Fronde, testified that the man who had married Magdeleine Dauplé in Normandy and Anne Allard in Saumur was a commoner called Michel Feydy de la Lérauderie. In contrast, those who had served with the foot soldier from the French Guards swore that he had always identified himself as Claude de Veré, and that he had always sported a scar on his forehead. Before the magistrate could take Michel Feydy into custody, however, he disappeared, never to be seen again; he was sentenced to death in absentia. In his wake, his wife, Anne Allard, sued the Dame de Chauvigny, alleging that she had entered into marriage and given birth to their children because she had been assured by the oaths and actions of the dame that the man she had married was her son. Now she found that her marriage was illegitimate, and her children disinherited. After three more years of tangled legal proceedings, the courts ruled in 1659 that Allard had married the impostor in good faith and that her children were legitimate, even though her marriage was not. Furthermore, the magistrates decided that the unfortunate Dame de Chauvigny owed Allard's children two thousand livres in damages.

Although separated by a century, the cases of the false Martin Guerre and the false Claude de Veré have much in common. Both involved a prodigal son who left the family embrace for more than a decade of war and adventure; both men remained incommunicado while gone. In their stead, gifted, opportunistic scoundrels learned of their absence and successfully insinuated themselves into the emotional and economic vacuums left behind. And both impostures were successful for a time because of the witting, or unwitting, connivance of an intimate family member. The historian Natalie Davis, in her account of the Martin Guerre affair, has argued that Bertrande de Rols, influenced by Protestant sensibilities, was fully aware of the imposture from the beginning. Nevertheless, she cooperated in the deception in order to restore her marital status and, possibly, to enjoy a companionate marriage with a man who was a better friend and husband than the youth who had abandoned her. In a brief from the late 1650s written on behalf of Anne Allard's two sons, a similar argument appears about the role played in the Veré affair by the Dame de Chauvigny. The mother of the missing son may have known from the outset that the man who had reappeared in 1650 claiming to be Claude de Veré was a fraud. But she so longed for her son, and was so taken by the newcomer, that she stifled her immediate doubts and allowed the impostor in. Over the next six years, until the reappearance of her true son, she "adopted" the newcomer as her offspring, enjoying his filial embrace, entrusting him with her property, and thereby recovering the dozen years of affection she had lost.

On one level, of course, the actions of Arnaud du Tilh and Michel Feydy were reprehensible; they had usurped the wealth and civil standing of the men they had impersonated. Even if one condemns Martin Guerre and Claude de Veré for the cruel absences that brought hardship to those close to them, it is difficult to argue that they deserved to lose their patrimonies to men who knowingly defrauded their families. On another level, however, these two temporarily successful impostors had something to recommend themselves: They were better than the originals. Neither Martin Guerre nor Claude de Veré brought their wife or mother, respectively, the kind of emotional commitment and financial stability that their impersonators offered. Interestingly, the courts concurred. The daughter of Arnaud du Tilh and Bertrande de Rols was made the inheritor of Arnaud after his death, and Anne Allard's two sons were proclaimed legitimate and granted a portion of their grandmother's estate, even though they were not her blood relations. In each case, the magistrates appear to have acknowledged that the material and emotional benefits provided by the impostors entitled their offspring to legitimacy and material compensation. Did these decisions constitute legal approval of deceptions that responded to the hardships of military absence or the impossibility of divorce?

Even in these clear-cut cases of imposture, therefore, the courts and other observers remained ambivalent about the demise of the usurpers; the doubts ran even higher in late 1698 in the seemingly unfathomable case of the missing Pivardière. An anonymous Parisian correspondent of Anne-Marguerite du Noyer, a Protestant who ultimately sought refuge in the Netherlands, summarized the case for her friend in a letter that fall. She noted that once the late July verdict was announced, most people who had followed the case expected Marguerite and the prior to be executed publicly in the Place de Grève. But the unexpected arrival of the self-proclaimed Pivardière had turned everything upside down. In spite of witnesses who claimed to have seen Louis' body full of dagger wounds, the Fort l'Evêque prisoner seemed to know all the answers to questions regarding the life of the missing man. Noyer's anonymous correspondent even claimed that an acquaintance named Madame Camus, who had supposedly attended school with Louis when both were children, was amazed when the prisoner recounted their childhood games. "Ultimately," the letter writer opined, "the judges understand nothing about this affair. We are assured that Mme de la Pivardière had her husband assassinated; nevertheless, they cannot avoid absolving her." No matter how much evidence the Chauvelin clan submitted to prove the identity of the Fort l'Evêque prisoner, Noyer's correspondent and many other observers that fall were still perplexed. The uncertainties created by past French impostors echoed in the debates that surrounded the Pivardière affair.

On September 3, shortly after the missing husband had incarcerated himself, the supposed Pivardière filed a *requête civile*, or appeal, in which he formally challenged the Parlement's July rul-

ing that he was an impostor. In this brief, the appellant reasserted
that he had not been murdered on the night of August 15; he argued that all other judicial activity in the case should be halted until his existence had been thoroughly and impartially investigated.
This *requête* continued the strategy employed by Louis Chauvelin
to undo the implicit verdict the Tournelle had issued in July. The
appeal went directly to the king, who alone had the power to re-
quire the criminal judges in the Parlement to review, and potentially overturn, their decisions. The king did not rule on the appeal until the beginning of December, but in the meantime the
case continued to be heard in the diffuse court of popular opinion.
Indeed, the affair became a cause célèbre in Paris that fall, a means
to ponder issues of marital fidelity and individual identity in an
uncertain age.

Chapter 5

STAGE PLAYS

⚜

$\mathcal{I}$n the beginning of 1699, as the Tournelle prepared to retry the Pivardière murder case, a pamphlet appeared in Paris bookshops written by a lawyer friendly to the cause of Marguerite and the prior. Before launching into his defense of the accused murderers, the author described the contemporary fascination with the case:

> Never has an affair had a bigger impact on polite society than that of the Dame de la Pivardière. The subject is similar to those invented topics that one sees onstage in every period, and which even today provide for the admiration and entertainment of many peoples. The novelty of the affair, the mixed nature of the intrigue, the juxtaposition of the characters, the uncertainty of the events. . . . This case has it all.

It is not surprising that the author of this work thought of the Pivardière affair in theatrical terms; two months earlier, the case had inspired a popular play, *Le Mari retrouvé* (*The Husband Returned*), which was performed at the Comédie-Française. The twists and turns of the affair, played out before Parisians in the second half of 1698, were well suited to the stage. Furthermore, playhouses were popular gathering spots where news and speculation about the case circulated rapidly. Paris boasted two year-round theaters in 1698, the Comédie-Française, which enjoyed a monopoly on the performance of French-language plays in the capital, and the Opéra, a royal academy that held a similar privilege for the staging of lyric drama. In addition, legal loopholes allowed for the appearance of makeshift stages on the grounds of the six-week trade fairs held in Paris every spring and fall. Minor troupes took advantage of these venues to perform acrobatic acts and slapstick works from the repertory of the Italian actors, a third year-round troupe that had been expelled from Paris in 1697 for alleged indecencies onstage. The same individuals who read both French and foreign periodicals, haunted the law courts in search of gossip and amusement, and visited Louis at Fort l'Evêque "out of curiosity" also made the capital's playhouses a necessary stop on their social circuits.

The playwright who adapted the Pivardière affair to the Parisian stage, Florent Carton Dancourt, was a writer, performer, and, at one point, the orator of the Comédie-Française. He was born in 1661, the same year as Louis de la Pivardière. He attended a Jesuit *collège* and passed the examinations to become a lawyer in his teens, but soon fell in love with Thérèse Le Noir de la Thorillière, an actress in an ambulatory provincial troupe and the daughter of a well-known Parisian actor who had been a member of Molière's company. They married in 1680, by which point Dancourt had abandoned the law for the stage; in 1685 they both joined the Comédie-Française, which then staged the first of many works he authored. By the late 1690s, he was the troupe's most important comic author, and he played some of Molière's greatest roles, such as Alceste in *The Misanthrope* and the title character in *Tartuffe;* he also performed young lover roles on occasion. Offstage, he was

Robert Gence, *Florent Carton Dancourt*, 1704. The artist has represented the playwright-performer as a man of letters. He is writing a dedication to his patron, the Duc de Bavière. The books on the right contain the works of the classical comic playwrights Aristophanes, Plautus, and Terence, lending a scholarly seriousness to the playwright.

rumored to have had dalliances with partners ranging from the dauphine to a maidservant he impregnated then abandoned. Early in the first decade of the 1700s, songs and rumors circulated alleging that Dancourt prostituted his wife and daughters for financial and social gain; the charges were undoubtedly fueled by the actor/ playwright's constant indebtedness throughout the 1690s and the first decade of the eighteenth century. Dancourt's dual public persona, therefore, verged from that of the elegant *amant* and public orator onstage to the promiscuous, irresponsible *roué* in the wings. Like Louis, his contemporary, his life was a constant improvisation: He moved between the aristocracy and the bourgeoisie, between town and country, albeit more artfully and with more success than the Berrichon gentleman.

Dancourt, therefore, was properly situated to script the story of Pivardière for the public stage, a task he undertook in the fall of 1698. Keenly attuned to his audience's interests, he wrote more than two dozen light, cynical, one-act romps, known to contemporaries as *dancourades*, which he set in a variety of bourgeois and peasant settings in Paris and the Ile-de-France basin. These plays were distinguished both for their direct, vivid language and their cynicism and loose morality. The mid-eighteenth-century governmental minister, bibliophile, and theater enthusiast René Louis de Voyer de Paulmy, Marquis d'Argenson, who was generally dismissive of Dancourt's theater, commented that "the marriages in Dancourt's plays always seem more like simple concubinage than anything else," while Voltaire in 1725 decried the coarsening effect he thought Dancourt had promoted among public theater audiences, accustoming them to the lowest common aesthetic and moral denominator.

Dancourt, however, was not solely responsible for the stage version of the Pivardière affair performed at the Comédie-Française that November. Theatrical performances, while often based on a written text by the end of the seventeenth century, took place in real time; they were an uneasy collaborative venture between writers, performers, and the spectators who responded instantaneously to the performance, constantly reshaping the work's meaning. This joint exercise in interpretation was materially different in late-seventeenth-century Paris from what it has become today. Spectators who wished to see a performance at the Comédie-Française, the royal company chartered less than twenty years earlier, had to fight their way through the crowded, dirty Parisian streets to the box office of the Left Bank building that housed the company. Ticket in hand, the spectator then pushed into a small foyer en route to the performance hall. When filled to capacity, the Comédie-Française theater held around seventeen hundred people, but the space could feel overcrowded on nights when a thousand people were in attendance. Most evenings, more than half the audience jammed into the theater pit, an open area without seating, where they would stand for three to four hours to watch the show. Other spectators found places in the boxes that ringed the pit, or on the benches of the raised amphitheater in back of the parterre. The available technology did not allow the troupe to dim the audience lights, so once the play started there was no significant visual distinction between the stage and the auditorium. In addition, wealthier spectators might purchase seats on the stage itself, further confusing the separation between spectators and performers. During the performance, audience members would comment loudly on the play, sometimes prompting players to break character to address their hecklers.

While the public theater of the late seventeenth century was undoubtedly more chaotic than playhouses today, it was also more interactive, and therefore more conducive to the broadest imaginable forms of interpretation. Molière, Dancourt, and other playwright-performers, in spite of their literary ambitions, understood that their scripts were a starting point for their spectacles, not the final word. The actors might modify characters and plots during the brief periods allowed for rehearsal, but even greater adaptations had to be made on the fly in front of live, highly critical audiences. At the most abstract level, each night's performance offered an occasion for a conversation between performers and spectators about matters of common interest. Audience response might prompt the performers to revise the playwright's staging of social relations or philosophical ideas. In short, it is not hard to see why the stage offered an attractive venue to explore the meanings of the Pivardière affair. Each evening's performance provided an opportunity for writers, performers, and spectators to examine the much-debated case within the parameters of the nightly give-and-take between players and audience.

The Husband Returned was not the only play derived from current events that the troupe staged that fall of 1698. Spectators in the 1690s enjoyed plays on topical themes. As one contemporary critic noted, "The style today is to make a comedy out of every noteworthy happening. . . . Everyone then runs to the playhouse, not for the sake of good theater, but to see a work that features some occurrence everyone has been discussing."

In the fall of 1698, in addition to the case of the mysterious Fort l'Evêque prisoner, the troupe and the spectators had military matters on their mind. The recently ended war, France's international standing, and the succession to the Spanish throne were topics that also appeared frequently in memoirs and newssheets throughout these months. Of particular interest were reports of the gargantuan, three-week-long war games that Louis XIV staged on the plains surrounding the town of Compiègne, forty miles north of Paris. On August 28, the same day the supposed Pivardière arrived in Paris, the Sun King and his court set out from Versailles to watch the exercises, which featured more than seventy thousand royal troops. The splendor of the army, the seriousness of the mock engagements, and the size of the exercises left an impression on observers; as a writer for the *Gazette d'Amsterdam* noted, "These are the games of the great, which often frighten their inferiors."

Although the military exercises were the ostensible focus of the event, the presence of the king and his court, including *les dames*, as well as some spies and other foreigners and *noblesse de robe* and bourgeois from Paris, meant that displays of conspicuous consumption were also central to the proceedings. Each memorialist

and journalist who reported on the exercises at Compiègne included extensive descriptions of the lavish military costumes ordered especially for the occasion and the sumptuous banquets given on a daily basis by the military commanders whose regiments participated in the affair. Writing forty years later, the Duc de Saint-Simon was still astonished by what he had seen:

> It is impossible to imagine anything, in any genre, that was lacking from these tables, for either the lowliest or the highest guest. These were houses of wood fitted out like the most superb Parisian townhouses, everything newly made for the occasion with a singular taste and gallantry. There were immense, magnificent tents, enough by themselves to house an army. The kitchens, the many locales and the diverse officers who attended these tables without interruption morning, noon, and night, the waiters and staff, all formed a spectacle in which the order, the silence, the exactitude, the diligence and the perfect propriety ravished the surprised and admiring viewer.

The camp at Compiègne, then, permitted Louis XIV, his army, and his court to stage the spectacles of military might and extravagance that typified his reign. But if one looks a little closer at the events of September 1698 on the Picardian plain, one sees both the actors and the spectators out of character at various moments. Troops fresh from the battles of the Nine Years War were made

---

Opposite page: The Camp and the Siege of Compiègne. In this almanac published after the games, the Sun King, flanked by the dauphin and a bevy of courtiers, points to his troops' maneuvers. The royal favorite, Madame de Maintenon, and the Dutch ambassador are situated in the foreground. Louis forces the ambassador, standing mute behind Madame de Maintenon, to witness this display of military strength. Thus Europe, in the person of Louis' longtime enemy, the Dutch, stares in awe at the might of the Sun King.

to harvest the fall crops before they could rehearse military maneuvers. This was done to avoid trampling the unharvested fields of grain four years after a devastating famine. Once the games began, a country still reeling from that famine was treated to an excessive display of culinary artistry and caloric consumption. Financially strapped noblemen spent money they did not have to feed one another and equip their regiments. Heavy rainfall that September meant that precision military maneuvers were impossible to execute due to the sloppy conditions. Beneath the façade of martial glory and conspicuous consumption, there was much to question. Back at the Comédie-Française in Paris, even as Dancourt and his troupe took note of the unfolding Pivardière affair, they couldn't resist first taking on the war games. Dancourt's one-act play *Les Curieux de Compiègne* (*The Curiosity-Seekers of Compiègne*) premiered at the Comédie-Française on October 4, a little more than two weeks after the camp had ended.

The playwright and his troupe most likely intended their Compiègne play to entertain the socially mixed audience of their Parisian theater, rather than the king and his courtiers; on the day of the premiere, as they did on that date every year in the late seventeenth century, the troupe's leading performers left for Fontainebleau, where the king and his court had gone after Compiègne. In order to compensate the Parisian audience for the "rump troupe" left behind, Dancourt had grown accustomed to providing a new play for his Parisian audience in early October. *The Curiosity-Seekers of Compiègne* capitalized on the event attended by many in the theater audience, but it also presented Dancourt and the troupe with an interesting dramaturgical dilemma: How should one stage an event that had already been overdramatized by its organizers? The playwright would face similar questions a month later when the company turned to the Pivardière case. In the instance of his Compiègne play, Dancourt's solution was to invert the official hierarchy of the event. Military parades, gaming halls, and delicacy-laden dining tables played no part in the one-act comedy, in part because the act of representing the actions of the king, his courtiers, and their armed forces on the comic stage threatened to offend some of the troupe's most powerful patrons. Instead, the playwright created a scenario that highlighted the actions of bankrupt aristocrats and status-seeking Paris merchants located on the fringes of the games.

At the outset of *The Curiosity-Seekers of Compiègne*, the audience learns that the Chevalier de Fourbignac and Clitandre, two military officers, are broke, presumably due to the expense of the camp. In addition, Clitandre is desperately in love with Angélique, the daughter of the cloth merchant Monsieur Valentin and his wife. The Valentins and another Parisian clothier named Mouflard, accompanied by his mistress, Madame Robin, have journeyed to Compiègne to watch the games. Valentin and Mouflard have outfitted themselves with swords and expensive attire in an attempt to pass as officers and courtiers. Taking note of their aristocratic pretensions, the two impoverished officers and their servants conspire to strip the two merchants of their money via a double-marriage scheme. The most comic, and at the same time most poignant and upsetting, moments in the play involve the exposure of the two Parisian merchants who aspire to higher social status. When Monsieur Mouflard (the name comes from the word *moufle*, or mitten; it is intended to remind spectators of his banal origins) first appears onstage, about two-thirds of the way through, he has already been humiliated for his efforts to counterfeit his social betters. He and three relatives, a mirror cutter, a hosier, and a notary, had been circulating among the soldiers in "fine clothes, with big swords and red plumes in their hats." No matter where they turned, however, the troops had mocked them, yelling that they should go back to their boutiques. Sergeants ordered maneuvers without warning, causing the troops narrowly to miss them. Finally, they chanced upon a battalion where the officers were dressed the same as two of Mouflard's relatives. The officers commanded their soldiers to strip the two merchants of their finery, accusing them of counterfeiting military officers; their act of imposture could not be allowed to stand. Mouflard recounts these woes then storms offstage, vowing never again to attend a military review.

Monsieur Valentin, the other bourgeois protagonist of the play, enters next, dressed in equally outlandish clothes, to recount his own miseries to his wife. Although he tries to put a positive face on his experiences, in part to disarm Madame Valentin who has complained bitterly throughout the play about being dragged to Compiègne, it quickly comes out that he too has been humiliated, receiving beatings, canings, and a kick in the stomach from a horse. His troubles have only begun, however; a rustic peasant enters to tell him that he is suspected of being a spy, and that if caught he will be forced to ride the *cheval de bois*, a stationary wooden horse with heavy weights attached to his legs. Before Monsieur Valentin can respond, the Chevalier de Fourbignac enters with four well-armed soldiers who take Valentin into custody. They are followed onstage by Clitandre, leading Monsieur Mouflard, whom he has also seized, and many peasants, bourgeois, and soldiers who ceremoniously transport the wooden horse onto the scene. At this point, the audience realizes that the two nobles and their followers have organized the threatened punishment to intimidate the two merchants into allowing Angélique to marry Clitandre, and Madame Robin, the well-dowered mistress of Mouflard, to marry the Chevalier. The merchants capitulate, and the play ends with singing, dancing, and the promise of two marriages.

Dancourt's dramaturgical strategy, then, was not to replicate the pomp of the games on the Parisian stage two weeks after the fact. Rather, he used the stage to mock the social pretensions of the urban merchants and financiers who had attended the military exercises. Whereas their betters had known how to perform in the military/courtly setting, the merchants had clumsily attempted to transgress their social station, suffering the ultimate humiliation of ridicule at the hands of the gentlemen officers. In *The Curiosity-Seekers of Compiègne*, Valentin and Mouflard are the heirs of Molière's Monsieur Jourdain, the protagonist of *The Would-Be Gentleman;* they try to pass themselves off as noblemen, but are ultimately exposed as usurpers. They forfeit money, a marriageable daughter, and a wealthy mistress to the actual noblemen and their servants, who outwit them.

But the meanings of the play are more complex. It is easy to imagine Dancourt, himself a notable social climber, heaping scorn upon the merchant class from which he wished to disassociate himself. But the army officers, with their unscrupulous schemes for wealth and women, are hardly more sympathetic than the merchants, and the peasants who help them defraud the bourgeois are scornful of their social betters. D'Argenson's accusation of concubinage appears accurate; when one considers the play in its entirety, there is little in the way of moral behavior that is worthy of emulation or praise. Dancourt's theater, intended in this case primarily for the mixed audiences of the capital, acts as the inverse of the spectacle staged at Compiègne. Whereas the military games and the courtly spectacle were supposed to provide a heroic view of French court life and military glory, the regime's officially sanctioned stage provided a space where the values trumpeted at Compiègne could be mocked. There was, of course, nothing especially revolutionary about Dancourt's stage; he disparaged all his characters equally, and he did so in the comic genre, where the author's main goal at the end of the seventeenth century was to entertain paying customers by provoking laughter in any way possible. Audience, actors, and playwrights all understood and abided by these conventions. But the implied mockery of royal pageantry was a defining characteristic of the declining years of the seventeenth century under the Sun King, when courtiers and would-be gentlemen alike grew weary of the rigid formality of court etiquette and welcomed the release provided by the low comedies of Dancourt and the farces and parodies of the Italian *commedia dell'arte* troupe and the fair performers on the Parisian public stage.

The Curiosity-Seekers of Compiègne bypassed military spectacle and aristocratic glamour to stress the uncertainty of class distinctions in the supposedly rigid society of orders. Onstage, the officers ended up with the merchants' women and money, but at Compiègne the lowly merchants made money, while the impoverished nobles paid a steep price for the glory of military association with the king. Each side wanted what the other possessed, as Dancourt humorously indicated onstage, but politics, economics, and culture worked against successful exchanges between the two. This frustrating situation, where neither aristocrats nor merchants could find satisfaction, also served as a backdrop for the bewildering saga of Louis de la Pivardière, a certified nobleman who had temporarily elected to pass as the son of a merchant.

The Husband Returned, which debuted on October 29 and played twenty-one more times before the end of its run in early December, was one of the most popular Dancourt plays performed in the late 1690s. The Comédie-Française staged thirteen of his one-acts from 1694 through 1698; only one of these plays exceeded *The Husband Returned*'s average of 761 paid spectators, or its 1,029 livres of revenue per night. The average figures for each of the twenty-five first-run performances of *The Curiosity-Seekers of Compiègne*, for example, were 634 spectators and 811 livres. In spite of the evident popularity of *The Husband Returned*, no direct testimony about audience response to the play during its run has survived. This absence is not surprising, because few spectators took the time to record their impressions of any Parisian productions in the seventeenth century. The few periodicals that covered the live stage confined themselves to plot summaries and dialogue excerpts without evaluating the staging or playhouse reception of a work; they were more interested in the literary qualities of the published text. The only direct mention of the 1698 production occurred twenty-seven years later, when a government-sanctioned monthly, the *Mercure de France*, noted that the play had been perceived during its initial run as a "fair and precise allegory of the false or true Pivardière, whose trial attracted the attention of all Paris at the time." This brief comment hints that spectators in 1698 saw the play as a telling, possibly truthful commentary on the baffling cause célèbre that was unfolding simultaneously, but it does not provide any further guidance to the meanings they ascribed to the play. In the absence of contemporary testimony, though, we can still examine the printed text of the play for clues about its initial reception, keeping in mind the context of the evolving legal case and the work's popularity with contemporary audiences.

Dancourt set the play in an imaginary rustic setting, a wily peasant world in the towns surrounding Paris where wealthy city-dwellers went to escape the density of urban life. The rustics Dancourt put onstage knew how to manipulate the city folk for their own purposes. They spoke in a patois that was a comic approximation of the dialects employed by country denizens such as Marguerite's maidservants, Marguerite Mercier and Catherine Lemoyne. Although Dancourt did not utilize these rural settings or quaint dialects in *The Curiosity-Seekers of Compiègne*, they appeared in many other one-act plays he penned. D'Argenson would later write that "one always likes to see Dancourt evoke the countryside around Paris . . . he stages it so well that one is delighted, one wishes to be there. While it is true that he is painting the morals of the peasantry, these morals smell of Paris; less innocence than in the provinces, a more subtle, urbane debauchery." Dancourt depicted this environment so often in other one-act

Les Vendanges des Suresnes. The engraving highlights the fictional world of Dancourt's stage, where the rural penury of the 1690s was transformed, for urban sophisticates, into an enticing scene of debauchery.

comedies of the 1690s that it became a kind of shorthand for the world beyond the halls of Versailles, the salons of Paris, or the banqueting and gaming tents of Compiègne. In these three sites, elites spoke proper French as it had been codified by usage at the king's court and in elite Parisian society, and followed rigorous rules of bodily comportment and manners. In the Suresnes of *The Suresnes Wine Harvest*, or the Besons of *The Besons Fair*, though, both staged in 1695, language, manners, and morals all took a back seat to the pursuit of physical love, food, and drink.

The Husband Returned is set at a country mill run by Julian and his wife, Julianne, who were intended to recall Louis and Marguerite at Narbonne. The choice of occupation is not accidental; the historian Steven Kaplan has argued that millers during the Old Regime held a special status in rural and urban communities because they performed an essential service by converting grain into flour. Millers were often figures of hatred, Kaplan claims, because it was thought they kept grain for themselves, or substituted substandard flour. Their clients speculated that they possessed extraordinary magical powers and sexual prowess, due to the transformative nature of their work and the earthy qualities of the mill. Dancourt's transformation of Louis and Marguerite into potentially subversive millers highlighted the rustic twist he brought to the onstage version of the cause célèbre.

Once Dancourt and his colleagues decided to situate their retelling of the Pivardière affair in this generic rural frame, they had to determine how to reduce the case's complexities to the one-act format. The troupe, knowing its audience would be familiar with the twists and turns of the story, had several moments from which to choose. They might have selected the point at which Marie learned from the Prior Charost's younger brother of her husband's first marriage. They might also have dramatized the return of the supposed Pivardière to the Berry in January 1698, culminating in the ill-fated confrontation with the two maidservants. Both scenarios, when translated to Dancourt's imaginary peasant world, offered substantial comic opportunities. The playwright and his troupe, however, chose to stage an earlier moment in the story: the point immediately prior to Louis' marriage to Marie, well before the alleged murder or the potentially corrupt investigations of the Châtillon judges. In other words, they chose to begin the play just before any misconduct had taken place, a moment when one could create a different ending to the case that held Paris in thrall.

As *The Husband Returned* opens, the audience learns that Julian and his long-suffering wife, Julianne, have become estranged after many years of squabbling; Julian is now absent from the country mill. Some locals are whispering that he has met an untimely end, while others claim that he has become engaged to an innkeeper named Margot in Nemours. Julianne, thrilled to be liberated from the yoke of her marriage, professes to be indifferent to Julian's fate. She is the boss now, she informs an interlocutor, and while she wishes Julian no ill, if he has kicked the bucket she won't shed any tears. Meanwhile, Julianne's niece, the young, beautiful, and wealthy Colette, has attracted the attention of three suitors: a dashing aristocrat named Clitandre, a local yokel called Charlot, and an oily, conniving Bailiff. About a third of the way through the play, Julian suddenly appears and confesses to a servant that he is, indeed, about to sign a marriage contract with a Nemours innkeeper; he has returned to the mill briefly to extract any financial resources he can from his business and his marriage to Julianne. He meets his wife, they quarrel ferociously, and Julian departs before Julianne can have him arrested on charges of bigamy. Elsewhere, Colette dismissively rejects the suit of the hayseed Charlot, who in his anger determines to take his revenge on the young woman and her aunt. He approaches the sinister Bailiff, who cleverly manipulates the credulous youth and Madame Agathe, a friend of Julianne, into stating that they watched Julianne murder her husband, Julian. The Bailiff, of course, hopes that once the aunt is out of the way, he will be able to marry Colette and enjoy her wealth and beauty. Just as it appears that the Bailiff's plot will succeed, Julian bursts upon the scene again. Although the

Bailiff and Charlot initially claim that Julian is an impostor, the handsome nobleman Clitandre sees through their stratagems. After he threatens to run the Bailiff through with his sword, and Julian appears onstage again, the evil magistrate relents. Clitandre and Colette, and Charlot and Madame Agathe, become engaged. To complete the happy ending, Julian vows to Julianne that he will not return to Nemours to sign the marriage contract with Margot; he proposes instead that they renew their marriage vows alongside the other two betrothed couples.

In *The Husband Returned*, then, all's well that ends well, at least on the surface. Julian, the putative Louis character, does not enter into a bigamous second marriage, and the corrupt judge is prevented from bringing a phony murder charge against Julianne, the Marguerite substitute. Dancourt's comic resolution avoids the morass of provincial investigations, the charges of murder and imposture, and the countercharges of judicial calumny that circulated at the Parlement. The sordid real-life tale ends on the familiar staged note of a triple marriage that satisfies everyone except the Bailiff, who slinks away during the final scene. Based on this plot summary, Dancourt and the Comédie-Française troupe appear to endorse the version of the affair put forth by Marguerite, the prior, and their supporters—that the man in Fort l'Evêque really was the missing Berrichon nobleman, and that the Châtillon judges were guilty of abusing their judicial authority.

But a dénouement to a stage play is not a legal verdict, and Dancourt's one-act omits important aspects of the real-life story. For example, the play has no counterpart to the prior, thereby eliminating the question of adultery and avoiding a potentially inflammatory reference to the Catholic Church, an institution that had long been hostile to the public stage because of the supposedly immoral lessons it imparted. Two other key figures in the case, the maidservants Mercier and Lemoyne, are not portrayed in Dancourt's play, although the credulity of Charlot and Madame

Agathe in the face of the Bailiff's machinations may constitute an oblique reference to the unfortunate servants. Finally, *The Husband Returned* does not include a character analogous to Louis' second wife, Marie, even though a confrontation between Julianne and Margot might have enlivened the comic proceedings. In all these ways, then, the stage version takes notable liberties with the real-life story, reminding us that Dancourt and colleagues did not set out to re-create the case verbatim.

In addition to these omissions, *The Husband Returned* is set in an imagined rustic setting that had little relation to Narbonne or the Berry at the end of the seventeenth century. It was perhaps an obvious commercial and comic choice for the troupe to tailor the topical tale of Pivardière to the contours of the rural milieux Dancourt and the troupe had popularized in earlier productions. But spectators in November 1698 would have been well aware of the discrepancy between the well-educated, well-spoken real-life couple and their naïve, semiliterate stage counterparts; some of the spectators, and perhaps even some of the performers, would have visited Marguerite and the supposed Louis in their jail cells. Beyond comic convention, another explanation for Dancourt's stage strategy might be that he sought to use theatrical stereotypes to eliminate the ambiguities of the real-life affair. In late fall 1698, playgoers at the Comédie-Française did not know whether the man imprisoned in Fort l'Evêque was really Louis or an impostor; they would have been uncertain whether Marguerite had plotted the murder of her husband, or whether she and the prior had been framed by corrupt judges. From one performance of the play to the next, audience members might have read reports or heard rumors about the case that swayed their opinions. Ironically, Julian and Julianne would have had more stability in the minds of spectators than the actual parties to the lawsuit; they had seen these "people" on Dancourt's stage before. Like the stereotypical figures of the Italian *commedia dell'arte* stage, such as Harlequin,

Scaramouche, or Pantalon, Dancourt's characters were set types who changed little from one production to the next. The conventions of his stage allowed Dancourt to establish concrete identities for Louis and Marguerite that proved elusive outside the playhouse; the comic certainties of the Comédie-Française stood in contrast to the judicial doubt that emanated from the Palais.

It is also possible that Dancourt's play explored the inconsistencies in the tale of the missing husband in a subtler fashion. The miller Julian, involved with a discontented wife at home and an unknown woman in Nemours, appears at first glance to be the play's surrogate Pivardière. But Dancourt and the troupe may have intended the character of Clitandre, the aristocratic lover, to incarnate some aspects of Louis' confusing life. *The Curiosity-Seekers of Compiègne* also featured a young aristocratic lover named Clitandre; in that instance, the character was willing to engage in shady activities to win the hand of Monsieur Valentin's youthful daughter, Angélique. The Clitandre of *The Husband Returned*, however, displays no moral ambiguities. In the opening scene, he informs his valet, Lépine, that he has fallen in love with Colette, Julianne's young, wealthy charge. His servant assumes that Clitandre is about to embark on another of his amorous adventures that have become legendary throughout the province, and he imagines that the conquest of the attractive niece will add another glorious chapter to this saga. But Clitandre assures him that he desires to marry Colette, not make her his mistress: "Is it birth which must determine the woman one marries? It is merit and virtue which makes marriages, and I find in the person of Colette everything that is needed to make me happy." In other words, there are characteristics beyond class which influence the fortunes of a marriage; the moral qualities of Colette are more meaningful to Clitandre than her wealth or social standing. In this scene, Dancourt offers his audience another explanation for Louis' bigamous marriage to Marie: Perhaps he was genuinely in love with her.

Of course, given the typical appetites of aristocratic rakes on the late-seventeenth-century French comic stage, spectators who saw *The Husband Returned* would have expected Clitandre to betray these fine sentiments by the end of the play. As it turns out, he remains true to them. After the opening scenes with his valet and with Julianne, who assures him she approves of the marriage, Clitandre heads off to arrange the details of his wedding. He does not return until the play's climactic moment, when he learns that the Bailiff is on the verge of arresting him and his valet for having helped Julianne to murder Julian. Not only will the Bailiff's plot result in Clitandre's arrest and Julianne's death, it will leave the path clear for the magistrate to marry Colette himself. Clitandre, pulling his sword, threatens to run the Bailiff through just as Julian returns. The Bailiff asserts that Julian is an impostor, but Clitandre, Julian, and the others quickly and effectively rebut this claim. In other words, Dancourt's play not only reproduces the alleged corruption of the magistrates, it also relies on Clitandre's aristocratic valor (and swordsmanship) to dismiss the murder charge before it seriously damages the livelihood or reputation of any of the protagonists. If only some virtuous local notable had stood up to the Châtillon judges at the outset of the affair, the play implies, things would not have progressed to the sorry state they had reached by late 1698.

Is it possible that the honorable Clitandre represents another aspect of Louis de la Pivardière, intended to complement the traits present in the character of Julian? No one who attended the play's initial run could say with certainty whether the man in Fort l'Evêque was a respectable gentleman or a scoundrel and an impostor. Dancourt's play allowed audiences to imagine either possibility. They could dismiss Louis as the opportunistic miller who had skipped out on his wife, but ultimately came to his senses by the end of the play. Or they could identify the Berrichon nobleman with Clitandre, a stage version of the frontispiece that had graced Louis' brief the previous summer.* This second Pivardière acted swiftly and decisively to thwart the miscarriage of justice, and behaved honorably toward the young woman he hoped to marry. Given the bifurcation of Louis' personality presented in the courtroom, in the legal briefs, and in conversation in fashionable Parisian society, it would not be surprising if Dancourt and his troupe used the possibilities of staged fiction to place dual Pivardières on the stage. Such a thesis, of course, is speculative, because we have no record of Dancourt's intentions. But its possibility suggests why the playhouse was a striking forum for examining the mysterious case in late 1698. *The Husband Returned* would never resolve the case with the certainty to which the judiciary aspired, but it did offer a nightly opportunity for performers and spectators to investigate its many possible interpretations.

The play ends with the promise of a triple reaffirmation of the merits of wedlock, even though in real life the Pivardière affair indicated that the institution of marriage was in disarray. A divertissement, or series of songs and dances, concluded the evening's entertainment. In Dancourt's theater, as on many other stages of the period, this musical interlude served as a point of transition between the liminal moment of the stage spectacle and the resumption of everyday life upon its end. The divertissement offered a chance for the players to thank the spectators for their patronage, and it also presented a final opportunity to reflect on the meanings of the spectacle just concluded. In the divertissement appended to the printed text of *The Husband Returned* in 1698, a series of dances featuring millers and their wives are interspersed with songs that comment on the events recounted in the play. The singing and dancing provided one final evocation of that imaginary rural world just beyond Paris, where city-dwellers and peasants could mingle amorously, yet harmlessly, for the space of an

*Compare the portrait of Louis, on page 89, with the representation of Clitandre on the far right of the illustration on page 136.

evening. The meanings of the final two sung stanzas, however, ventured beyond rural love trysts to remind the audience of the specific events that served as inspiration for the evening's entertainment. A Mademoiselle Lolotte, a singer affiliated with the troupe who did not perform in the play, sang the penultimate stanza of the divertissement; a Monsieur Touvenelle delivered the final lines:

> MLLE LOLOTTE: Having two lovers in Nature,
> Well, her laws permit this;
> But one profits doubly,
> By having two husbands at once.

> M. TOUVENELLE: You, destined by Love for marriage
> Listen well to this lesson:
> Those who think they have gotten flour,
> Often end up with nothing but bran.

This couple, not a part of the main performance, sings a duet that offers a reflection on the merits of bigamy. Mademoiselle Lolotte sings to the spectators, as they prepare to make their way out of the playhouse, that while nature's laws permit more than one lover at a time, women who marry two husbands simultaneously are even better off. Touvenelle, however, quickly responds with a different interpretation: Millers and their wives (i.e., Louis and Marguerite) who think that adultery or bigamy is beneficial will end up not with flour to sell, but its worthless byproducts. Moral censure and knowing approbation mixed in the dueling stanzas sung by the couple serves as a final reminder of the tensions evoked by the Pivardière case: horror and bewilderment at the possible explanations for the behavior of the Berrichon gentleman and his wife combined with libidinous fascination at their actions. Critics at the time and since have often pointed to Dancourt's stage as a mirror of the conflicting trends toward more austere religious devotion emanating from the court of Louis XIV, and the moral laxity displayed by his subjects in the wake of the troubles caused by his wars and natural disasters. In creating *The Husband Returned*, Dancourt and his colleagues took the raw material provided by the Pivardière affair at the moment of its greatest uncertainty in late 1698 and fashioned a theatrical amusement that reflected the case's ambiguities back at the audience.

Spectators who left the theater after seeing the play during its initial run surely experienced a variety of sentiments: mirth and voyeuristic titillation, perhaps, alongside a renewed interest in the troubling social and cultural issues raised by the affair. Outside the playhouse, in the rounds of speculation about the case that took place throughout the capital, debates about the identity of the prisoner in Fort l'Evêque continued. Soon, though, it would be time for the robed magistrates of the Tournelle to determine the fates of the affair's protagonists.

Chapter 6

JUDICIAL DOUBT

While *The Husband Returned* played to packed houses at the Comédie-Française during the month of November, curiosity-seekers continued to visit the prisoner whose puzzling saga had inspired the play. The prior and the maidservants, upon the decree of the King's Council, had been transferred from Chartres to Paris at the start of winter. On December 7, three days after the last 1698 performance of *The Husband Returned*, ministers to Louis XIV confirmed the *requête civile*, or appeal, that the attorneys for Louis had submitted upon his arrival in Paris three months earlier. The king then ordered the Parlement to retry the case as though the July 23 verdict had never been issued. The path was opened for the magistrates to address the possibility that the Fort l'Evêque prisoner was actually the missing aristocrat.

In principle, the court should have begun to investigate the identity of the prisoner. In practice, the Tournelle judges allowed the early 1699 phase of the trial to become a referendum on the prisoner's appeal, which they felt the king had improperly upheld.

When the hearings began again in January, the barristers representing the Châtillon magistrates returned to an argument they had advanced the previous summer, claiming that the identity of the prisoner was, in the context of the proceedings, a *fait justificatif* — an issue subsidiary to the murder trial itself. They claimed that it was not necessary to determine the prisoner's identity in order to identify Louis' murderers, and they argued that the 1670 ordinance confirmed that a murder investigation took precedence over legal wrangling about a subsidiary matter. Simply put, lawyers for the Châtillon judges were still insisting that a murder had been committed, regardless of the prisoner's identity or the king's desire that it be investigated.

The barristers defending Marguerite, the prior, and Louis launched a counterattack. Their lead attorney, a respected lawyer named Louis Nivelle, told the magistrates that he was prepared to present a brief, authored by an unnamed source, that would prove that the Châtillon judges themselves had retroactively sprinkled blood around the room at Narbonne where Louis had slept on the night of August 15. And once this fact had been established, Nivelle continued, it might not be hard to demonstrate that the vengeful Châtillon judges and their henchmen had actually killed an innocent bystander to produce evidence of the Berrichon nobleman's death. In this version of the affair Bonnet and Morin, rather than Marguerite and the prior, were guilty of murder. Given the Châtillon judges' determination to prevent Marguerite and the prior from clearing their names, Nivelle argued, it was imperative that the provincial magistrates also remain at risk of criminal conviction in this phase of the trial.

Nivelle never produced the threatened memoir, nor is there any credible evidence to support his insinuation that the provincial magistrates had turned murderers themselves to pursue their vendetta. Onlookers in attendance at the Tournelle hearings in January and February 1699, however, were struck by the eloquence of the oral pleadings. The jurist Pierre-Jacques Brillon, who attended the sessions, was so taken by the force of the lawyers' pleadings that he sought to publish them twenty-seven years later in his *Dictionary of Verdicts*. In this way, he wrote, a curious public might have full access to these "masterpieces of eloquence." The attorney general Henri-François d'Aguesseau was impressed with the "vigorous male eloquence" of Nivelle, which "seemed to grow from day to day." In particular, he remarked on the "vehemence" with which Nivelle had claimed that the case was not about Louis de la Pivardière, but about allegorical notions of justice and truth. In Nivelle's view, according to d'Aguesseau, the entire public seemed to become Louis' protector, to file a communal *requête civile* on his behalf.

While one can find the notion that justice itself was on trial in other French cases in this period, and indeed in the legal annals of many other times and places, the overblown courtroom rhetoric did not diminish the interest in the case among the Parisian public. As the *Nouvelles extraordinaires*, another clandestine Dutch journal, noted at the end of January, "This most unusual case continues to hold the public's attention." With each twist and turn, with each new legal maneuver unleashed by the wily barristers, the stakes grew. Would the Tournelle magistrates yield to the king's request to nullify their earlier verdict, thereby paving the way for a full-scale investigation into the identity of the man in Fort l'Evêque? Once the barristers for each party had finished their pleadings, attention turned to Attorney General d'Aguesseau, the king's representative at the bar, whose task it was to summarize the case and recommend a verdict to the judges. In so doing, both judges and observers hoped this celebrated jurist would finally resolve the year-and-a-half-old case. D'Aguesseau would eventually satisfy their expectations, but not before he had introduced his own authoritative blend of juridical, philosophical, and theological concerns into the mysterious case.

Henri-François d'Aguesseau was the most spectacularly successful member of one of the great administrative dynasties of the Old Regime. His grandfather had been an intendant under Louis XIII, and his father had served the Crown as a magistrate at the Parlement of Alsace and as an intendant in three different provinces. Educated by his learned, Jansenist-leaning father, d'Aguesseau became a barrister at the municipal Paris law court in 1690. A year later, rapidly promoted as a reward for his evident judicial talents as well as his family pedigree, he became attorney general at the Parlement of Paris. There he represented the interests of the king, and therefore those of the "public." He remained in this position until 1700, when he became procurator general at the Parlement, a post in which he oversaw the work of the attorneys general in Paris and the king's representatives in lesser courts throughout the kingdom, and he corresponded directly with the lord chancellor and the secretaries of state at Versailles, the most powerful ministers in the kingdom. In 1717, two years after the death of Louis XIV, the regent promoted him to the position of lord chancellor itself, the highest judicial office in France, a rank he held until 1750, the year before his death.

D'Aguesseau published little while alive, but soon after he died interested publishers collaborated with his sons, who possessed his papers, to bring out his *Complete Works*, a thirteen-volume edition that serves as the basis of his intellectual legacy. The man who emerges from these writings was deeply influenced by Renaissance humanism, Cartesian epistemology, and the more austere Jansenist elements of the French Catholic Reformation. He was an impressive linguist, with a command of ancient Hebrew, Greek, and Latin, as well as English, Italian, and Spanish. His orations to his legal colleagues, and his meditations on education, philosophy, and theology, emphasize a profoundly Christian pessimism about human capacity for knowledge of the self or the world one inhabits; at the same time, he was imbued with a Cartesian confidence in rational human inquiry. The result was a tension, which manifested itself in much of his legal writing, between perpetual suspicion of human capacity to perceive final truths and supreme confidence in the use of reason as a means to resolve conflict in human affairs. While this tension might have paralyzed a less worldly thinker, d'Aguesseau managed to keep these tendencies in balance in both his earlier judicial career and his later political one, although his determination to consider all aspects of a problem served him better in the legal world than at Versailles. He was celebrated during his life and afterward as a model of the sage jurist, but contemporaries often perceived him as a weak and vacillating politician.

His intellectual and spiritual formation also imbued him with a deep mistrust of the stage, and therefore of theatricality and attempts to experiment with identity. Unlike many of his most distinguished French contemporaries at the bar and in the Republic of Letters, d'Aguesseau never attended a Jesuit *collège*, and therefore had never received exposure to that order's passion for drama as a pedagogical device. From an early age, he had refused to attend the theater; in his writings, he often denounced the frivolity and the artifice of the stage as counter to virtue and seriousness of purpose. In his first *mercuriale*, or occasional speech, delivered to the magistrature in November 1698, d'Aguesseau chided those judges who failed to take their responsibilities with the gravity they demanded. Such magistrates, he wrote, spent brief intervals on the bench between their pursuits of worldly pleasure, but as soon as curtain time approached, they fled the courtroom for the playhouse. Plaintiffs and defendants who encountered these

An engraving of Henri-François d'Aguesseau from 1764, which is based on a portrait of the jurist done in 1703, not long after the Pivardière affair.

judges at the theater, after having observed them in the court-house, despised them, "and the Public that sees them in both places does not know in which location they do a greater disservice to Justice." Like his contemporary the abbot Jacques-Bénigne Bossuet, or the most influential antitheatricalist of the following century, Jean-Jacques Rousseau, d'Aguesseau viewed the theater as an institution corrosive of moral virtue; more specifically, he saw the illusions of the stage as antithetical to the search for truth that occupied the law.

D'Aguesseau was only thirty years old in early 1699, younger than all the main figures in the affair and, probably, most of the magistrates called upon to adjudicate the case; the *Gazette de Rotterdam* noted his youth in its February 13 report from Paris. In spite of his age, however, in the eight years he had been an attorney general he had impressed observers as a sage orator and a powerful jurist. This reputation rested in part on a series of seasonal addresses he made in his capacity as attorney general to the court's barristers and magistrates. "The Independence of the Barrister," delivered in 1693, outlined the exacting standards demanded of that profession. "For the public good," d'Aguesseau declaimed, "you are placed in the midst of the tumultuous conflict between human passions and the Throne of Justice." In order to navigate those troubled waters, barristers had to achieve absolute independence from the concerns that drove others, especially their desire for wealth and social status. Emotion had to be subjugated: "Man is never more free than when he has subjected his passions to his reason, and his reason to justice . . . the most free and independent men are all-powerful only to do good; their infinite power is bounded only by the evil to which they do not descend."

Two years later, in "The Knowledge of Man," d'Aguesseau noted that barristers had to be persuasive orators as well as solid reasoners: "To convince people, it is sufficient to address the mind, but to persuade them, you must go directly to the heart." Reason had also to be disguised with the language of imagination at times, and the clever orator must seem to imitate nature itself in the minds of those listening. To achieve this elevated state of persuasion, and to avoid public censure, the barrister had to know himself: "He will sense that the surest method to please others is to be true to his own character, and to never speak with the voice of anyone other than himself." Credible jurists should avoid at all costs the false personae necessarily adopted by stage professionals. In these orations, and in others delivered in this period, d'Aguesseau stressed the necessity of reason and moral probity for those engaged in a legal career. He urged magistrates and barristers to perfect themselves, while simultaneously asking them to reform human imperfections found outside the courthouse.

By the late 1690s, in addition to these soaring orations, he owed his stature to the summary pleadings he delivered before the court in some of the most high-profile cases of the decade. In one instance, the 1696 confrontation between the Duc de Luxembourg and many of the kingdom's most prominent noblemen, his pleadings clarified a thorny matter of aristocratic rank based on historical precedent. In another, the 1700 dispute over the validity of a sixty-year-old marriage contracted in Brussels between the Duc de Guise and the Comtesse de Bossu, he took up the legitimacy of foreign legal traditions in France and the power of the French king to annul or otherwise alter marriages contracted by members of the royal family. But the high-stakes case in which d'Aguesseau most distinguished himself was the 1695–1698 case of the *Prince de Conti v. the Duchesse de Nemours*, an inheritance struggle over the substantial estate of the House of Longueville. The Abbot d'Orléans, last in the Longueville line, had descended into dementia prior to his death; the parties to the case disputed which of the two extant wills was prepared while he still had his wits about him. In four lengthy pleadings before the Parlement, d'Aguesseau evaluated the mental competence of the testator by examining testimony from those who had known him in his later days, and by an exhaustive study of the wills. His second pleading in particular took place before an assembly of France's most important nobles, who filled the Great Hall of the Parlement and, according to Saint-Simon (who was present), greeted his eloquent oration with "cries of joy and applause." The clarity and analytic quality of the pleadings in all these affairs impressed his contemporaries and subsequent legal commentators, further enhancing the already substantial reputation built upon his professional orations.

In addition to these closely followed cases, d'Aguesseau provided summary pleadings for more than a hundred other cases during his decade as attorney general. While most of them did not attract much attention, d'Aguesseau treated them all with equal care and exactitude; he considered it his responsibility to the Crown, the Crown's subjects, and the law to follow the same rigorous standards in all the cases he handled. These concerns were evident in a 1695 paternity suit between Alexandre de Lastre, the son of a minor Amiens administrative family, and his wife, Marie-Magdeleine Courtois, daughter of a family of similar standing in the same town. In 1686, three months after their marriage, Courtois gave birth to a son; due to this awkward timing, the child was not baptized until three years later. At first de Lastre cared for the child as though he were his own, a fact confirmed by many neighbors at the trial. Over time, though, things worsened between the couple. The wife began to claim that her husband was a gambler and, worse, impotent. She assigned paternity to another man and filed for separation. In turn the husband, who had secured his marriage seven years earlier by telling the bride's parents that he had impregnated their daughter, now claimed he had never fathered a child with his wife, and that his wife had falsified her pregnancy seven years earlier and never given birth. The child he had raised was not his, and perhaps not his wife's. Because of Courtois' infamous conduct, he claimed he was entitled to her dowry and other assets. The wife, now fearful of losing both her wealth and her reputation, reasserted that her husband was the father of her child. In his summary pleading, d'Aguesseau typically began with an explicitly antitheatrical statement, saying that the case seemed more likely "to entertain the vain curiosity of people in a public spectacle, than to merit the serious attention of ministers of justice." He then carefully reconstructed the chronology of the case, considered various legal precedents, and weighed the evidence gathered in more than fifty depositions from people with knowledge of the case. In the end, in spite of the wife's inconsistent story, d'Aguesseau concluded that the child belonged to de Lastre, and that his false testimony justified a legal separation financially favorable to the wife.

In its uncertainties, the de Lastre case resembled the Pivardière affair that d'Aguesseau would be called upon to summarize four years later. While the principal figures were not well known or powerful, the case was of interest because of its unusual circumstances, and its seeming insolubility. D'Aguesseau, through his knowledge of the law, his methodical application of reason, and his powers of oratory, all of which were tempered by an awareness of human failing, proposed to reveal the truth. "No matter how heavy the veil that hides this mystery, we believe it will fall away of its own accord, once we begin to establish the real principles that will . . . reveal the true status of the child who appears before this Court, whether it be that of a shameful bastard or that of a legitimate son." This statement, like many others found in the jurist's speeches and pleadings, demonstrated an assumption that the truth in legal matters existed, and could be determined by virtuous, diligent, magisterial inquiry. But it was also the legal authority of his office and the intellectual and moral weight of his reputation that strengthened his claims to identify the truth of the matter. The attorney general's task was to overcome his own very human limitations in order to peel away the layers of confusion and misdirection that had obscured the once certain paternity of the child. As d'Aguesseau rose in the Tournelle on February 13,

1699, to pronounce on the Pivardière affair, the packed chamber waited anxiously to see if he would be able to resolve an even more convoluted case.

✣

D'Aguesseau, no doubt aware of the popularity of the previous fall's production of *The Husband Returned*, began his pleading in the Pivardière affair with a reference to the theatrical nature of the case. Unlike Dancourt and the Comédie-Française troupe, however, he distanced himself from the conventions of the stage:

> The singularity of the facts; the contrariety or the bizarreness of the events; the surprising turns that the artifice of the accused, or the force of truth, has caused to appear in this case; the perpetual opposition between the true and that which seems to be true [*le vrai et le vraisemblable*] that characterizes the parties; and all that a curious people, who love prodigal events and novelty, have come to see played out in your Courtroom, *are not that which occupy me as I begin this discourse.* A more elevated purpose, a nobler and more important object, requires all our attention from the outset.

Predictably, d'Aguesseau refused to sensationalize the case in order to play to the desires of a restless public. Dancourt and the Comédie-Française might jocularly recast the principals in the affair as millers and bumbling peasants, but the king's high court could not play the story for laughs. D'Aguesseau's opening salvo had another effect: His magisterial stance worked to distance him from his audience. *The Husband Returned* invited spectators into the knowing circle of those who could laugh at the dilemma in which Louis and Marguerite found themselves. In contrast, the attorney general proclaimed that he would not fall prey to the same easy assumptions that people had previously made. He did not invite his listeners to mock or to idealize the figures he was about to present. Instead, he relegated his audience to a passive, spectatorial position as he set out on a sober quest for truth.

D'Aguesseau's purpose in reporting the Pivardière case to the magistrates, then, was not to entertain. He also made it clear in his opening remarks that one would not be able to derive much of moral value from the affair. By the time the magistrates reached a verdict, there would not be any innocent parties left. Either Marguerite and the prior had committed adultery and assassination, or the provincial magistrates were guilty of calumny and prevarication. Either the man in Fort l'Evêque was an impostor, hired by the accused to absolve them of murder charges, or he was a bigamist and possibly a cuckold incapable of managing his own affairs. Interestingly, this point was also one of the lessons of the stage version; the underlying cynicism of *The Husband Returned* prevented spectators from imagining a redemptive resolution to the story. The tale of Pivardière contained no heroes, only humans who behaved in inexplicably dark and contradictory ways. Dancourt's moral cynicism masked in comedy and d'Aguesseau's lament for the absence of virtuous exemplars defined the conceivable contemporary responses to the case.

Freed from the demands of the stage or the printed page, and gravely aware of the potential crisis of judicial authority that an unfair verdict might provoke, d'Aguesseau began to lay out the factual and legal issues in the case for the magistrates. He started with the uncertainties surrounding the identity of Louis de la Pivardière. Even before the night of the alleged murder, Louis had presented an impossibly contradictory figure. He had been an impoverished noble *and* an obscure Parisian bourgeois, an officer in the king's armies *and* a minor police official in Auxerre, the husband of two women at once. "Louis de la Pivardière, if he still breathes," proclaimed d'Aguesseau, "assembles within himself qualities that are so incompatible, and contradictions that are so astonishing, that he seems to unite in his person two minds and two bodies, in a word, two different men." Later in the pleading, while describing the experience of Pivardière after the supposed assassination, d'Aguesseau employed a Christian vocabulary. Having "died" on August 15, 1697, he was "resurrected" in January 1698 when he reappeared in the Berry, only to fade once again into a purgatory-like state "of doubt, of cloudiness, of uncertainty, where he is, so to say, suspended between life and death." Christ-like, Louis had risen from the grave, but in 1699 resurrections appeared as improbable as dual personalities inhabiting the same body. The central narrative of the Christian faith also appeared inadequate to explain the mysteries surrounding the Berrichon gentleman. "Phantoms," "shadows," and "uncertainty" were all that one could expect from the passion of Louis de la Pivardière. In both these passages, d'Aguesseau employed contemporary vocabularies, in one case that of seventeenth-century secular psychology, in the other that of Christian theology, to explore Louis' bewildering identity crisis.

Having recounted the biography of the mysterious nobleman, d'Aguesseau then presented the proofs offered by each side in support of their respective explanations for the puzzling saga. His purpose in offering these parallel theories was not to privilege one over the other, but to demonstrate that the public rush to judgment over the previous half year had been misguided: "I dare say that, surprised, suspended like me between assumptions that are so contradictory, you will recognize that there is not yet anything certain about this case except doubt and uncertainty. In such a juncture, the more judicious spirit is that which is wise enough to suspend judgment." The case affirming that Marguerite, the prior, and their accomplices murdered Louis rested on a number of presumptions, including the suspected adultery of Marguerite, the cries and gunshots the evening of August 15, the traces of blood at Narbonne following the supposed murder, and Louis' personal effects left behind at the manor. In each instance, d'Aguesseau acknowledged the plausibility of these circumstances.

The best proofs of the murder, he suggested, were the interrogations of the maidservants, which contained eyewitness testimony of the murder and the dead body. How would one know if the two maidservants were providing false testimony against their innocent mistress and the prior? D'Aguesseau examined the case against their reliability, arguing that if they had given misleading testimony, it must be for one of three reasons: They had been misled, they had wished to trick others, or Bonnet and Morin had forced them to perjure themselves. He argued persuasively that the domestics were neither duped nor had sufficient motivation to dupe others. Did the judges, in particular Bonnet who had hated the prior's family for so long, force the servants to lie? Unlikely, claimed d'Aguesseau. Bonnet, seventy-four years old, would die soon and be constrained to account for his actions before his maker. Why risk such an odious act? Why would Bonnet and Morin bring a false accusation against the brother of their superior, the lieutenant general of Châtillon? If they were serious about altering evidence, why did they wait almost six weeks before investigating Narbonne? And why, in January 1698, did the maidservants testify that the man presented to them was a false Pivardière, when they were surrounded at that moment by a small army of men who believed they had led the real Louis to the Châtillon prison cell? For all these reasons, d'Aguesseau argued, the testimony of the maidservants regarding the murder appeared credible from a remove of a year and a half, possibly even decisive.

At the same time, however, d'Aguesseau acknowledged that the case against assassination was equally believable. Not only was no body discovered, but the investigating magistrates had not undertaken a thorough investigation to find it; they had relied instead on the maidservants' testimony as decisive. Beyond the issue of the body, even if Marguerite was guilty of adultery, it would be faulty reasoning to argue that she was therefore also guilty of murdering her husband. The cries in the night, the children locked in rooms where they normally did not sleep, and the bloodstains all might plausibly be explained in ways that excused Marguerite and the prior from suspicion. Furthermore, as soon as Marguerite learned that Bonnet and Morin might press charges, she sought proof of the continued existence of her husband; surely she would have hesitated in this endeavor if she had in fact plotted his murder. Even if she and the prior had decided to present an impostor as her husband, they could not have found a look-alike and assembled so convincing a case in the four months between the start of the investigation in September and the appearance of the man claiming to be Louis in January. It was not possible for an impostor to have fooled so many people who had seen Louis in person only months before. The false Martin Guerre case, the Veré affair, and other examples of imposture had featured the return of the false person years, sometimes decades, after the disappearance, long after precise memories of facial features and body types had faded.

In short, d'Aguesseau asserted, exhaustive critical examination of the known facts after more than a year of investigation proved inconclusive: "When we consider the first argument [that Louis was murdered], it seems almost impossible to doubt that the death occurred; but when we regard the second, we find it equally difficult to believe he is not still alive." All paths led to obscurity, all inquiry to doubt. Having arrived at the culmination of his summary, the young attorney general admitted to the criminal judges that he did not have a recommendation to make. Rather than throw up his hands in despair, however, d'Aguesseau turned this affirmation of the case's troubling uncertainty into a virtue. With Christian humility, but with an equal dose of Cartesian methodology, he told the judges, "We doubt everything in this case; *but it is this doubt itself which will surely lead us to the certainty of a final deci-*

sion." These words established doubt as a procedural principle in the Pivardière affair. In the *Discourse on Method* (1637), René Descartes had argued paradoxically that the only sure way to knowledge of oneself and the world beyond one's mind was through doubt. Not content to rely on any form of authority external to his own mind to prove he existed, not even sure of the existence of his own mind, Descartes had ultimately asserted his own existence precisely because he could doubt everything. In the act of doubting, he affirmed his independence of all authority and all thought that had preceded his being. Once received authority had been called into question, human beings were in a position to build, step by step, a rational understanding of themselves and their world through a logical, deductive process. In 1699, legal Cartesianism allowed d'Aguesseau to suspend judgment long enough to consider all sides of the case; it would permit the judges to explore different arguments before arriving at the definitive conclusions required in the highest court in the kingdom.

The role of doubt was more in evidence in the Pivardière affair than in any other trial d'Aguesseau handled in his years as attorney general. He took the opportunity of his summary pleading to sift through more than a year of investigations and legal wrangling. He weighed the facts, considered the possibilities, and came out in favor of the fundamental uncertainty of the case. It was an extraordinary moment, one that at first glance appears to be evidence of yet further dithering and delay in a case that had already revealed disheartening weaknesses in France's criminal justice system. This was the interpretation endorsed by Voltaire when he looked back at the case three-quarters of a century later. The elderly *philosophe* was outraged that anyone had found the maidservants' testimony credible, and dismayed that Louis' return to the Berry in January 1698 had not ended the affair. The fact that the case lasted so long before the high court was yet further evidence of the inadequacies of Old Regime justice. But Voltaire had his own ax to grind with the Parlement in 1777, and his comments should be interpreted in light of his highly publicized campaigns against the pre-Revolutionary legal system.

While it is hard to argue that the case represented one of the Old Regime's finer moments of criminal jurisprudence, d'Aguesseau's injunction to doubt did allow the magistrates to redress their errors, negligence, and ill-considered conclusions. After the obvious biases of the Châtillon magistrates, after the mistakes of the Romorantin judge, after the Parlement's too hasty judgment the previous summer and the king's rebuke in the fall, the attorney general's summary pleading, delivered with the moral authority he had acquired over the previous decade, allowed the judges to reexamine the case without directly acknowledging earlier miscues. The procedure d'Aguesseau laid out might conceivably allow the high court to save face in the wake of the royal decision to overturn the July judgment, and it also offered the hope that the court might redeem itself in the eyes of an increasingly skeptical public. Justice in an allegorical sense was not on trial, as the barrister Nivelle had claimed, but the judiciary's authority at this moment was at stake. D'Aguesseau's integrity, learning, and intelligence offered the court a way to restore confidence in its functions.

If all was in doubt, however, how was the court to proceed? Here d'Aguesseau harkened back to the court's first verdict in July 1698 and subsequent developments. At that time, the court had been unable to examine Louis de la Pivardière in the flesh; if he existed, he had been unwilling to appear without a safe-conduct indemnifying him of charges of bigamy. At the same time, the Parlement had declared its suspicion that the "phantom" hiding in the provinces was an impostor, and insisted that he be seized for interrogation. Accordingly, in the name of the king, he recommended that the Parlement undertake its own intensive, impartial investigation into the continuing existence of Louis de la

Pivardière, rather than relying on the investigations of the provincial judges who had furnished the evidence considered the previous summer. In its second verdict in the case, handed down on the same day that d'Aguesseau delivered his summary pleading, the Parlement magistrates wisely agreed with his conclusions and ordered that the investigation begin without delay. Finally, the court agreed to suspend all other issues in the affair pending the outcome of an examination into the "existence" of Louis de la Pivardière.

Chapter 7

INTERROGATION

$\mathcal{T}$he Tournelle judges assigned one of the court's councilors, a veteran jurist named Jean Bochart, to conduct a three-pronged inquiry into Pivardière's identity. First, they directed him to take testimony from witnesses who knew Louis from before August 1697, as well as any other witnesses Bochart deemed appropriate. Second, the judges asked Bochart to interrogate the alleged Pivardière, posing questions that would be supplied by the procurator general. Third, they ordered Bochart to gather testimony from three court-designated handwriting experts, who would evaluate documents signed by Louis before and after his alleged murder on August 15, 1697. The result of these procedures, the magistrates expected, would decisively determine whether Louis de la Pivardière still existed. Fortunately, the paper record generated by Bochart's investigations in the spring of 1699 has survived intact in the National Archives in Paris. The transcripts, which consist of about two hundred pages of tiny, irregular handwriting, are filled with deletions, corrections, and abbreviations. They are challenging to read, but once deciphered they offer fresh insights into the case. Within their pages, we catch glimpses of handwrit-

ing experts laboring over Louis' signatures. We hear the echoes of
Bochart's conversations with men and women who had known
Louis in his provincial obscurity, before his name found a place
on the tongues of thousands of Parisians in the middle of 1698.
We gain access to the discussions the court's councilor held with
the maidservants, and with Marguerite and the prior, whose lives
hung in the balance as the investigation ground on.

The most tantalizing document, however, is a seventy-page
transcript that records Bochart's interrogation of the Fort l'Evêque
prisoner. This sheaf of browning paper documents the results of
eight encounters between the interrogator and the captive. It is
not a window allowing us a transparent view of the prisoner, of
course. The words spoken by Bochart and the man he interviewed
were transcribed by a third party, then reviewed and corrected by
both speakers. The demands of a criminal investigation colored
both the questions and the responses, so that the prisoner in particular had good reason to tailor his story to the circumstances of
the moment. The handwritten transcript does not capture hesita-
tions, or facial expressions, or tones of voice. But over the course
of their meetings, Bochart asked the prisoner many of the questions that had been on the minds of the judges and those who followed the case since its inception. From August 1697 onward, the
Berrichon gentleman, or his impersonator, had managed to avoid
accounting for his actions, but he could delay no longer. The prisoner had to convince a seasoned interrogator that he was Louis de
la Pivardière. It would be a difficult task, because no one in Paris
could imagine that one person might embody so many apparent
contradictions.

❧

Before interrogating the prisoner, Bochart gathered fourteen documents signed by Louis de la Pivardière before August 15, 1697,
as well as ten letters written after that date by the supposed

Pivardière to his first wife and other family members and friends. He then made these two dozen documents available to three hand-writing experts appointed by the court to examine Pivardière's signature before and after the disputed murder. Their task was to determine whether the signatures before August 1697 were penned by the same hand as those after that date. Today this pro-cedure seems like an unreliable method for establishing fact in a capital case. The spread of e-mail and word-processing programs has meant that we write less frequently by hand; as a result, an in-dividual's handwriting style is too untutored and inconsistent to provide the type of evidentiary certainty required in a criminal case. Furthermore, in an age of online passwords and scannable identification devices, individual signatures appear to be an in-creasingly irrelevant indicator of identity.

Not surprisingly, however, these issues looked different to ob-servers three centuries ago. In the first place, only about a quarter of all men in France circa 1700, and only one in ten women, knew how to sign their names. Those who possessed this hard-won skill were unlikely to alter their signature substantially over the course of their lives; their signatures often stood in for their corporal presence on letters of credit, property transfers, and other legal and financial transactions. Second, like many other facets of ev-eryday activity in pre-Revolutionary France, the skill of teaching and evaluating handwriting had been transformed into a bureauc-ratized monopoly controlled by a small number of guild masters. Since the sixteenth century in Paris, the corporation of *maîtres écrivains jurés,* or master scriveners, had successfully staked their claim as the exclusive designers and teachers of standardized, hand-written alphabets authorized by the Crown. Claiming that calligraphy was an art that required training and expertise, just like painting and sculpture, the master writers "policed" the handwrit-ten page on behalf of the king's interests and their own corporate privileges.

La Grande Chambre du syndic pour la vérification de la fausse et bonne écriture. This late-seventeenth-century engraving depicts master scriveners at work in their guildhall, verifying handwriting samples. The charter of their guild hangs on the wall behind them.

By the mid-seventeenth century, the courts were increasingly soliciting the scriveners' opinions on handwriting samples submitted in civil and criminal legal cases, although not without controversy. The scriveners themselves thought that their practice of handwriting comparison was logical and rigorous, but when pressed, they had a difficult time convincing critical observers that their procedures measured up to emerging standards of legal proof. These debates were damaging to the scriveners' claims to expertise, but not lethal; the criminal ordinance of 1670 required royal magistrates to seek their expert advice in any criminal matter dealing with written forgery. The judges in the Pivardière affair therefore asked Bochart to oversee an official handwriting comparison as one aspect of his investigation. The court appointed

three of the most senior members of the Parisian Scriveners Guild
to examine Louis de la Pivardière's handwriting. One of them had
just published a treatise in support of handwriting verification
in criminal cases the previous year, while another had recently
authored a luxurious folio volume of exemplary calligraphy.

After taking the necessary oath, they noted that in some of the
signatures the name *Pivardière* appeared with two *r*'s at the end
rather than one. Nevertheless, they observed, the handwriting on
display in the ten post–August 1697 letters was internally consistent and clearly matched the hand of the man who had signed the
fourteen pre–August 1697 letters. The guildsmen explained the
orthographical error as the result of an understandable rush to
complete tedious clerical chores combined with a lack of space for
a proper signature, something they had observed on many previous occasions. In addition, each expert went beyond the claim that
the pre– and post–August 1697 documents showed technical similarities, to assert that the calligraphy itself bore the imprint of a
distinct human personality. Their use of words like *aura* and *spirit*
suggested that handwriting was a medium that expressed the
moral and psychological uniqueness of an individual. In this case,
without ever having met Louis, all three men argued that they
could discern his presence, before and after the alleged murder, in
the dried lines of ink he had left on the page. In their view, the
man who had signed the fourteen earlier documents was still alive
and wielding a quill.

How did the criminal magistrates receive this testimony? Again,
we lack knowledge of the judges' internal deliberations regarding the handwriting evidence, but the debates begun a generation earlier made it likely that they approached the scriveners' testimony with caution. Half a century later, in an article in the
Encyclopédie on handwriting comparison, the Chevalier de Jaucourt
asserted that handwriting resemblances were often just as misleading as facial similarities in cases of imposture. "Handwriting," the

encyclopedist suggested, "is nothing more than a painting, which is to say an imitation of traits and characters. A great painter in this genre can imitate others so well, that he can dupe the most discerning critics." It was unlikely that any of the criminal magistrates in 1699 were willing to base a decision on handwriting evidence alone.

While the handwriting experts were examining the documents that he provided them, Bochart was also gathering testimony from those who claimed to have known Louis de la Pivardière before August 1697. The ordinance called for a two-step process; first, Bochart was to depose the witness without the Fort l'Evêque prisoner present. Then, if the witness appeared to be in a position to pass judgment on the identity of the imprisoned man, Bochart scheduled a second session in which he would "confront" the witness with the man who claimed to be Pivardière. During this procedure, both parties were offered the opportunity to make statements and question each other about their assertions; these confrontations were recorded by court secretaries. Bochart was given a list of sixty potential witnesses; the final roster of twenty-seven individuals, interviewed between mid-March and mid-May 1699, included neighbors from the vicinity of Narbonne, merchants with whom Louis had conducted business in the Berry, officers from his dragoon regiment in the early 1690s, and others in Paris who had known him before the alleged assassination and had come to see him in Fort l'Evêque out of curiosity.

One of the first witnesses deposed by Bochart was Dame Elisabeth du Gripon, who had served as Louis' godmother when he was baptized as an infant. In the absence of his parents or his godfather, Gripon might reasonably be expected to have the longest, and possibly most accurate, memories of Louis. In her deposition, however, she testified that she had almost no knowledge of

Pivardière in his childhood and adolescence. She had held the newly born Louis on the baptismal font during a brief trip she had made through the Berry with her now-deceased first husband, but after that moment she had not seen him again as a youth. At some point in the mid-1690s, while she was in residence in Paris, a gentleman who said he was named Pivardière had come to her door. She allowed him in, and during the course of their conversation he claimed to be her godson. Gripon did not see the man again until she learned that someone claiming to be Louis de la Pivardière Dubouchet was imprisoned at Fort l'Evêque. "Everyone was discussing his case," she noted, so she resolved, as his godmother, to offer him her services. The man she saw in prison was, she asserted, the same man who had knocked on the door of her Parisian abode four years earlier.

Charles Carré de la Bru, a Berrichon gentleman from near Vierzon, was typical of the dozen or so witnesses who had known Louis as a country gentleman during his marriage to Marguerite. He had first met Louis at his wedding to Marguerite; a neighbor, he had frequently gambled and caroused with him, and had attended the marriage of Marguerite's eldest daughter by her first marriage. Unlike Gripon, he claimed a "perfect knowledge" of the man who had become the Lord of Narbonne in 1687. More than a decade later, he had heard that someone claiming to be Pivardière was in Fort l'Evêque; furthermore, the rumor was that this man was not the "real" Pivardière. Curious, he went to the prison, where he and the man recognized each other and embraced as soon as he entered the room. They chatted, fondly recalling their younger days. In the deposition, Carré de la Bru swore to Bochart that he had no doubts about the identity of the Fort l'Evêque prisoner, a certainty he confirmed during his confrontation the following week with the alleged Pivardière.

In addition to the Berrichon nobility who had socialized with Louis and Marguerite in the late 1680s and early 1690s, Bochart also sought testimony from military officers who had known Louis during the war. Louis Coquard de la Mothe, thirty-four years old, a lieutenant colonel in the St. Hermines dragoon regiment, had received money from Pivardière's military patron, the Duc de la Feuillade, who had requested that Mothe and his superiors take care of Louis. About three weeks before his interview with Bochart, he and some gentleman friends, including another officer from the St. Hermines regiment who had known Louis, had gone to Fort l'Evêque "out of curiosity," to see if the prisoner was their former military colleague. They had immediately recognized him, a fact to which Mothe swore in his deposition. Mothe's verification was echoed by the dragoon regiment's supply master, the major to whom Louis had directly reported, and the regiment's chief, Elie de St. Hermines, who recognized the man in Fort l'Evêque as his former subaltern officer "not only by his face, but also by his body and by the knowledge of the regiment's affairs he had displayed during their conversation."

In contrast to these immediate identifications, a few of the witnesses examined by Bochart hesitated when asked to swear to the identity of the incarcerated nobleman. Dame Marie-Anne Leger de St. Ciran, a thirty-two-year-old widow, told Bochart that she had seen Louis once before his alleged murder, at a gathering of local notables at Narbonne around 1690. The men and the women had socialized separately, and she had seen Louis up close only at the end of the day, when he had given her his hand to lead her to a waiting carriage. She recalled that he was of "medium height, without a wig." After that encounter, their paths did not cross again until late August 1698, when she received word from her friend the lawyer Baudran that a man claiming to be the missing Louis was at his house in Paris, and that she could stop by to see him if she were curious. The two exchanged courtesies upon her arrival, after which she asked the man if he remembered the visit she and her late husband had paid to Narbonne. Louis told her that he remembered her husband, but not her. The Lady of St. Ciran observed him carefully, but honestly could not say whether the man at Baudran's house was the same individual she had met eight or nine years earlier, in part because the prisoner now wore a wig.

Louis Douault, a gentleman from the Touraine and lieutenant of a cavalry regiment, had similar misgivings about his ability to identify the prisoner in Fort l'Evêque. Douault had also met Louis only once, at the home of Louis' neighbor the Sieur de Preville, on the eve of Louis' wedding to Marguerite Chauvelin more than a decade earlier. In December 1698, learning that the supposed Pivardière was imprisoned at Fort l'Evêque, he had paid him a visit. Even though the prisoner answered his questions in a convincing fashion, Douault still hedged his testimony before Bochart. In both his deposition and his confrontation with the prisoner, he carefully stated that "he believed he was not mistaken" in thinking that the man was the same person he had met a decade before in the Berry. A third witness, the priest Joseph David, also hesitated before the investigator. The cleric had known Louis a decade earlier when he performed the ecclesiastical duties at the Château of Valançay; among other rites, David had conducted the investiture ceremony for Louis' two sisters when they entered the town's Ursuline convent. In September 1698, while at the residence of the lawyer Baudran, he learned of the man claiming to be Louis de la Pivardière in the Fort l'Evêque prison. He immediately went to visit the prisoner, but had such doubts about his identity that he returned six weeks later to question him more closely. During this second visit, the man recalled many more details of their mutual encounters and acquaintances, including incidents the priest had forgotten. Unlike the Lady of St. Ciran or the Chevalier Douault, David had no hesitation confirming Pivardière's identity during their confrontation.

If St. Ciran, Douault, and David expressed uncertainty about the identity of the Fort l'Evêque prisoner, two of the twenty-seven witnesses deposed by Bochart flatly denied that he was the missing Berrichon nobleman. Not surprisingly, both of them were from Châtillon-sur-Indre. Jean Chenu, one of the archers who had assisted with the raid on Narbonne in September 1697, as well as many other key incidents in the affair, provided Bochart with a rambling deposition claiming that he had first encountered Louis five or six years earlier when he had been assigned the task of collecting a debt from him. It had taken him six months, he stated, to collect the money. Chenu had next seen someone claiming to be Louis in January 1698, when the lieutenant general of Romorantin had escorted the missing nobleman around the province. Chenu argued, however, that the man in the custody of the Romorantin judge was "smaller, and had a leaner face" than the man from whom he had collected an outstanding debt four to five years earlier. Furthermore, according to Chenu, when pressed about the details of his earlier debt, the man with the Romorantin magistrate was unable to recall the details of the affair correctly. In spite of this highly detailed deposition, it is likely that Bochart was already suspicious of Chenu; the maidservants Mercier and Lemoyne, already interrogated by Bochart, had accused Chenu of threatening them with violence if they did not stand by the murder story. When the Parisian magistrates wrote to Châtillon requesting more information about Chenu, they learned of a suspended 1690 sentence to row in the king's galleys which left him indebted to Jean Bonnet. Given these facts, Bochart decided not to allow Chenu to challenge the prisoner face-to-face in Fort l'Evêque, effectively dismissing Chenu's allegations.

Bochart, however, permitted the second Châtillon witness, an Augustinian monk affiliated with that order's monastery in Châtillon, to visit the prisoner. The cleric, named Paul Chauvin, recounted that he had met Louis once, at a two-day gathering of the Berrichon aristocracy at an estate outside Châtillon in 1690 or 1691. Then, in January 1698, the Romorantin magistrate had brought the alleged Pivardière to Chauvin's monastery in Châtillon. The latter was certain that this man was not the same person he had encountered at the gathering of the nobility in the early 1690s. The man who came to the monastery did not speak to the monk and never raised his eyes. Furthermore, the week before his deposition, Chauvin had gone to Fort l'Evêque to view the prisoner who claimed to be Pivardière. He had seen him from afar, in a large room after morning Mass; the prisoner, who according to Chauvin was much smaller than the man he had seen a decade previously, had withdrawn from the room before Chauvin could speak with him. Chauvin's testimony, like Chenu's, was suspect. His lone contact with the assumed Pivardière, like that of the Lady of St. Ciran, had been a fleeting encounter among a group of provincial gentlemen ten years before; if St. Ciran had been unsure of her identification, why should that of Chauvin be any more credible? In addition, during the course of the investigation Bochart was given a letter from Chauvin's Châtillon superior in which the author impugned Chauvin's motives. Among other charges, the letter asserted that close relatives of Bonnet and Morin had provided Chauvin with the funds for his trip to Paris to testify in the affair.

In spite of these doubts, Bochart allowed the interview between Chauvin and the man in Fort l'Evêque to go forward. This encounter led to an inadvertently hilarious exchange. Facing the prisoner, the Augustinian monk repeated his skepticism that the man before him was the Berrichon aristocrat he had known a decade earlier. In response, the prisoner insisted that Chauvin describe in detail the man he had seen in the Berry, and list the others who had been present at the gathering. The monk then stated, like the Lady of St. Ciran, that the man had not worn a wig. In addition, his hair had been lighter and curlier, and his body much larger than that of the prisoner before him. He then listed the

names of a dozen people who had attended the meeting of local notables. This story was more than the prisoner could bear:
"Although the witness claims that he does not know me, Louis de
la Pivardière, husband of the Lady Chauvelin, who incarcerated
himself in this prison nine months ago to prove his existence, I declare nevertheless that I am the real Louis de la Pivardière, husband of the Lady Chauvelin. I request that the witness be arrested,
given that he is attempting to pass as an impostor!"

If the prisoner was himself an impostor, as the Châtillon magistrates had argued for more than a year, his outburst was almost
comical; his only defense was to accuse the cleric of the same
crime. The investigation had seemingly taken a detour into a hall
of mirrors, where no one could be identified with certainty. In
making this allegation, the prisoner had taken a risk that his
charge of imposture would backfire; after all, who better to sniff
out an impostor than someone who was well versed in that art?
There is no indication that Bochart placed the Augustinian monk
under arrest. But when the time came, he did subject the prisoner
to a withering interrogation, in an effort to determine his identity.

The author of the January 1699 pamphlet that likened the Pivardière affair to a stage play had also predicted that the interrogation
of the prisoner would provide convincing evidence that Louis still
existed. "We have found no better way in France to discover the
truth about a crime than a face-to-face interrogation," he wrote.
The suspect, under sacred oath, would be interrogated by a seasoned judge trained to expose inconsistencies in the witness's testimony and note telltale facial tics, awkward gestures, and false
tones of voice. He would be forced to reveal the most minute details of his family history, his marriage, his fortune, and other aspects of his life unlikely to be known even by the best-prepared
impostor. These interrogations had reached such a state of art,

the pamphleteer claimed, that they were like "a speaking portrait which revealed the most hidden secrets." The record of the encounter between Bochart and the prisoner, however, was anything but. It reads instead like a performance composed of several hundred variations on a theme, each one including a question, or set of questions, by Bochart, and a response by the prisoner. Over the course of the interrogation, which totaled more than twenty-four hours, Bochart asked the alleged Louis 338 questions. Yet we might reduce them all to a simple exchange:

> Q: Are you an impostor?
> A: No.
> Q: Prove it to me.

It took the entire interrogation to begin to articulate an answer to this second question, yet in a larger sense it had taken almost two years to be able to pose the query in its most pristine form, and to create a setting where one might expect a credible answer.

Bochart questioned the suspect in the day room of the concierge at Fort l'Evêque, toward the back of the first floor of the prison, which was reserved for interrogations and judicially sanctioned torture. The two men sat with a court secretary who recorded their proceedings, undistracted by the bustle of prisoners and their visitors in the adjoining courtyard. For eight solid sessions over five days, twice a day on March 2–4, 1699, and then only in the morning the final two days, the court official posed questions about the life of Louis de la Pivardière from before his birth to his alleged assassination, and beyond. There was no chronological or thematic consistency to the topics covered by Bochart; part of the interrogator's art was to skip around the facts of the case, returning to issues raised earlier in an effort to catch inconsistencies on the part of the accused. Bochart listened carefully to the responses, and observed the comportment of the prisoner as he answered. The prisoner adopted a variety of sentiments, ranging from an aristocratic nonchalance about his leisure habits, to regret and repentance for his act of bigamy, to exasperation with the examiner's repeated skepticism about his identity. In these exchanges, influenced by each man's agenda and mutually shaped by their unspoken understandings of the stakes involved, a "portrait" did indeed emerge, as the Merville pamphleteer had predicted, though not necessarily that of a fixed identity consistently present across the entirety of Louis de la Pivardière's adult life.

On the first day of questioning, the prisoner stressed his participation in the provincial aristocratic networks of the lower Berry, even though Louis had not resided in the region for any significant length of time since 1690. For example, when Bochart asked the respondent to name the gentlemen who lived near Narbonne, the latter listed more than a dozen names, then offered to supply even more if needed. Bochart then asked "if some particular occasion" had given rise to the acquaintance he claimed to have with these provincial nobles; the court officer was fishing for a civil or criminal violation whose confession would have unnerved the man under interrogation. His respondent replied, however, that there had been no single incident that had led to his acquaintance with the region's notables, other than the frequent occasions when they had assembled "as good friends." The words he used, *bons amis*, were a code that suggested the distinctive sociability among provincial elites. These cultural attributes contributed to efforts to differentiate themselves from the peasants and servants among whom they lived. Later in the same session, when asked about his relations with the neighboring Prior Charost, the prisoner denied that there had ever been any cause for complaint between the two men. He and the prior had never filed any criminal or civil actions against each other, and they had always lived together "as good friends." The prisoner was at great pains to draw on the language of elite friendship to describe his social world. Yet as Bochart knew, and as the respondent's answers over the course of the eight sessions would reinforce, it had been a number of years since he had lived within the friendly embrace of the Berrichon aristocracy. While he never entirely abandoned his Berrichon origins, his marriage to Marie in Auxerre had constituted a repudiation of the network in which he now reasserted his membership.

On the first day of questioning, in addition to stressing his identity as a provincial aristocrat, the prisoner also argued that the irregular aspects of his behavior over the previous four years stemmed from his second, bigamous marriage. Bochart, in one of the initial questions he posed during the first session, asked the prisoner why he had hidden in Etalante after being discovered in Auxerre by Sousmain and Charost's younger brother. The prisoner claimed that it was because of the "unfortunate" second marriage he had been forced to contract after his "encounter" with Marie. Furthermore, employing a formula he would use two more times, he admitted that this ill-conceived adventure forced him to the "extremity" of marrying a second wife, an action that "he repented, and would continue to repent for the rest of his life." When asked why he had returned to Narbonne on August 15, 1697, he replied that he had done so to ask Marguerite for money to buy his way out of his second marriage. Had he succeeded in this aim, he told the interrogator, he would have offered Marie, whom he now claimed "he had a great desire to leave," enough money to terminate their relationship, and would then have returned to his first wife. Later, during the second day of the interrogation, when explaining how he had passed himself off in Auxerre as the son of a Parisian merchant, he added that he hoped the king would pardon him his faults, just as His Majesty had already granted him the safe-conduct that had allowed him to appear in person before the court. And in the next-to-last session of the interrogation, the prisoner even claimed that it was "a particular joy" to incarcerate himself in order to exonerate his first wife.

The prisoner wished these statements of contrition to be viewed as part of a stable, unchanging persona that would render the facts of the case plausible. He claimed that he had played his proper role in provincial French society up to the moment when, swayed by the charms of Marie, he had made his only mistake and agreed to marry her while his first wife was still alive. If he could count on the goodwill of the king, he would now return to his first marriage, and his proper place in the social hierarchy of the Berry. This self-presentation was likely crafted in conjunction with Marguerite and her family, who had paid for his return to Paris, his lodgings in Fort l'Evêque, and the dissolution of his second marriage to Marie in the hopes that he would definitively exonerate his first wife. The prisoner probably agreed to this strategy because it was the best option he possessed after the revelation of his bigamous actions. But his expression of repentance raised as many questions as his continuing claim to belong among the gentlemen of the lower Berry. His second marriage, while perhaps inspired by physical desire, had also been motivated by a wish to escape his stalled military career, his mounting debts, and his unsatisfactory first marriage. In other words, the facts of the case worked against the prisoner's assertions of fidelity to his Berrichon life. The magistrates, and those following the case beyond the courtroom, might well have been reassured to learn that this bizarre affair did, after all, fit within an essentially conservative pattern of behavior that upheld basic assumptions about individual identity, the importance of marital alliance, and the fixity of the French social order. But Louis' decision to return to Marie in the summer of 1698 left his desire to repent the bigamous marriage in question.

Over the five days of the interrogation, Jean Bochart's circuitous mode of inquiry continuously probed the inconsistencies in the prisoner's story. At the start of the second day of questioning, for instance, Bochart delved into the details surrounding Louis' return to Narbonne on August 15, 1697. When asked if he arrived at Narbonne that day accompanied by a valet, a reasonable assumption given the prisoner's claims to noble status, the latter responded that he entered the gates of Narbonne with only a broken-down horse. Bochart, however, found the response inconsistent with the prisoner's earlier answers: "You're not telling me the truth, because it is unlikely that an officer like you would make such a long journey without someone to serve him and care for his horse." The prisoner, however, simply repeated his assertion: "I did not have anyone in my service." Later that same day, Bochart asked him why, after fleeing Narbonne in the middle of the night on August 15, 1697, he had stayed a whole day at Châteauroux, only a few hours away from Narbonne. When the prisoner referred Bochart to an earlier, incomplete answer, the interrogator again claimed he was not telling the truth: "If you had fled the estate before sunrise because you were afraid Marguerite Chauvelin would have you arrested for bigamy, why did you remain in Châteauroux where you might easily have been seized?" The prisoner replied that bad weather that day had prevented further travel, and that in any event Marguerite did not know the direction he had taken after leaving Narbonne. These exchanges showed Bochart at his most skeptical, highlighting the illogical elements of the story the prisoner had fashioned. In the face-to-face confrontation between the interrogator and the interrogated, the former pointed out the inconsistencies that had previously led many observers to conclude that the prisoner was an impostor.

At times, however, Bochart's suspicions appeared unjustified, and his questions made him look too eager to identify the prisoner as an impostor. At the start of the afternoon on the third day of questioning, Bochart began by asking the prisoner how much money he had been promised in January 1698 to swear in front of the Romorantin lieutenant general that he was Louis de la Pivardière. Essentially, he asked the man under interrogation to admit he was an impostor and disclose the financial arrangements that persuaded him to undertake the charade. The prisoner quickly dismissed the allegation: "I am the real Pivardière, husband of the Lady Chauvelin; beyond that, I have no idea what you are asking of me." Earlier in the same session, Bochart had implicitly compared him to Arnaud du Tilh, the false Martin Guerre, when he asked if he had served in the army with the now-deceased Sieur Dubouchet, "husband of Marguerite Chauvelin." Dubouchet, the interrogator implied, would have told him the details of his personal history. But the prisoner rapidly rebuffed this suggestion as well, reaffirming that he was the "real Louis de la Pivardière, Sieur du Bouchet," who had served in the king's armies during the recent war. And during the final session, Bochart asked the prisoner if he had served as a tutor to Marguerite's children from her first marriage, thereby giving him an opportunity to learn Louis' biographical details. The prisoner responded, almost scornfully, that he was the real Louis, not an itinerant pedant passing through the provinces. In each of these instances, the prisoner quickly countered the interrogator's assertions of imposture.

In this fashion, the two men sparred verbally over the course of the eight sessions. During the second day of the interrogation, a pattern emerged. Bochart would pose questions to the prisoner that overtly suggested his imposture; the prisoner would begin his response with an explicit denunciation of this premise:

Q: Is it not true, and does it not belie your claim to be the real Louis de la Pivardière, that during the night of August 15, 1697, many people entered your bedroom, including the Prior of Miséray and his two valets, in order to kill you, in spite of the fact that you claim to be the true Pivardière?

A: I don't know what you are talking about. I am the real Pivardière, and no one wanted to kill me.

Q: Even if you are the real Pivardière, isn't it the case that a rifle was fired at you, that it wounded you, that you were also wounded by a blow from a sword or dagger? In what parts of your body were you wounded, and by whom among the people in the bedroom?

A: As I told you before, I am the real Pivardière, and none of these facts are true except that this is a false accusation made against my wife, Marguerite Chauvelin, and the Prior of Miséray by the Châtillon judges, who have a hatred of the prior and wish to attack him. . . .

Q: I am telling you again that you cannot be the same person who was assassinated by gunshots and blows from a saber or bayonette on the night of August 15, 1697, in the room where Pivardière slept, because he was seen in the bedchamber lying in his own blood.

A: As I said before, I am the real Pivardière. I was not assassinated; it is a story invented by the Châtillon judges to attack my wife and the Prior of Miséray, and anyone who says otherwise is perjuring themselves.

Bochart's line of questioning categorically rejected the prisoner's claim that he was Louis de la Pivardière, in spite of the wealth of detail about Louis' life provided by the prisoner. Instead, he insisted on the argument put forth by the Châtillon judges that the man who came to the Berry in January 1698 and who now resided in the Fort l'Evêque prison was an impostor, coached by Marguerite, the prior, and their accomplices to impersonate the murdered nobleman. At one point, Bochart even implied that Marguerite was currently disguising herself as a maidservant, leaving her own cell in the Conciergerie, and coming to Fort l'Evêque to tutor the prisoner in preparation for his interrogation. The prisoner, in response to Bochart's repeated assertions of imposture, stated each time that he was "the real Louis de la Pivardière."

It was Bochart's task, of course, to maintain his skepticism about the prisoner's identity throughout the interrogation; if the man was an impostor, the magistrate needed to employ every tactic available to uncover his deceit. This was why he prefaced his initial question on the first day by noting that he had summoned the "supposed" Louis de la Pivardière before him for questioning, and it was why he began the last session four days later by asking the prisoner to identify the moment at which Marguerite had learned that Marie-Elisabeth Pillard of Auxerre was married to a man who resembled Marguerite's deceased husband. In spite of Bochart's persistence, the prisoner did not crack; at the end of the last session, he continued to affirm that he was the "real Louis de la Pivardière." Were his repeated assertions grounded in fact, and did they, therefore, constitute incontrovertible proof that he was the missing Berrichon aristocrat? Or did the fifty-two repetitions of the phrase "I am the real Louis de la Pivardière" simply demonstrate that the prisoner was an able actor who had discharged his part well? After reading this transcript, evaluating the testimony of the witnesses who had known Louis before August 1697, and considering the opinions of the handwriting experts, d'Aguesseau and the criminal magistrates would have to pass judgment on the evidence.

The interrogation of the Fort l'Evêque prisoner raised another problem that, while not central to the criminal trial, was equally interesting. D'Aguesseau mentioned the issue in his summary pleading, when he noted the seemingly impossible fact that Louis de la Pivardière "assembles within himself qualities that are so incompatible, and contradictions that are so astonishing, that he seems to unite in his person two minds and two bodies, in a word, two different men." Bochart posed a similar query during the interrogation when he asked the prisoner how a man of quality and an officer in the king's army could have stooped to buying the office of a huissier. The prisoner answered in the context of his regret at having committed an act of bigamy; he had accepted the post to mollify Marie and her mother, and to better hide himself from the repercussions of his second marriage, should his first become known. But this answer begged other questions. It did not explain why he had become so disenchanted with his aristocratic privileges and his military career that he willingly gave them up, nor did it explain how he had expected to maintain his two separate identities once the war ended.

In fact, some of the details provided by the prisoner during the interrogation only deepened the mystery. For instance, there was a period in 1697, between Louis' visits to Narbonne in May and August, when his whereabouts were unknown. Marguerite told Bochart that her husband, whom she still believed at the time to be an army officer, had said he was heading to the port town of Bayonne in the southwest corner of the kingdom to join his dragoon regiment. But given the St. Hermines regiment's consistent presence in Flanders and on the Rhine throughout the war, such a move by French military strategists as the conflict was winding down was unlikely. Bayonne was a port town unthreatened by Spanish forces to the south; dragoon regiments were not necessary for the town's defense, and most of the action on land along the Spanish border in the last year of the war took place in Catalonia, on the Mediterranean end of the Franco-Spanish frontier. Furthermore, the city was a minor French port without a naval garrison; the Crown's major naval operations were located in Rochefort and Brest on the Atlantic coast, and in Toulon along the Mediterranean. The town's merchant marine was also inconsequential.

Why then did Louis head for this Atlantic coastal city, far to the south of Burgundy and the Berry? Under interrogation by Bochart, the prisoner claimed that he had traveled to Bayonne at the recommendation of a "Sieur Planque, *Lieutenant du Roy à Bayonne*," who had promised to help him find employment on one of the king's frigates that sailed out of Bayonne to protect French merchant vessels. This work, Louis hoped, would allow him to amass a significant amount of money. His need for funds was real, of course; the grain official Curne was waiting back in Auxerre with a warrant for his arrest. Faced with two unappealing prospects (debts and a position he disliked in Auxerre, or a wife and struggling estate he hardly knew anymore at Narbonne), Louis may have found Bayonne appealing because it promised an escape from both unsatisfactory domestic situations. He had already tried to invent himself anew in the St. Hermines regiment and in Auxerre; on the high seas, maybe he could begin the process again. Unfortunately, the prisoner testified to Bochart, Planque had passed away by the time he arrived in Bayonne in the summer of 1697. Although he stayed in the town for a while in the hope of making another acquaintance who might find him a naval post, he failed to secure employment, perhaps because naval officers and merchant marines in Bayonne and other French ports suspected that the end of the war would prompt the Crown to cease using privateers as naval surrogates. By July at the latest, he had decided to return to Narbonne, in part to plead for more funding from Marguerite. His arrival there on August 15, of course, began the fateful series of events that led to his Fort l'Evêque jail cell.

Of all Louis' schemes for advancement, the Bayonne interlude must rate as the most fantastical, and perhaps the most desperate. It is so far-fetched, in fact, and yet so detailed, that it is hard to imagine how the prisoner could have invented it, or why, if he was Louis de la Pivardière, he would have mentioned it unless it were true. Nor was this revelation the only one during the interrogation that prompts questions. At one point, Bochart quite reasonably asked the prisoner where the man who claimed to be Pivardière had gone in late January 1698 after the Romorantin lieutenant general had dismissed him. The prisoner responded, of course, that he was Louis de la Pivardière, and that he had quickly fled the province. He did not, however, head back immediately to Pillard and her mother in Burgundy. Instead, he traveled to the town of Blaye, upstream from Bordeaux near the mouth of the Garonne River, far to the southwest of the Berry and Burgundy. When questioned about this distant, unlikely destination, he responded that he had gone there to retrieve some clothes and personal effects worth around one hundred fifty livres that he had left with an innkeeper the previous summer while returning from his failed attempt to find a naval post in Bayonne.

This action, like so many others undertaken by Louis, seems implausible. Why would he set out on a trip hundreds of kilometers in the opposite direction of his hideout when he knew he would be safest deep in the Burgundian hinterlands with his second wife? Perhaps we should take Louis at his word; he was already part of the way to Blaye from Burgundy, so this was a good opportunity to retrieve the valuable clothes. (Though it is still unclear why he left them there in the first place.) In addition to this economic motivation, one might also hazard a psychological explanation. Throughout his escapades in Auxerre and Bayonne, he had scrupulously maintained his former Berrichon identity in the event he needed to fall back on it. His repudiation by the maidservants that January, and the confusion that ensued, underlined how difficult it would be to reestablish himself as Louis de la Pivardière in the wake of the murder investigation. At the same time, after his flight from Auxerre in the fall of 1697, he could no longer live there as Louis Dubouchet. Who could he be now, and how could he avoid the severe penalties attached to the crime of bigamy, not to mention the string of creditors chasing after both Pivardière and Dubouchet? Perhaps it seemed comforting to temporarily leave both of his shattered identities behind to retrieve a set of clothes that were material and symbolic markers of a time when his identity was still intact.

These two details that emerged during the hearings, the Bayonne adventure and the dash back to Blaye, are puzzling when considered in isolation from the other facts of Louis de la Pivardière's life. They make no more sense than the decision to marry Marie as a commoner, yet simultaneously maintain a noble identity in the Berry. When we think about them in the global context of everything known about the life of Pivardière, we are left with several conclusions. For one, Louis seemed constitutionally incapable of imagining how decisions he made on the fly might impact family and financial arrangements already in place. At every turning point, he seems to have blundered forward with little consideration of the consequences. For another, Louis appears to have put little stock in the social or professional categories, or moral obligations, that contemporaries valued — at least in principle. He liked to hunt and live nobly, yet he had no problem telling everyone he met in Auxerre that he was a commoner. He had an intermittent but lifelong flirtation with the army, yet he easily walked away from his commission to become a low-level municipal policeman, and then contemplated starting anew in the navy. The Christian sacrament of marriage meant so little to him that he willingly contravened it by entering into a bigamous marriage. He casually ignored the financial debts he accumulated as a royal military officer and as a townsman in Auxerre. Taken individually, each of these transgressions was common enough, but taken together they created a portrait that was deeply unsettling.

D'Aguesseau and the Tournelle judges wanted to know about the existence of Louis de la Pivardière so that they could resolve the thicket of legal charges and countercharges that had resulted from the alleged assassination plot on the night of August 15, 1697. But the interrogator's investigation must have reinforced the judges' incredulity. In the series of choices he faced from his marriage to Marguerite Chauvelin in 1687 until his alleged murder in 1697, we see a man who appears to have little regard for the social norms of the day. He ignored Christian morality, Old Regime social hierarchy, and financial obligations at many critical moments in his life. Why he operated independent of these principles is a question open to speculation. Perhaps he failed to absorb these ideals in childhood. Perhaps the desperate circumstances in which all French men and women lived in the 1690s made it easier for him to act in a moral vacuum. Perhaps, as some historians have speculated, this was a period in France, indeed in all of Europe, where older religious, scientific, and ethical principles had broken down, and had yet to be replaced by new formulations. Or, perhaps, historians have focused too much on normative ethical statements made in the seventeenth century, and not enough on the actions individuals actually took when confronted by ethical challenges. It is easier to define Cartesianism or Jansenism than it is to study their relationship to lived experience.

By the end of May 1699, three months after d'Aguesseau had urged the court to undertake an entirely new investigation into the affair, Bochart had completed all the necessary interrogations in the case, as well as the depositions and confrontations with those who had known Louis prior to August 1697. He had also secured testimony from the three court-approved handwriting experts. Although Bochart's investigations into the affair were not open to the public, interest in the case had not waned. In early April, the clandestine newssheet *Histoire journalière* noted that both Louis and Marguerite had been interrogated, and that such respectable witnesses as Louis' commanding officers, the Count of Valençay, Louis' godmother Gripon, and the Father David had given depositions. The journal further reported that Louis' half brother and daughter would soon arrive in Paris to testify in the case. The latter two witnesses did not, as it turned out, appear before Bochart, but their mention in the news of the day suggests that rumors concerning the affair continued to swirl. "It won't be long," the author of the account opined, "before we are better informed about this affair than we are at present."

Chapter 8

VERDICTS

*O*n an overcast summer day in 1699, a horse-drawn cart containing a middle-aged woman dressed in a simple white shift and bound in chains rolled into the Place de Grève in central Paris. The occupant of the cart had just lost her appeal on charges of conspiracy to murder her husband. The square, the traditional site of public executions in the capital during the Old Regime, was already overflowing with people intent on witnessing the beheading of the convicted prisoner. Windows overlooking the plaza were equally full of curious spectators, some of whom had spent extravagant sums to rent apartments for a day with a prime view of the execution site. Before the guard could march the prisoner from the cart to the scaffolding erected for her death, a thunderous storm burst forth, forcing the spectators in the square to seek shelter. The torrent passed, however, and the armed men escorted the woman to her fate. Many in the crowd remarked upon the composure of the convicted prisoner, who had waited out the frightful storm with stoic dignity, then mounted the scaffolding and offered her hand to the executioner in a gesture of refined civility. One commentator wrote later: "[O]ne might almost say that she had studied her role, since she . . . performed all the rituals of the occasion as if it were nothing more than a scene in a stage play."

Her studied theatrics were betrayed, however, by the inexperience of the nervous executioner, a last-minute replacement from the provinces called in after the usual Parisian executioner had been imprisoned for an infraction. The flustered substitute required at least half a dozen swings of his ax to sever the woman's head from her body. With each effort, the crowd in the square grew more agitated, until finally a riot broke out in which "a few observers were killed, many viewing stands collapsed, carriages were broken, horses were abused, and numerous people were robbed." As the police tried to quell the disturbance, the executioner placed his victim's head, finally detached from her torso, on the edge of the scaffolding for the people to see. A female spectator present that day wrote that she was "astonished" by the beauty of the severed head as it rested on the platform, lifelessly presiding over the chaos unleashed in the square.

The central character in this disturbing scene was not Marguerite Chauvelin, the first wife of Louis de la Pivardière, but Angélique-Nicole Carlier de Tiquet, the wife of a lawyer in the Parisian courts. But the two had much in common. Like Marguerite, Madame Tiquet had been accused of plotting to murder her husband after enduring endless rumors of her infidelity. Because of her marriage to a Parlement councilor, she also had close connections to the Parisian judicial establishment. On April 8, 1699, while Bochart was deep into his investigation of the Pivardière affair, his colleague Claude Tiquet had been accosted in the street by two men while returning from dinner at a relative's house. The two attackers shot Tiquet with a pistol and plunged a sword several times into his body, then left him bleeding in the street. Eventually, the lawyer was dragged back to his relative's house, where, miraculously, he survived the next twenty-four hours and ultimately regained consciousness. The inspectors conducting the investigation, which was assiduously followed by Tiquet's legal colleagues, quickly settled on his attractive, estranged wife as the primary suspect. The couple's incompatibility had been common knowledge at the Palais and beyond for over a decade: In the early 1690s, for example, Claude Tiquet had obtained a decree from the king allowing him to imprison his wife for suspected unfaithfulness, although he never enacted the king's orders. By the middle of the decade, Madame Tiquet's affair with the Sieur de Montgeorges, a commander in the King's Guard, was the subject of widespread comment; their potential liaison had proven so scandalous that the king himself threatened to reassign Montgeorges far from Paris and Versailles if he did not act in a more circumspect fashion. Some commentators alleged that Madame Tiquet had tried to have her husband murdered three years before, but he had supposedly thwarted the plot. Now, in the spring of 1699, the investigation into the April 8 attack moved swiftly; four days after the assault, a criminal lieutenant and a squadron of fifty huissiers appeared at Madame Tiquet's residence to take her into custody. A little more than two months later she died on the block.

The case was an ominous precedent for Marguerite, who awaited final judgment in the Conciergerie, where Madame Tiquet had also spent the final two weeks of her life. Contemporary observers were aware of the similarities; one journalist writing in the Dutch papers reported on May 1 that Madame Tiquet's case was not going well, and that it seemed like her only hope was a royal pardon. By June 15, a week before the execution, the same journal reported that there was "almost no doubt" that Madame Tiquet would meet a tragic end on the scaffold. On July 20, only days before the verdict in the Pivardière affair, the same reporter noted that "one is beginning to have a bad feeling about the trial of Madame de la Pivardière," in much the same way that rumor had seemingly consigned Madame Tiquet to the executioner's block.

The two notorious women were linked in popular song as well. One eighteenth-century compiler of popular airs noted that the following bit of doggerel, sung to a popular vaudeville tune, had been current in "the time of the adventures of Mesdames Tiquet and de la Pivardière":

> It's a sad thing these days,
> That he who marries a well-behaved girl
> Finds her to be another woman once married.
> The husband tries to control her in vain,
> Pleas only make her laugh.
> And if the husband scolds her,
> He winds up dead!

This mocking tune displayed more than a bit of nervousness about a seeming epidemic of spousal assassinations. Picking up on this unease, one commentator on the Tiquet case argued that the wife had been framed by a husband who wanted full control of her dowry, and by the king and the archbishop of Paris who feared that other discontented wives would take out contracts on their husbands. Whatever Madame Tiquet's guilt while alive, or the status of her posthumous reputation, the comparison between her case and that of Marguerite Chauvelin did not augur well for the latter.

The Tiquet execution offered uncomfortable lessons for the Tournelle magistrates as well. Although they had only confirmed the verdict rendered by a lower criminal court, they could not have been pleased with the breakdown in public order the day of her execution. On one level, everyone understood that the scene in the Place de Grève was typical of crowds who witnessed Old Regime executions, who often turned these occasions into raucous public festivals. In addition, no matter how heinous the crime, observers often yearned for the condemned person to be spared, both to avoid the awful spectacle of death, and also to imagine that divine justice, a higher authority than earthly magistrates, had intervened at the last minute. But there was also an undercurrent of uncertainty surrounding the Tiquet verdict. While undergoing torture the morning of her execution, Tiquet had confessed to the crime, implicating two other men as her accomplices. One source noted that her confession under duress had been cause for relief among the criminal magistrates, who may have had second thoughts about the verdict. Furthermore, according to the Dutch reporter, d'Aguesseau himself twice put off the delivery of his second summary pleading in the Pivardière affair, the first time only days after Madame Tiquet's execution. Did the young attorney general and his judicial colleagues find it imprudent to rule on another case of alleged spousal homicide so soon after the ghoulish dénouement of the Tiquet affair and the violent reaction it provoked?

After Jean Bochart finished his inquiries in May, he turned the transcripts over to the court for analysis. The Tournelle resumed hearings in the case the following month, offering barristers for both sides the chance to state their case one final time. Just as the hearings began, however, Jean Bonnet, the septuagenarian lieutenant who had conducted the investigations at Narbonne and interrogated the maidservants in 1697 and 1698, died. His Châtillon colleague François Morin notified the court of this development, and Marguerite and the prior agreed to indemnify Bonnet's modest heirs against any judgment convicting their deceased relative. Bonnet's demise significantly altered Morin's legal strategy, because it allowed his attorneys to shift the blame for calumny and corruption to the dead investigator who could no longer defend himself. It also gave the Tournelle judges an out, should they decide to rule that Louis was still alive; the guilt could be assigned to the dead magistrate, allowing them to avoid the spectacle of rebuking a provincial officer of the law.

The lawyers spoke before the court for four sessions. Predictably, the advocates for Marguerite, the prior, and the prisoner in Fort l'Evêque argued that Bochart's investigation decisively demonstrated the continuing existence of the Berrichon gentleman and demanded that the court dismiss the charges. Morin's barrister chose not to contravene the conclusion that Louis was still alive. Instead, he claimed that Morin's actions in the investigation that followed the supposed assassination had been strictly determined by his judicial responsibilities in Châtillon. He would have been negligent if had he not asked Bonnet to look into the rumors emanating from Narbonne. Furthermore, he argued that the July 1698 verdict had vindicated his client's actions, and that he could not be retried on those grounds.

On July 22, five months after his first pleading and almost exactly a year after the court's first ruling in the case, Attorney General d'Aguesseau rose to address the court again. He began by invoking the astonishing history, "or perhaps the fable," of the life and death of Louis de la Pivardière, which "has become one of those events that we are not permitted to ignore." He briefly retraced the complicated factual and legal history of the case, but wasted no further time before stating what he believed to be the inescapable conclusion to the affair. "Today the veil is lifted, the work of darkness has been undone. . . . the existence of the Sieur de la Pivardière, certain, solid, palpable, is the grand dénouement of this fraudulent intrigue." The magistrates, he urged, would have to withdraw the July 1698 verdict, now shown to be based on incomplete facts; their indignation in the matter should be directed to Morin, the remaining Châtillon magistrate, or perhaps to the maidservants who had given misleading testimony. It was no longer vague noises and popular rumor, nor the discredited procedure of the Romorantin lieutenant general, which constituted the primary proof that the missing aristocrat was still alive; it

conspired to murder Pivardière. Others reported that Nicholas Mercier, Marguerite's father, had knowledge of large bloodstains in the room where Louis had slept only days after the fact. Residents of Romorantin, Luçay, and other nearby towns also swore under oath that Mercier or Lemoyne had regaled them with the story of their master's demise before they were taken into custody by Bonnet. While it is plausible that one or two of these witnesses might have spoken against the servants out of personal animosity, it is unlikely that dozens of people, whose testimony was recorded by three investigators at different times, would have done so. Once in custody, Mercier and Lemoyne initially stopped repeating the story of their master's murder, perhaps fearing that they would perjure themselves. But this quickly changed; the transcripts of their October and November 1697 interrogations show them once again recounting the lurid tale of their master's death. Mercier claimed that she had denied the murder in these sessions only to have the court recorder falsify her testimony. However, the recorder, Louis Breton, told the investigators in 1699 that he was a cousin of the prior, and that the prior's mother had prevailed upon him to serve as Bonnet's recorder to ensure an accurate transcript; it was unlikely he would have made up a tale that threatened the family's reputation. In short, Morin presented enough evidence to undercut Mercier's claim that she never told anyone her mistress and the prior had killed her master.

What prompted the servants to spread this misleading rumor? We will never know for sure, but we can imagine the tensions at Narbonne between Chauvelin, the Parisian-educated daughter of an important judicial family, and the local maidservants who toiled on her estate. Louis' sudden disappearance might have seemed like a prime opportunity for the girls to strike at their mistress for real or perceived slights. Local peasants in Jeu and the surrounding countryside would have been more than willing consumers of tales about Marguerite's adultery and treachery. The crescendo of rumors that reached Châtillon by September 5, prompting Morin to ask Bonnet to investigate, is entirely plausible in this scenario. But even if the maidservants shortsightedly exploited the unusual situation, the Châtillon judges also bore responsibility for the debacle. Why did they hasten to plunder Narbonne four weeks after the alleged assassination, but wait two more weeks to investigate the scene of the crime? Why did they not approach the servants' testimony with more skepticism, particularly when they could not find any other eyewitnesses to the murder, or a corpse? When the huissiers arrested Marguerite Mercier in Romorantin, they heard her tell Louis' stepsister, the Dame des Fosses, that she had not seen her master perish on August 15. In retrospect, it is clear that Jean Bonnet's fortuitous death in 1699 released him from having to answer questions the next year about his role in the Pivardière affair.

Factual discrepancies were not the only way in which Morin cast doubt on Mercier's testimony during the investigation. In the brief his lawyers published, Morin noted that "the dignity and the gravity of a witness adds weight to a deposition, just as the baseness of a witness' condition, the weakness of her sex, or her poverty can expose her to the influence of those who have authority over them." He reminded his readers that Louis and Marguerite had already characterized the servants as "imbeciles who were easy to intimidate by threats or corrupt by promises." And throughout the pamphlet he referred to his opponent as "La Mercier," a formulation reserved for common women and prostitutes. During the investigation that year, the court recorder Breton charged that Mercier was *une fille* whose views should not be given any credence, and the ecclesiastical judge Jacquemet expressed his "pain and sadness to find himself confronted by a person such as Mercier." Now that the Châtillon investigation had been declared a failure and the investigators themselves were suspect, they resorted to ad hominem attacks that appealed to the social hierarchy and gender bias of the day.

The court took note of all these arguments. No longer pressed to act swiftly by public curiosity, however, it did not render a verdict in the perjury phase of the trial until June 14, 1701, almost four years after the supposed killing. D'Aguesseau was by then procurator general, and the words of the attorney general who delivered the final summary pleading in the case have not been preserved. We do not have transcripts of the judges' deliberations leading to their decision. But the verdict survives: The magistrates found Marguerite Mercier guilty of false testimony. They condemned her to perform the *amende honorable*, the Old Regime's ritual of humiliation imposed upon convicted criminals. She was sentenced to kneel in front of the main church in Châtillon-sur-Indre, barefooted and with a cord around her neck, holding a heavy torch. She was ordered to declare that she had willfully and maliciously made false declarations to the Châtillon judges, for which she had to repent, and demand pardon from God, the king, and the law. Then she was to be whipped, branded on her right shoulder with the fleur-de-lys, and made to perform the same ceremony of repentance in the town's other main squares. She would forfeit her possessions to the Crown, pay a fine of fifty livres, then be banished from the jurisdiction of the Parlement of Paris, which covered more than half of the kingdom, including all of the Berry, for the remainder of her life. Morin and the Bourges officials did not escape punishment; they were ordered to provide compensation, to be determined at a later date, to Louis and Marguerite for the damages to Narbonne. The Bourges officials were also ordered to restore the Prior Charost's benefices lost during his incarceration. The damages that Marguerite and the prior had claimed the previous summer were finally awarded. But the high court allowed the provincial judges to return to their posts without further penalty.

Marguerite Mercier was no innocent in this affair, but when she and Catherine Lemoyne began to spread word in August 1697 that their master was dead, she could not have imagined that she would lose her possessions, her honor, and her place in the rural Berrichon milieu as a result of the events of August 1697 and their aftermath. The fleur-de-lys burned onto her body symbolized not only her misfortune, but also the inequities of a system that stigmatized its weakest members while allowing those with greater status to avoid public shaming and destruction of their lives. The uplifting oratory of d'Aguesseau, which had encouraged the criminal magistrates to acknowledge their fallibility and engage in humane judicial practice, went unheeded by the high court magistrates when it came time to judge Marguerite Mercier.

We know nothing about the lives of the Prior Charost or the substitute procurator general Morin after the great affair had run its course, but some evidence survives about Marguerite Chauvelin. The 1701 verdict that condemned Mercier to the *amende honorable* also erased Chauvelin's name from the sentence passed against her and the prior by the Bourges judges, clearing her of the adultery charges that had accompanied the initial murder accusation. By the time this final vindication was published, she had already thanked the Parisian relatives who had seen her through her trials and returned to Narbonne, where she undertook the sizable job of rebuilding her ruined estate. In November 1699, at the request of the Parlement, a police lieutenant from Issoudun arrived at the estate with a mason, a carpenter, a locksmith, and other artisans, whose task it was to estimate the costs of restoration that Morin and the Bourges officials would be assessed. No record of the final accounting has survived, but Narbonne eventually returned to its minimal level of productivity, allowing Marguerite and her children from both marriages to resume their unadorned existence. The task of reestablishing the manor house and its domains would not have been easy even under normal circumstances: The livestock was gone, the interior furnishings had disappeared, doors and windows had to be repaired, and at least two, possibly all three, of her maidservants had to be replaced. But it is hard to imagine that Marguerite returned to Narbonne under normal circumstances. The novelty of the events that had touched so many local lives would have made it hard for the mistress of the manor to resume her existence as she had led it before August 1697. "When one has had a scandalous adventure," wrote François Gayot de Pitaval in 1734, "one cannot present oneself again to others without making a stir."

Yet return she did, perhaps with the assistance of Louis' older brother Antoine, perhaps with help from her Parisian family. It is unclear how successful she was at her task, or how well she was able to reintegrate into the social world of the lower Berry. The parish register for Jeu-Malloches indicates that she died at Narbonne on February 21, 1708, at the age of forty-eight. Did she ever speak of her experiences in Paris during the murder trial? When she returned to Narbonne, how did she interact with the neighbors whose loose tongues had contributed to her difficulties? The scandalous events of the late 1690s that drove her from her threadbare estate to a yearlong confinement in a Paris prison constituted her moment of greatest notoriety. But they should be placed in the context of a full life that saw her take up a position in rural society while still a teenager as the head of a small country estate, give birth to at least seven children, and endure two unsatisfactory marriages. Her journey was not an easy one, but it was remarkable, as she preserved until her death a degree of autonomy within a legal and institutional system that was unfavorable to women.

And what of Louis de la Pivardière, the calculating adventurer whose subterfuges and missteps affected the lives of so many others? Our last glimpse of him is at Marguerite's side at Narbonne in November 1699, observing the efforts of the artisans who had come to calculate the damage done to the estate. How much longer did he stay there, playing the devoted husband he had portrayed himself to be during his interrogation by Bochart eight months earlier? All we know with certainty is that he is not buried in Jeu alongside his first wife. A legend that first surfaced in print in the 1730s claimed that he perished in the first years of the eighteenth century as a member of the royal army fighting smugglers in the Jura mountains. In this scenario, dissatisfied with his lot as a member of the impoverished provincial nobility, unable to pass as the son of a bourgeois merchant, Louis gave his life to defend the Crown's protectionist economic policy that was also under attack at the outset of the eighteenth century. He would have died just as he had lived, on the uneasy borders of Old Regime France. But it is an unverifiable tale. After November 1699, Louis' life trails off into uncertainty, becoming a series of blank pages upon which one might write many endings. Perhaps he headed back to the Atlantic coast, once again in pursuit of a marine career. The onset of the War of the Spanish Succession in 1701 undoubtedly created other options. Almost any sequel is possible for a man who had already changed course so many times that his contemporaries could not perceive any pattern in his actions.

The life of Louis de la Pivardière is disconcerting because it upends our received notions of identity in the age of Louis XIV. Every other individual we encounter when telling his tale has a readily identifiable position in the ordered society of late-seventeenth-century France. Marguerite Mercier cannot transcend the baseness of her servitude in the eyes of the judges. Florent Carton Dancourt is always a sinful stage impersonator, even if he cleverly works theatrical convention to explore the meanings of the Pivardière affair. Henri-François d'Aguesseau can evoke a jurisprudence of doubt and bring finality to the confusing case, because he plays the role of the judicial oracle with such authority.

Only Louis de la Pivardière continually, casually, steps outside the frame that contains his portrait. The engraver creates a likeness for his legal brief that cannot possibly be accurate. D'Aguesseau, relying on Bochart's investigations, conjures up a triptych composed of Louis' handwriting, witness testimony, and the interrogation, yet admits its potential inaccuracies. Dancourt, in *The Husband Returned*, creates two different characters that evoke the curious provincial aristocrat, but neither Julian nor Clitandre lay to rest the many questions surrounding the man in the Fort l'Evêque jail cell.

A generation earlier, while creating Monsieur Jourdain, his send-up of social imposture, Molière also offered his audiences a seeming antidote to Jourdain's buffoonish insincerity. In the climactic moment of the comedy, Cléonte, the bourgeois suitor, asks Monsieur Jourdain for permission to marry his daughter. The latter, desperate to ally his daughter with a man of quality, responds with a curt question: "I pray you, tell me if you are a gentleman?" The answer Monsieur Jourdain receives is unexpectedly profound. Momentarily abandoning the work's rich comic repertory of wordplay, physical humor, and stock character conflicts, the playwright has Cléonte speak sincerely:

> Monsieur, most people would not hesitate to respond boldly to your question. Few have any scruples when taking this name, and current usage appears to authorize its theft. As for me, however, I must admit I have somewhat more complicated feelings on this matter. I find all imposture beneath the dignity of an honorable man. It is cowardly to disguise that which Heaven has given us at birth, to parade a false title before the eyes of the world, to pass oneself off for what one is not. I was born to parents who have, without a doubt, held honorable positions. I have had the honor of serving for six years in the army, and I have worked hard enough to hold a respectable rank in the world. But even with all that, I would

never want to take a title that others in my place would falsely assume. So I will tell you frankly that I am not at all a gentleman.

At one level, of course, the speech provides a critique of Monsieur Jourdain's ludicrous behavior. It grounds the play's comic extremes in a more rational morality one might encounter outside the playhouse. But Cléonte's unvarnished response to Monsieur Jourdain also condemns all imposture as a betrayal of one's birth, parents, and station in life. There is merit enough, he implies, in living honorably no matter what rank one holds. "Heaven" has provided all the markers of identity one might need; we disregard these signposts at our own peril. The play's moralizing moment is fleeting; later Cléonte himself impersonates a Turkish potentate in order to trick Monsieur Jourdain, a device intended to recall the visit of an Ottoman entourage to Louis XIV the previous year. But the burlesque send-up of the Muslim Other does not entirely negate Cléonte's earlier avowal that individual merit contains reward enough for those not born to the aristocracy. Hidden amid the comic stage antics of Monsieur Jourdain and the spectacle of the ballets, Molière hints that he and his contemporaries were also familiar with an alternative to the façade of nobility that social elites had learned to erect. Decent parents, service to the state as a rank-and-file soldier, and a record of honest productivity after military service conferred their own substantial moral and material rewards, a point confirmed when Cléonte finally wins Lucille's hand at the end of the play.

A generation later, after the wars and famines and religious intolerance that had marked three decades of the Sun King's reign, it was more difficult to pinpoint a moral foundation upon which to make sense of the case of the would-be commoner. D'Aguesseau's juridical doubt, which ultimately ceded authority to an inaccessible, divine judge, was as close as any of Pivardière's contemporaries would come to resolving the mysteries of the case. From a perspective three centuries removed, it is tempting to cling to Cléonte's common-sense rejection of imposture, to assert that identity has stable boundaries that are apparent to men and women of goodwill and discernment. But it is also difficult to deny the fascination engendered by that Berrichon rogue, Louis de la Pivardière, as he tripped through the 1690s flouting all the rules that would have limited him to one identity, one wife, and one set of life experiences and expectations.

Epilogue

REWRITING
A CAUSE CÉLÈBRE

$\mathcal{S}$ometime in 1733 or early 1734, a sixty-year-old lawyer and marginal man of letters named François Gayot de Pitaval sought an interview with a Madame Leroux, the wife of a judicial official in Chaillot, a village outside the Paris city limits. Gayot de Pitaval was researching the celebrated Pivardière affair that had been heard in the Tournelle a generation earlier, and Madame Leroux had critical information for him. Much had changed in France since the high court had ruled in the case. The Sun King had died in 1715, in the seventy-second year of his reign. The War of the Spanish Succession had ended two years before, bringing to a close the almost constant warfare of the latter half of Louis XIV's reign. The British emerged as France's chief geopolitical competitor in the Atlantic and Indian oceans, but the two countries' overseas rivalry did not shut off the flow of new ideas across the channel. The physics and mathematics of Isaac Newton and the epistemology and political theories of John Locke found an appreciative audience in the salons and academies of Paris and the major provincial centers in the first half of the eighteenth century. Voltaire's *Letters on England*, which praised British freedoms while im-

plicitly criticizing French absolutism, appeared in the same year
that the lawyer Gayot de Pitaval sought his audience with Madame Leroux.

Among the central figures in the Pivardière affair, the one who
led the longest and most interesting life after the Parlement rendered its final verdict in 1701 was the woman Gayot sought to interview, who had been known in her youth as Marie-Elisabeth
Pillard. Unlike Marguerite Chauvelin, worn out before her fiftieth
birthday by her marital mishaps and the demands of running Narbonne, and unlike Marguerite's maidservant Marguerite Mercier,
who alone suffered the stigma of judicial punishment, Marie was
not ruined by the chaos that Louis had wrought. None of the
three children she had conceived with the bigamous husband of
her youth survived infancy; the last one, a daughter also named
Marie-Elisabeth, died at the age of three in April 1699 while her
father was still locked away in Fort l'Evêque. Sometime no later
than October 1705, her union with Louis no longer an obstacle,
she married a Parisian named Mathurin de la Rey, a royal tax
collector at the city gates. She was to marry twice more over the
next thirty-four years, according to a 1739 document in which she
was identified as the widow of a Sieur le Brasseur and then of the
Sieur Leroux. Only once do we have evidence of her presence in
Auxerre after 1700, a signature in an Auxerrois parish register
identifying her as the godmother of the recently born Jean Pillard,
son of one François Pillard, shoemaker. Beyond these details, we
can only speculate about how a young woman who had survived
the scandal of a notorious marriage parlayed the lessons she
learned into three advantageous matches.

What is certain, though, is that sometime in the early 1730s
she sat down to discuss the great affair in which she had once
played an important role with Gayot de Pitaval, who was writing a
multivolume compendium of famous court cases. Before he hit on
the novel idea of a work devoted to unusual criminal trials, Gayot

had authored several collections of bons mots and curiosities, including a *Collection of the Most Curious Enigmas of Our Times* (1717) and *The Spirit of Agreeable Conversations* (1731). One literary historian has noted that "his goal in his conversation manuals is to provide both a model of the most agreeable conversational tone and a collection of noteworthy anecdotes." The same objectives applied to his twenty-volume collection of *Causes célèbres et intéressantes*, published between 1734 and the author's death in 1743. Gayot's *Causes célèbres*, by far his most famous work, became a bestseller. A typical volume contained a short preface, followed by discussions of two to six "celebrated" cases and analogous examples from the annals of French law. Critics complained that the work lacked structure; Gayot did not organize the volumes chronologically, nor is there an overall logic, legal or otherwise, to the order of their presentation. A reader browsing casually through the work might be reminded of famous fictional compilations of amazing stories, such as Giovanni Boccaccio's *Decameron* or Geoffrey Chaucer's *Canterbury Tales*.

In the first five volumes, Gayot recounts many of the most notorious cases from the storehouse of Old Regime criminal jurisprudence. The initial volume begins with the Martin Guerre case, and includes the scarcely credible affair of the Comtesse de St. Geran, who, after a nine-month pregnancy and an arduous labor, was duped by jealous heirs into believing she had never been pregnant or given birth to a son. The fifth volume contains the tale of the Marquise de Gange, a beautiful, virtuous, wealthy young woman who was ultimately murdered by her sordid brothers-in-law; Gayot's version of the story later inspired a novel by the Marquis de Sade. The Marquise de Brinvilliers, who poisoned her father and brothers early in the reign of Louis XIV, the priest Urbain Grandier and the bewitched nuns of Loudun, the convicted husband-killer Madame Tiquet, the bigamist Jean Capé, and the calumnious magistrates of Mantes all grace the pages of these first five volumes along with Louis, Marguerite, and the prior.

Gayot's *Causes célèbres* should be situated at the crossroads of early-eighteenth-century literature, philosophy, and jurisprudence; they are a reminder of the emergence of a literate, engaged public in France, one that was avid for new knowledge, yet wished to approach it through the literary traditions of the seventeenth-century plays and novels that had amused the subjects of Louis XIV. This public hunger, as much as anything written by Montesquieu, Voltaire, or Diderot, was responsible for the spread of the eighteenth-century intellectual and cultural phenomenon called the Enlightenment. Neither mindless entertainment nor pure pedantry satisfied this audience; its members sought a combination of distraction and self-improvement in their reading, spectating, and polite conversation. In the time of the Pivardière affair at the end of the 1690s, this tendency to fuse entertainment and instruction was not yet possible with respect to the law and the stage; Dancourt's comical one-act and d'Aguesseau's solemn judicial reports could find no middle ground. A generation later, however, Gayot and his publisher had the insight to realize that the genre of the *cause célèbre* could bridge stage and courtroom, thereby uniting fiction and fact.

It was within the context of these literary and cultural changes that Gayot undertook his narrative of the Pivardière affair. Even among the extraordinary examples he had assembled, he thought the case stood out; as he remarked in the introduction to volume three, "the epithet 'singular' was coined expressly for this adventure." He titled the case "A Woman Accused of Having Had Her Husband Killed, and Who Proved Her Innocence by Presenting Him," thereby making Marguerite, and not her wandering husband, the protagonist of the affair. On the second page of his account, however, he also lets the reader know that the version of events he is about to recount has added credibility: "Happily, in this wondrous case, wanting to go to the source, I found people who were eyewitnesses to the events and who, being without passion, faithfully instructed me in the truth of the matter." Not until the end of his narrative does he reveal the identity of his primary informant: "[W]ith respect to the second wife [of Louis], she has had other true husbands since her false one. . . . she is still alive, and she recounted to me many of the particulars of this story."

The influence of the former Marie-Elisabeth Pillard is evident in several key passages of Gayot's account of the Pivardière affair. The opening pages of the text detail the marriage of Louis and Marguerite and the subsequent cooling of their affection for each other; Gayot might have easily cobbled these pages together from the printed briefs. When Gayot claims that Louis knew about his wife's infidelity with the prior, however, the narrative begins to present new interpretations and events that are not mentioned in any of the accounts from the late 1690s. According to Gayot, a chagrined Louis abandoned his wife to her extramarital pursuits, fearful of the ridicule often heaped upon a jealous husband. He was traveling from town to town, "seeking to efface the idea of his domestic affliction, when he arrived in Auxerre one summer's evening." Strolling along the city's ramparts, he happened across a group of young girls amusing themselves by playing games. His view fell on one of them, "and he felt himself suddenly disposed to love her. She was one of those people whose charms unite everyone's opinion in her favor; she had a rare wisdom about her." The young girl in question, of course, was Marie, Gayot's "eyewitness" informant. Nowhere in any of the sources of the late 1690s can one find an account of Louis wandering heartbroken from town to town, waiting for Cupid's arrow to strike; the fiction must have come from Marie, or perhaps from Gayot's embellishment of her account.

Gayot next suggests that the happy couple married and settled into their lives in Auxerre, where he claims they lived in harmony for four years, producing four children. Either Marie's memory failed her, however, or Gayot altered the facts she related to him, because no more than two and a half years elapsed between the couple's marriage in April 1695 and the start of their final troubles in the fall of 1697. Gayot then shifts his narrative back to Narbonne, relating the events of August 15, 1697, and their immediate aftermath. When Marguerite's emissaries track down Louis, convincing him to sign notarial documents attesting to his existence, Gayot repeats the narratives from the late 1690s that recounted the wayward husband's sympathy for his falsely accused first wife. But he adds another reason, again unmentioned in the contemporary sources, to explain Louis' decision to cooperate with Marguerite in October 1697: "His second wife came generously to the rescue of the first; far from conceiving a hatred for the man whom she might have said had abused her trust, and jealousy against a rival who might steal him away, she encouraged her husband to come to the aid of his legitimate wife." This interpretation of Marie's response to her husband's bigamy is surprisingly generous, if one stops to consider Marie's circumstances in October 1697. She, her husband, and her mother had been in financial difficulty since at least the beginning of the year, a hardship that Louis' August trip to the Berry had clearly failed to ease; she and Louis had ceased to live together at some point during the previous summer; and their second child, and first son, had died shortly after his birth the previous year. Under these circumstances, it is difficult to imagine Marie receiving the news of her husband's duplicity with the grace Gayot attributes to her. It is more likely that the mature Marie, in the calm and security of a legitimate marriage in the 1730s, recast that desperate moment from her youth for her inquisitive interlocutor.

Gayot and Madame Leroux, though, saved their most striking revision for a later moment in the narrative. After a lengthy analysis of the first round of pleadings before the Parlement in the summer of 1698, Gayot turns to the safe-conduct that Louis XIV granted in late August 1698. Contemporary documents and accounts do not detail the way in which the Chauvelin clan approached the Crown to request the safe-conduct. Gayot's 1734 version presents an account of this request in which Marie, "supported by the credit of powerful people," travels to Versailles to solicit a safe-conduct for her husband. Finding herself in the presence of the monarch, she throws herself at his knees. The Sun King, "not one to allow a beautiful supplicant to languish long in that state, raised her to her feet. He learned her business and then, because indulgent words flowed from the lips of this Monarch, especially in all that concerned the fair sex, he said to her, 'A girl as beautiful as you deserves a better fate.'" He then grants her the safe-conduct for her husband.

Did Marie's audience with Louis XIV take place? If it did, no account of it from the late 1690s has survived. None of the court memorialists, from Sourches to Saint-Simon, recorded the interview. Madame du Noyer's aristocratic correspondent, who provides her with dozens of similar details of court life, was silent. The Dutch journalists, who followed the case attentively from June 1698 onward, made no mention of Marie at court, although one of them reported a rumor in late July 1698, weeks before Marie's supposed trip, that Louis' second wife "will cease her marriage claims if given a sum of money, which will remove the obstacle [a charge of bigamy] that prevents him from appearing." A little more than a month later, the same newssheet matter-of-factly reported that the king had granted Louis a safe-conduct, but did not report on the circumstances under which it was obtained. If Gayot's account is true, it is curious that no contemporary report of this colorful encounter between monarch and young female subject survives. The interview, which showed the king at his most benevolent, was the type of incident that royal hagiographers eagerly seized upon to bolster the image of a king who attended to the needs of his deserving subjects. The following spring, during the trial of Madame Tiquet, her husband took the couple's three children to Versailles to plead for their mother's life at the feet of the king; their goal was to avoid the public shame the family would experience because of her execution. Louis XIV refused to grant a pardon, but the scene, just as sensational as that recounted by Gayot, was reported in every one of the sources that remains silent on Marie's moment at court.

Marguerite Chauvelin's 1699 interrogation transcript reveals a different role for Marie and her mother in the late summer of 1698. Marguerite had first made contact with Marie in the fall of 1697, when she had sent the prior and his brother to Auxerre in search of Louis. The following summer, while the Parisian trial was in progress, Marie and her mother traveled to Paris to visit Marguerite in prison. According to Marguerite, she met only once with her husband's young second wife; Marie told her that she was "quite happy with her husband, and that they loved each other a great deal," but also admitted she was distressed that Louis had not disclosed his previous marriage. This single-sentence account surely does not capture all the dimensions of this encounter. Perhaps the two women empathized with each other; likely there was some degree of jealousy. Both were no doubt upset that Louis was causing such turmoil in their lives. But there is no mention of Marie's heroic, selfless gesture as it was reported by Gayot a generation later. In her interrogation, Marguerite granted that Marie's mother, Marie Caillant, "had contributed a great deal" to Louis' eventual appearance in the capital. Caillant, of course, was inspired to cooperate because his arrival in Paris resulted in a payment of twelve thousand livres, after which she and her daughter returned to Burgundy and appear to have had no further involvement in the affair. There is no contemporary evidence to corroborate Marie's fairy-tale interview with the Sun King.

The details of Marie's involvement in the case occupy only a few of Gayot's ninety-two pages of text, yet they alter the moral meanings of the affair. D'Aguesseau had claimed in February 1699 that the case boasted no exemplary figures, but Gayot had discovered a heroine for his tale in the figure of the wronged, but generous, second spouse. Young, beautiful, and carefree when Louis first spied her on the town ramparts, Marie had provided him with the domestic harmony that had been absent from his marriage to the more senior Marguerite. When he had been forced by events to confess his deceit to her, she had thought not of herself, her marriage, and her children, but of the innocent first wife whose life was in jeopardy. When Louis' January 1698 return to the Berry failed to quiet the charges against Marguerite and the prior, she had amazingly taken it upon herself to travel to Versailles to seek an audience with the king. And in a moment that served as the emotional climax of Gayot's narrative, her beauty, charm, and courage resulted in a success where the efforts of Louis, Marguerite, and their lawyers had come up empty. The complexities of the case that had resulted from months of magisterial wrangling were simply, gracefully, untangled in the moment when the young wife asked the absolute monarch to intervene directly in the trial. Only the self-sacrificing virtue of Marie and the all-knowing wisdom of Louis XIV together could undo the Gordian knot of the Pivardière affair.

Although too little is known about Marie after 1700 to hazard a guess about when and why she came to reformulate her role in the Pivardière affair, it was obviously in her interest to dress up her role in the case. Gayot also had reasons for casting Marie as the chaste heroine of the tale. In several of his causes célèbres, he offers accounts that were sympathetic to the women involved. In his version of the Martin Guerre case, for example, he imagines that Bertrande de Rols is complicit in the deception with Arnaud du Tilh because "it pleased her" and served her interests. And in his narrative of the Pivardière case, he describes Louis' supposed jealousy over Marguerite's involvement with the prior, then comments: "Do men who are unfaithful to their wives have the right to demand of them a chastity they do not maintain? If women had the right to reform the laws, they would begin with this one." Gayot's feminist leanings no doubt pleased some of the "ladies" among his readers whom he sought to entertain and instruct; these tendencies may have also led him to empathize with the version of the Pivardière affair he heard from Marie in the early 1730s.

Beyond the question of Gayot's intentions lies the issue of his readers' perceptions. Every subsequent eighteenth-century edition of Gayot's *Causes célèbres*, and each of the four rewritten versions of it, gives Marie a central role in the salvation of Louis, Marguerite, and the prior. By the early twentieth century, the story of Marie's trip to Versailles had been so embellished that the king invites her to stay at Versailles for several days after granting her the safe-conduct; she is lavishly attended by the ladies-in-waiting, and then sent back to Auxerre, Cinderella-like, in a royal carriage and courtly dress. While it is certain that many elite women were reading fiction and other types of narratives in the eighteenth century, an appeal to this audience is not necessarily the only reason for the appearance of Marie as the sole sympathetic character in the Pivardière affair. In the 1690s, efforts to turn the case into a comprehensible narrative had focused on the figure of Louis and the puzzle of his self-imposed social demotion; why had he chosen to live a bourgeois lifestyle in Auxerre, and what were the implications of this choice for the declining figure of the chivalric nobleman? Almost every observer, from the Dutch news gatherers to Madame du Noyer's correspondent, had registered their bewilderment with the case, offering no coherent explanation.

For Gayot, however, writing in the 1730s when the wars of Louis XIV were almost two decades in the past, the challenge the case posed to the privileges of the military nobility was less significant. When placed alongside the false Martin Guerre, the ill-fated Marquise de Gange, and the befuddled Comtesse de St. Geran, Louis' unusual behavior seemed less in need of explanation, simply a historical curiosity that had given rise to an unusual legal case. Furthermore, the new masculine heroes for the reading public Gayot courted were at times not virile military leaders, but intellectuals and popularizers of their ideas, men like the Montesquieu of the *Persian Letters* (1721), or the Voltaire of the *Letters on England*. If anyone involved in the case deserved heroic treatment, it was the wise d'Aguesseau, a member of the robe nobility and now lord chancellor of France, whom Gayot praised generously for his meticulous resolution of the case. Gayot, by claiming that his compendium was a handbook of jurisprudence, also sought to emulate these figures. The moment of the heroic military noble, stoically serving his king and lord on the battle-field, had passed.

The figure of the young, chaste, selfless second wife, however, had more cultural resonance in the early 1730s, particularly when set against Marguerite's implied infidelity. Louis, of course, had created the unfortunate situation by contracting a second marriage while his first wife still lived. He had been forced into doing so, according to Gayot's narrative, by the shrewish unfaithfulness of Marguerite, who had driven him from his proper role as seigneur of Narbonne to wander the French countryside. In Gayot's version, not only had Marie provided him with a happy, successful domestic life in spite of his duplicity; after he had revealed his treachery, she stepped forward twice to save the alleged adulteress and the unhappy bigamist. Marie's selfless actions provided the virtuous heroine the story had lacked in the late 1690s. The troubling affair now had a resolution that renewed its interest for the increasingly large, no longer exclusively aristocratic public that had emerged by midcentury.

Gayot's Marie anticipates the great moral heroines of the eighteenth-century sentimental novel, Samuel Richardson's Clarissa or Jean-Jacques Rousseau's Julie. These feminine exemplars, wildly popular in an age when new rules for encounters between the sexes were sought, stood for virginity and moral purity prior to marriage, in the case of Clarissa, or the accommodation of natural attraction to marital conventions, in the case of Julie. In both instances they were women who stubbornly insisted on shaping their fate, even if their wishes placed them in potential conflict with powerful male figures. Gayot's Pillard, virtuous in the face of marital adversity, successful in later marriages, also fit the mold of a woman who overcame unfortunate circumstances, yet did not repudiate the institution of marriage. She triumphed over individual misfortune, but ultimately did not disrupt the patriarchal transmission of wealth and status upon which marriage strategy and state finance depended during the Old Regime. The narrative transformation of Marie-Elisabeth Pillard in his *Causes célèbres* allowed Gayot to refashion the uncertainties of the Pivardière affair into a politically and culturally resonant tale for the eighteenth century. In an ironic twist, Marie, the unwitting dupe of Louis' bigamous activity in the 1690s, became the affair's only virtuous figure in the eyes of posterity.

Gayot admits to another purpose in his telling of the Pivardière tale, one that is consistent with his desire to instruct his readers in the subtle science of Old Regime jurisprudence. In the preface to the volume in which the Pivardière case appears, Gayot mentions that there are still, in the 1730s, many people who believe that Marguerite and the prior murdered Louis. But Gayot argues that the verdict in the case is not only clear, but enlightened:

> Although there was no physical evidence of a murder, the innocents [Marguerite and the prior] were accused of a homicide; the absent man, thought to be dead, returned to put himself on display to an infinity of persons. But the investigat-

ing magistrate, who knew him, continued to pursue murder charges, pretending that the man was a phantom, or an illusion. Here is perhaps the strangest bias to ever take hold of the spirit of man. This is what we will see in the story we will recount in all its details, up to the verdict in the Parlement that allowed innocence to triumph.

With these words, Gayot shapes a second aspect of his cause célèbre. The Pivardière case is not only about the triumph of Marie's virtue in the face of Louis and Marguerite's vices; it is also about the victory of an enlightened judiciary over a superstitious provincial investigation. D'Aguesseau alluded to the deficiencies of Bonnet's procedure in his second pleading, and the trial that resulted in the guilt of Marguerite Mercier hinted at judicial wrongdoing. Nevertheless, the timely death of Bonnet allowed the errors of the Châtillon judges to be swept under the rug in 1701. Now, a generation later, with Morin most likely gone as well, the improprieties of the Châtillon investigation could be hauled out into the light of day, to be contrasted with the truths uncovered under the direction of d'Aguesseau in 1699. The light of that magistrate, now one of the most powerful ministers in France, overturned the superstitious frame of mind that led Bonnet and others to think that Louis was a ghost in January 1698.

The burden of Gayot's narrative is to highlight the triumph of innocence facilitated by the use of reason in criminal investigation. The author returns to this theme again at the end of the text:

> The prejudice of the people, and that of many others who do not think like the people, against Pivardière, is in truth exceedingly strange. Given these miraculous events, why is it that the minds of men, having bent in one direction, cannot bend the other way when presented with the most striking truth? . . . Nothing is more shameful to Reason than this illness of an incurable spirit. The hidden Truth demands that we render it homage once it appears ringed by [Truth's] rays.

Gayot's account of the Pivardière affair, therefore, also served in the battle against ignorance and superstition, one that was still evident, he claimed, as he wrote. His narrative, based on excerpts from legal papers and eyewitness accounts, would further dispel doubts about the propriety of the verdict reached by the Parlement. The moral example of Marie and the ringing confirmation of reason's victory over superstition and human inertia justified the retelling of the tale in 1734. In the pages of Gayot's *Causes célèbres* we find an affair crafted to speak to the sentimentality and the confidence in reason of the new age. D'Aguesseau's residual Christian apprehensions about human fallibility had been left behind.

Both Gayot's rewrite of the Pivardière affair and Dancourt's one-act play kept the case alive in the minds of the French during the eighteenth century. There were at least seven full or partial editions of Gayot's compendium within two decades of its appearance in the 1730s and 1740s, and the success of the work inspired revisions, continuations, and abridgements in the second half of the century. Dancourt's comic send-up of the case may have benefited from Gayot's work, for *The Husband Returned* held the stage of the Comédie-Française throughout the century, and then found renewed interest among audiences during the revolutionary decade of the 1790s. According to the most recent tabulation, Dancourt's one-act was the most popular of all his plays during the Revolution; 107 of the 545 performances of his works were stagings of *The Husband Returned*. The reason for the play's success a century after its premiere was almost certainly the scene in which the sinister Bailiff, bent on marrying the wealthy niece, suborned witnesses and manufactured evidence in an effort to convict the Marguerite character of assassinating her husband. Dancourt's provin-

LE MARI RETROUVÉ

LE BAILLI.

Je, les ferai arrêter sur votre déposition,
et je vais, tout de ce pas, faire chercher le
greffier pour la venir recevoir.

Scène XV.

"The Bailiff," from an undated nineteenth-century edition of *Le Mari retrouvé.*

cial magistrate, a figure who had lightly played upon the perceived excesses of Bonnet and Morin in 1698, appeared more ill-intentioned at a time when revolutionaries often exaggerated the evils of the Old Regime to legitimize the new one. A play in which

Bourbon judicial corruption was thwarted was bound to find favor with elements of the Parisian theatergoing public in the 1790s. In one nineteenth-century volume of selected plays by Dancourt, the publisher chose to illustrate the Bailiff rather than any other major character in the play, thereby suggesting that he had become the most important figure in the play for post-Revolutionary readers and spectators.

The last performance of Dancourt's play at the Comédie-Française took place in 1835, but Gayot's version of the cause célèbre had a longer shelf life, both within France and without. His account, with embellishments, was translated into German in 1822 by E.T.A. Hoffman, the author of the children's story that inspired Peter Tchaikovsky to create *The Nutcracker Ballet*. A century later, the future Nobel Laureate Hermann Hesse published another version in a high-end edition of criminal tales called *Mordprozessen* (*Murder Trials*). In France, the trajectory from criminal trial to romantic fiction that Gayot had initiated reached completion in 1886 when an obscure author named Philibert Audebrand published a novel titled *La Pivardière le bigame* (*Pivardière the Bigamist*). In its pages, Narbonne was transformed into a huge estate run by an attractive, childless Marguerite, and the king pardoned Louis as he stood on the scaffold accused of bigamy. After World War II, two more French authors tried their hand at refashioning the story: In 1967, Robert Gaillard turned the tale into a series of lurid adventures in which a sex-crazed Louis bedded every woman he met, including the two maidservants, and in 1984 Eric Deschodt created a brooding psychological exploration of Louis' unusual history. In between, in 1972, French viewers were treated to a one-hour made-for-TV costume drama called *L'Etrange Trépas de Monsieur de la Pivardière* (*The Strange Demise of Monsieur de la Pivardière*), which was aired in a series that also featured a dramatization of the life of Casanova. This version was subsequently published the same year in a book called *Les*

Evasions célèbres (*Famous Evasions*); both the TV and the print version reduced the complexities of the past to a simple fairy tale, as a critic in the Communist newspaper *L'Humanité* noted at the time.

The story also continues to circulate in the northwest corner of the Berry, where it has intrigued amateur historians and become the stuff of local myth. A Capucin monk and archivist, Jean Mauzaize, published perhaps the most accurate twentieth-century account of the affair in 1993; he carefully examined the surviving print sources, and made a trip to Auxerre to consult the town's marriage registers. His contemporary, a Berrichon parish priest named Michel Borderioux (d. 1991), hoarded documents related to the affair, including the missing marriage contract between Louis and Marguerite prepared by a Valençay notary in 1687. When I asked the priest's heirs if I might consult his treasure trove of Pivardière documents, I was refused access. Would Louis, Marguerite, and the prior take any comfort in learning that the details of their misfortunes were jealously protected and interpreted by the prior's clerical successors three centuries later?

Outside church circles, an account in a Berrichon periodical in the 1950s, labeled "Legend Admits the Murder, but History Refuses to Speak of It," asserted that the lusty Marguerite and her lover, the prior, had, after all, succeeded in murdering the helpless nobleman and deluding d'Aguesseau and the high court into proclaiming their innocence. The article concluded by assuring readers that every year on the evening of August 15, the ghost of Marguerite appeared at Narbonne, wringing her bloodstained hands in a futile effort to wash away the traces of her crime. Far from the Paris media, storytellers and their audiences continued to make "public noise," similar to that which first prompted Morin to have Bonnet investigate the case. These modern-day gossips resurrected the unfortunate protagonists of the great affair, placing them in the service of nostalgia-laden efforts to preserve local identities against the onslaught of a nationalizing mass media.

Readers in both the Francophone and Anglophone worlds may wonder why a North American at the outset of the twenty-first century would devote so much effort to a local legend that is now more than three centuries old. In part, of course, I undertook the task for the satisfaction of correcting the historical record through extensive archival research. The results might seem meager to some; an extended exploration of the mystery of Louis de la Pivardière's alleged murder will not obviously alter our understanding of the military and diplomatic history of the second half of the Sun King's reign. Others might complain that even after intensive archival labors, too many key documents are missing to write the definitive version of the affair. Some skeptics might even ridicule the notion that the past is knowable in the detail I have attempted here. But there is something to be gained, I would argue, by stripping away the layers of myth that over time became fact in the tale of the would-be commoner. We may never know exactly why Louis married a second time, or why the maidservants lied about his supposed murder, or how so many contemporaries could believe that the prisoner in Fort l'Evêque was another in a legendary line of impostors. But there is a great deal to be learned about the past — and, in comparison, about the present — when we rid the story of its mythical qualities and observe judges, lawyers, journalists, and curiosity-seekers struggling with uncertain, contradictory accounts of a single event. It is a cautionary tale that reminds us to acknowledge the limits we encounter when exploring the past. In this sense, it is an even more powerful critique of human fallibility than d'Aguesseau's jurisprudence of doubt. And it should inspire us to look beyond convenient half-truths wherever we may find them.

NOTES

SELECTED BIBLIOGRAPHY

INDEX

✐Notes

ABBREVIATIONS USED IN NOTES

ADC: Archives départementales du Cher (Bourges)
ADCO: Archives départementales de la Côte d'Or (Dijon)
ADI: Archives départementales de l'Indre (Châteauroux)
ADLC: Archives départementales du Loir-et-Cher (Blois)
ADY: Archives départementales de l'Yonne (Auxerre)
AN: Archives nationales de France (Paris)
BA: Bibliothèque de l'Arsenal (Paris)
BnF: Bibliothèque nationale de France (Paris)
Char. Fac.: BnF 4 Fm 3516, *Factum pour Mre Silvain François Charotz, Prestre, Prieur de l'Abbaye de Miseré, prisonnier, appellant & demandeur en prise à partie.* . . .
Char. Int.: AN X²B 1283, Interrogatoire de Sylvain François Charost, 6–13 avril 1699.
Chauv. Fac.: BnF 4 Fm 17548 (1), *Factum servant de requeste, contenant demande en Réparation d'honneur de la Dame de la Pivardiere.*
Chauv. Int.: AN X²B 1283, Interrogatoire de Marguerite Chauvelin, 20–27 mars 1699.
D'Aguesseau: Henri-François d'Aguesseau, *Œuvres de M. le Chancelier d'Aguesseau* (Paris: Chez les libraires associés, 1764), Vol. 4, pp. 399–541. [Full text of d'Aguesseau's two summary pleadings before the Parlement in the Pivardière case.]
Info.: AN X²B 1283, Information à l'existence de Louis de la Pivardière, 17–30 mars 1699. [Depositions of twenty-five witnesses who claimed to know Louis before August 1697.]
Morin Fac.: BnF 4 Fm 17548 (8), *Mémoire, pour Maître Jean Bonnet sieur de Bigorne, Lieutenant Particulier au Siege Presidial de Châtillon sur Indre, & Maître François*

Morin, Substitut de Monsieur le Procureur General, Intimez pris à partie, Deffen-deurs & Demandeurs. . . .

Piv. Fac.: BnF 4 Fm 17548 (5), *Factum pour Louis de la Pivardiere Ecuyer Sieur du Bouchet, Demandeur, tant en son nom que comme prenant le fait & cause de Margue-rite Françoise Chauvelin sa femme. . . .*

Piv. Int.: AN X²B 1283, Interrogatoire de Louis de la Pivardière, 2–6 mars 1699. [N.B.: Although the final folio of the transcript is numbered 69, two consecu-tive pages are numbered "7," so that the interrogation transcript is actually sev-enty pages long. In the notes, I have added one to each folio number after the first "page 7" to take account of this scribal error.]

Prologue: *The Mystery of Louis de la Pivardière*

xv Late in August 1698: For details on Dubouchet's trip from Tournus to Paris, and his reception in the capital, see Piv. int., 56, 60–61; and Chauv., int. 34.

xvii "greatly surprised those": BnF G 4286, *Gazette d'Hollande*, Sept. 11, 1698. All translations from the French are mine.

The second turning point: Two recent studies of identity in Europe before 1700 are John Jeffries Martin, *Myths of Renaissance Individualism* (Palgrave MacMillan: Basingstoke, 2004); and Valentin Groebner, *Who Are You? Iden-tification, Deception, and Surveillance in Early Modern Europe*, trans. Mark Kyburz and John Peck (New York: Zone Books, 2007).

xix Since then, dozens of scholars: See the selected bibliography for a list of these works. All previous versions of the Pivardière affair ultimately derive from one of three print sources: the four legal briefs published in the summer of 1698 during the first round of hearings before the Parlement of Paris, the two sum-mary pleadings by Henri-François d'Aguesseau, drafted and delivered in the first half of 1699 but only published posthumously in 1764, or the account of the case found in François Gayot de Pitaval's 1734 *Causes célèbres et intéressantes* and its many eighteenth-century reprints. In the preface to his 1926 book, Maurice Soulié claims to have worked with the archival documents, but he provides no citations or bibliography and fabricates many details.

xx In the following century: On his contemporaries' response to Molière, see Larry F. Norman, *The Public Mirror: Molière and the Social Commerce of Depic-tion* (Chicago: University of Chicago Press, 1999); and Joan DeJean, *The Re-invention of Obscenity: Sex, Lies, and Tabloids in Early Modern France* (Chicago: University of Chicago Press, 2002). For subsequent response, see Jean-Jacques Rousseau, *Politics and the Arts; Letter to M. d'Alembert on the Theatre*, trans. Allan Bloom (Ithaca, NY: Cornell University Press, 1960); Robert Darnton, "The Facts of Literary Life in Eighteenth-Century France," in *The French Revolution and the Creation of Modern Political Culture*, vol. 1, *The Political Culture of the Old Regime*, ed. Keith Michael Baker (Oxford: Pergamon Press, 1987), pp. 261–91; Susan Maslan, "The Comic Revolution: Molière, Rous-seau, Fabre d'Eglantine, and Revolutionary Antitheatricalism," in *Revolution-ary Acts: Theater, Democracy, and the French Revolution* (Baltimore: Johns Hop-kins University Press, 2005), pp. 74–124; and Sheryl Kroen, "Tartufferie," in *Politics and Theater: The Crisis of Legitimacy in Revolutionary France, 1815–1830* (Berkeley and Los Angeles: University of California Press, 2000), pp. 229–84.

xxi "Jourdain: What? When I say": Molière, *Le Bourgeois Gentilhomme*, act II, scene iv, ll. 158–64; on issues of class and deception in another Molière play, *George Dandin*, see Roger Chartier, "From Court Festivity to City Spectators," in *Forms and Meanings: Texts, Performances, and Audiences from Codex to Computer*, trans. Lydia G. Cochrane (Philadelphia: University of Pennsylvania Press, 1995), pp. 43–82. But see also Nicholas Paige, "*George Dandin*, ou les ambiguïtés du social," *Revue de l'histoire littéraire de la France* (Sept.–Oct. 1995): 690–708.

xxii It was one thing: *Le Bourgeois Gentilhomme* was performed on the stage of the Comédie-Française on Aug. 30 and Sept. 7, and again on Dec. 18 and 21. See Henry C. Lancaster, *The Comédie-Française, 1680–1701: Plays, Actors, Spectators, Finances* (Baltimore: Johns Hopkins University Press, 1941), 176, 179. The reigning, increasingly dated formulation: Paul Hazard, *La Crise de la conscience européenne* (Paris, 1935); English translation: *The European Mind, 1680–1715*, trans. J. Lewis May (New York, 1963). Revising Hazard is a task that is underway. See Margaret Jacob, "The Crisis of the European Mind: Hazard Revisited," in *Politics and Culture in Early Modern Europe: Essays in Honor of H. G. Koenigsberger*, eds. Phyllis Mack and Margaret Jacob (Cambridge: Cambridge University Press, 1987), pp. 251–71; Jean de Viguerie, "Quelques réflexions critiques à propos de l'ouvrage de Paul Hazard: La Crise de la conscience européenne," in *Etudes d'histoire européenne. Mélanges offerts à René et Suzanne Pillorget* (Angers: Presse universitaire d'Angers, 1990); and Jonathan Israel, *Radical Enlightenment: Philosophy and the Making of Modernity, 1650–1750* (Oxford: Oxford University Press, 2001). For the theater of the period, see Guy Spielmann, *Le Jeu de l'ordre et du chaos: Comédie et pouvoirs à la fin de règne, 1673–1715* (Paris: Honoré Champion, 2002).

1. Becoming a Gentleman

3 Estimates based on tax rolls: Jacques Dupaquier, *La Population rurale du Bassin Parisien à l'époque de Louis XIV* (Paris: Editions de l'Ecole des hautes études en science sociales, 1979), p. 191; for Jeu-Malloches, see Christian Poitou, *Paroisses et Communes de France. Dictionnaire d'histoire administrative et démographique. Indre.* (Paris: Editions du CNRS, 1997), p. 358.
"If the people": The quotes from Dey de Séraucourt and Lambert d'Herbigny, the earlier intendant, are from Claude Michaud, *L'Intendance de Berry* (Paris: Editions du CTHS, 2001), p. 78; on Dey de Séraucourt's intendance, see Jean Néraud, *Les Intendants du Berry* (Paris: Editions de la vie universitaire, 1922), pp. 72–137. An anonymous manuscript in the AN, dating most likely from the 1760s or 1770s, describes the deterioration of the province by the second half of the eighteenth century, and offers suggestions for reinvigorating the region: "Mémoire sur la Province du Berry," *Revue archéologique, historique et scientifique du Berry* (1897), pp. 332–76.

4 A 1691 report: ADC 2G 13, *Visites des paroisses de Châteauroux, 1691.*
5 "Siberia of France": Guy Devailly, et al., *Histoire du Berry* (Toulouse: Editions du Privat, 1987), p. 223.
The situation of Louis' father: J. Pierre, "Maison de la Pivardière," *Revue du Berry et du Centre* 43 (1914): 24–28; ADI 3^{E}162/3, *Registres paroissiaux de Poulaines,* 1657–92; Piv. int., p. 6; E. Duroisel, "La Seigneurie de Poulaines," *Revue du Berry* (1904), pp. 150–58 on the activities of the Pivardière family in the parish of Poulaines.
6 The priest noted: ADI 3^{E}162/3, f. 40; Piv. int., p. 4; Info., pp. 1–2; George D. Sussman, *Selling Mother's Milk: The Wet-Nursing Business in France, 1715–1914* (Urbana: University of Illinois Press, 1982).
7 After Louis' mother died: Piv. int., pp. 7–10.
In these settings: On elementary schooling in seventeenth-century France, see Jean de Viguerie, *L'Institution des enfants: L'Education en France, XVIe–XVIIIe siècles* (Paris: Callman-Lévy, 1978), pp. 124–32; and Bernard Grosperrin, *Les Petites écoles sous l'Ancien Régime* (Rennes: Ouest-France, 1986). On the *collèges,* see Roger Chartier, Dominique Julia, and Marie-Madeleine Compère, *L'education en France du XVIe au XVIIIe siècles* (Paris: SEDS, 1976), pp. 147–206; François Lebrun, Marc Venard, and Jean Quéniart, *Histoire générale de l'enseignement et de l'éducation en France. Tome II: de Gutenberg aux lumières* (Paris: Nouvelle librairie de France, 1981), pp. 513–57; and Lawrence Brockliss, *French Higher Education in the Seventeenth and Eighteenth Centuries: A Cultural History* (Oxford: Clarendon Press, 1987). On the academies, see Mark Motley, *Becoming a French Aristocrat: The Education of the Court Nobility, 1580–1715* (Princeton, NJ: Princeton University Press, 1990), pp. 123–68.
9 Later, after their father's death: During his interrogation, Louis gives both 1680 and 1682 as the year of his father's death, but ADI 3^{E}162/4, f. 69, the Poulaines parish register, indicates that Antoine de la Pivardière was buried in the churchyard there on Aug. 21, 1679. On the agreement between the half siblings and the arrangements made to cloister the sisters, see Piv. int., pp. 18–19. I have been unable to find the legal instrument described by Louis in his interrogation. The Valençay convent played an important role in the social and economic life of the town and the surrounding area, so the sisters were not entirely cut off from the life of the region. But Antoine de la Pivardière's small estate, and the rights of his sons by his first marriage, made it difficult, and most likely undesirable from their brothers' perspectives, to find suitable matches for his daughters. On the Ursuline convent of Valençay, see R. P. Raoul (aka Jean Mauzaize), "Valençay pendant le Grand Siècle," in *Pages d'histoire sur Valençay et sa région* (Issoudun: Laboureur, 1968), pp. 99–101.
Upon his father's death: On living with his uncle and the Battle of Chiny, see Piv. int., pp. 7–9.
The following year: On the cadet companies, see John A. Lynn, *Giant of the Grand Siècle: The French Army, 1610–1715* (Cambridge: Cambridge University Press, 1997), pp. 272–75; Guy Rowlands, *The Dynastic State and the Army Under Louis XIV: Royal Service and Private Interest, 1661–1701* (Cambridge: Cambridge University Press, 2002), pp. 181–86.
10 In 1685, he was party to a lawsuit: Piv. int., pp. 14, 68.
11 Marguerite Chauvelin's family was from: On the House of Chauvelin, see

François-Alexandre Aubert de la Chenaye-Desbois et Jacques Badier, *Dictionnaire de la noblesse . . .*, 3rd ed. (Paris: Schlesinger, 1870), vol. 5, pp. 528–37; Gustave Chaix d'Est-Ange, *Dictionnaire des familles françaises anciennes ou notables à la fin du XIXe siècle* (Evreux: Charles Hérissey, 1911), vol. 10, pp. 188–92; François Bluche, *L'Origine des magistrats du Parlement de Paris au XVIIIe siècle (1715–1771). Dictionnaire généalogique* (Paris: Faculté des lettres de l'Université de Paris, 1956), pp. 128–29.

11 In the second half: Contemporary descriptions of the buildings and lands of Narbonne include Piv. int., pp. 10–13; Chauv. int., pp. 3–4; and ADI 2^{B}43, *procès-verbal du 5–10 novembre 1699*, a report on the degraded condition of the estate immediately after the Parisian trial of 1699. Piv. fac., p. 3, provides the 800–900 livre revenue figure. No account books exist for Narbonne, and the few tax rolls from the late seventeenth and early eighteenth centuries still in existence are too sketchy to re-create the revenues generated by the estate. E. Delaume, *Notice monographique sur Jeu-Malloches (Indre)* (Châteauroux: Mellotée, 1914), pp. 11–12, reproduces a detailed description of Narbonne in 1790 undertaken by the Revolutionary government for tax purposes that estimates the annual revenue of its lands, forests, and ponds at 767 livres, 10 sols. Michaud, *L'Intendance du Berry*, pp. 248–72, for noble incomes in the Berry; the Marquis de Valençay at 260. James Wood, *The Nobility of the Election of Bayeux, 1463–1666: Continuity Through Change* (Princeton, 1980), pp. 323–24, presents evidence for a district in Normandy showing that the mean income for the 553 noble families of this district was 1,880 livres per annum, although 204 of these families enjoyed less than 500 livres a year.

14 In Paris, she might have been tutored: Martine Sonnet, *L'Education des filles au temps des Lumières* (Paris: Editions du Cerf, 1987); Elizabeth Rapley, *A Social History of the Cloister: Daily Life in the Teaching Monasteries of the Old Regime* (Montreal: McGill-Queen's University Press, 2001), pp. 219–56; and the works listed for p. 8.
In 1672, however: Chenaye-Desbois, *Dictionnaire de la noblesse*, vol. 5, pp. 532–33; Delaume, *Notice bibliographique*, pp. 20, 53–57, on Marguerite's marriage and the family's possession of Narbonne.

15 There is reason to believe: ADI 5^{B}582, "Justice de Narbonne" for the 1679 judgment and the 1685 cases. More generally on marital separations, although in an urban context, see Julie Hardwick, "Seeking Separations: Gender, Marriages, and Household Economies in Early Modern France," *French Historical Studies* 21 (winter 1998): 157–80.
The next mention: *Commune de Jeu-Malloches, registre 1663–1681*, unpaginated entries for 1685. (In spite of the label on the register, it contains parish data through the first decade of the eighteenth century.)

16 In 1687, however: Info., pp. 17–19; Piv. int., p. 44. There is no other contemporary trace of this story, but Archambault did tell the interrogator in 1699 that when he had seen the Fort l'Evêque prisoner he had mentioned this incident, which the prisoner had acknowledged. Because both Archambault and the prisoner knew the interrogators might check with the other to verify the story, and because each was unaware of the contents of the other's testimony, it would seem unlikely that the story is fabricated.

17 "one of the most sterile": Michaud, *L'Intendance du Berry*, p. 223.

17 A list of assets: ADI 5ᴮ648, Jan. 10, 1688. I have been unable to find the marriage contract, drafted the day of the marriage by a Valençay notary named
Étienne Argy. Argy's files for 1687, maintained in the office of a current
Valençay notary named Francis Challeau, no longer contain a copy of the document. For the amount of cash Louis brought to the marriage, see Piv. int.,
p. 42; and Chauv. int., p. 2–3.
18 Miséray, like Narbonne: Michaud, *L'Intendance du Berry*, p. 96.
19 While his eldest brother: Chauv. int., passim, and Char. int., passim, for information on the Prior Charost's siblings.
The three of them: Piv. int., pp. 19–20, 66; Chauv. int., pp. 6–7; Char. int.,
pp. 3–4.
20 Marguerite managed the daily affairs: Piv. int., pp. 12–13; Chauv. int., p. 4;
Info., p. 8; AN X²B 1283, Convention des pièces de comparaison, Apr. 28,
1699 (for a list of contracts signed by Louis in 1690); D'Aguesseau, p. 403. In a
series of important articles over the past two decades, Sarah Hanley has emphasized that Old Regime marriage was often understood by spouses, jurists,
and the state as a legal relationship that the French state worked hard to support and control, more than an affective bond between two individuals; see
in particular Hanley, "Engendering the State: Family Formation and State
Building in Early Modern France," *French Historical Studies* 16 (spring 1989):
4–27; Ibid., "Social Sites of Political Practice in France: Lawsuits, Civil
Rights, and the Separation of Powers in Domestic and State Government,
1500–1800," *American Historical Review* 102 (1997): 27–52; and Ibid., "The
Family, the State, and the Law in Seventeenth- and Eighteenth-Century
France: The Political Ideology of Male Right versus an Early Theory of Natural Rights," *Journal of Modern History* 78 (June 2006): 289–332.
22 The war he inadvertently initiated: The best English-language account of the
war from the French perspective is John A. Lynn, *The Wars of Louis XIV, 1667–
1714* (London: Longman, 1999), pp. 191–265, which magisterially puts the
conflict in the context of Louis XIV's half century of bellicosity; the phrase
"the Great Miscalculation" is his.
this figure had shot up: French military personnel figures from the Middle
Ages to the seventeenth century in Lynn, *The Wars*, pp. 50–1; and Guy
Rowlands, *The Dynastic State*, pp. 171–72; recruitment practices in Lynn, *Giant*, pp. 347–96; and Rowlands, *Dynastic State*, pp. 204–8, 257–58.
The terms of service: Ibid., *Giant*, pp. 369–71, and Marcel Marion,
Dictionnaire des institutions de la France aux XVIIe et XVIIIe siècles (Paris: Picard,
1923), p. 34.
24 But even the best-paid lieutenants: The discussion of French military structure and officer ranks in this paragraph is based on Lynn, *Giant*, pp. 224–28;
and Rowlands, *Dynastic State*, pp. 161–71, 227–30.
Louis sought an initial appointment: Piv. int., p. 44, asserts that he began his
cornet post in 1690; documents from the period collected by court investigators, however, make mention of rents and contracts he signed at Narbonne
throughout the summer and fall of 1690, which would suggest he may not
have returned to the army until the following year.

25 Although his initial foothold: On his efforts to secure a commissioned post, see Piv. int., p. 44; Info., p. 24. On the Duc de la Feuillade, see Chenaye-Desbois, *Dictionnaire de la noblesse*, vol. I, pp. 974–77; and Sharon Kettering, *French Society 1589–1715* (Harlow: Pearson, 2001), pp. 136–37.
   Military encounters under the Sun King: The discussion of warfare in this period and issues of supply is based on Lynn, *The Wars*, pp. 47–104 ("forbearance" quote on p. 66); and Lynn, *Giant*, pp. 107–83.
26 by his own account: Piv. int., p. 44.
27 One historian has calculated: Rowlands, *Dynastic State*, p. 252.
   These fiscal difficulties: Piv. int., p. 66; Char. int., p. 4; Info., pp. 6, 21–22, 24.
28 This increased frequency of death: World War I, commonly perceived as a period of similarly catastrophic demographic loss for France, saw the national population decline by three million people from 1914 to 1918. Although this drop was twice as large as that experienced in 1693–1694 in absolute terms, it represented a population decline of 7.2 percent, a figure comparable to that experienced in the earlier period. Furthermore, it occurred in more than double the period of time, making the demographic impact of famine and disease far more precipitous in 1693–1694 than that of combat mortality and disease during the Great War, and certainly greater than it was during other periods of national crisis in modern French history such as the Revolutionary era, 1870–1871, or 1939–1945. Population statistics for 1693–1694 and 1914–1918 are from Marcel Larchiver, *Les Années de misère. La Famine au temps du Grand Roi, 1680–1720* (Paris: Fayard, 1991), pp. 205–6. They can be tabulated as follows:

Crisis Years	Starting Pop.	Ending Pop.	Numerical Change	Percent Change
1693–1694	22,247,000	20,736,000	1,511,000	6.8
1914–1918	41,700,000	38,700,000	3,000,000	7.2

2. The Murder Narrative

30 Marguerite received a troubling letter: Chauv. int., p. 8. For more on the solicitor, François Vigan, see Info., pp. 15–16.
31 He arrived at the compound: For accounts of Louis' return to Narbonne that day, see Piv. int., pp. 20–23; Chauv. int., pp. 11–13; Char. int., pp. 11–12; and d'Aguesseau, pp. 404–5. The evening of Aug. 15, 1697, at Narbonne is the key moment in the story of Louis de la Pivardière, but every previous account of that night is at best thirdhand. Furthermore, the investigations by local magistrates in the fall of 1697, including depositions of people present at Narbonne that night, have been lost. In the narrative that follows, I rely solely on the eyewitness accounts provided by the central participants in the affair during their testimony in Paris in the spring of 1699, two years after the fact. I supplement this testimony with the narrative of the case constructed by Henri-François d'Aguesseau, the impartial attorney general who had access to the now-missing judicial investigations when preparing his summary of the case for the Parisian court in Feb. 1699. There are obvious problems with these sources. The principals related their well-rehearsed versions of events two years later under

the pressure of a life-and-death court hearing, and their memories may have been conveniently faulty on some points. We cannot check d'Aguesseau's version against the depositions given days and weeks after the events they recount took place. I have tried to take these qualifications into account when constructing my version of the events that evening.

31 Some of the guests: d'Aguesseau, p. 404, for the officious peasant; Chauv. int., p. 11, for Marguerite's reaction to her husband's return. In their 1699 interrogations, Marguerite and the prior both explicitly denied that Louis had said that evening that his wife was not his companion. Among the sources still existent, the phrase first appears in the published legal briefs in the summer of 1698.

32 According to her: Piv. int., p. 21; Chauv. int., p. 13; and AN X²B 1283, Interrogatoire de Catherine Lemoyne, Apr. 18, 1699, p. 2, for the details in this paragraph. It is likely that Louis and Marguerite neglected to mention Louis' accusation of infidelity against his wife because the charge that she had cuckolded him was part of the trial proceedings two years later. The maidservant Lemoyne had no reason to conceal this aspect of their confrontation. A second maidservant, Marguerite Mercier, claimed that she was eating in another room with Lemoyne and heard Louis and Marguerite laughing and chatting with each other, but this account of joviality seems unlikely in light of the eyewitness testimony recounted here and the general circumstances of the encounter. (AN X²B 1283, Interrogatoire de Marguerite Mercier, Apr. 16–17, 1699, p. 3.)

33 The residents of Narbonne: Piv. int., pp. 21–23; Chauv. int., pp. 14–16; AN X²B 1283, Interrogatoire de Catherine Lemoyne, Apr. 18, 1699, pp. 2–3; AN X²B 1283, Interrogatoire de Marguerite Mercier, Apr. 16–17, 1699, pp. 1–3, for the information in this paragraph.

34 No one knew the whereabouts: Piv. int., pp. 22–23; Chauv. int., pp. 16; d'Aguesseau, pp. 405, 459 for the information in this paragraph.
Less than three weeks: AN X²B 1283, Interrogatoire de Nicholas Mercier, Apr. 18, 1699, pp. 1–2, for his visit to Narbonne the day after the feast; AN X²B 1283, Interrogatoire de Me. François Morin, Mar. 19, 1700, p. 2, for N. Mercier's claim to have seen bloodstains days after the feast, and for the rumor of the severed head; ADI 5B 648, Sept. 10, 1697, for the naked, wounded body in the ditch.

35 Breton worked in the *siège présidial*: The *présidial* in Châtillon was one of many judicial seats in the kingdom that the Crown established as early as 1551 in an effort to relieve the caseload of the Parlements, the sovereign courts within the kingdom. But the Crown also created the *présidiaux* to raise funds for the royal treasury through the sale of their venal offices, an investment that purchasers strove to recoup through the collection of *épices*, or fees they charged to plaintiffs. These magistrates also viewed a venal office in a *présidial* as a steppingstone to higher judicial or administrative posts that would eventually grant their families perpetual ennoblement. A *présidial* usually boasted one or two *lieutenants généraux* who stood above the other local judges and officers; they were sometimes referred to as *présidents*. A judicial seat might also have a *lieutenant civil*, a *lieutenant criminel*, or a *lieutenant particulier*. In French, the title of *lieutenant* had assumed the meaning of judge toward the end of the fif-

teenth century, when the king decreed that *baillis* and *sénéchaux*, the judicial representatives of the king, the nobility, and the Church throughout the Middle Ages, had to be schooled in legal practice or had to be replaced by legally educated *lieutenants*, literally those who "held their place." By the late seventeenth century, *baillis* and *sénéchaux* were mostly figures of derision who wielded little judicial authority; it was the various *lieutenants* who handled most civil and criminal investigations at the level of towns and districts. For background on the history and social status of these legal institutions, see the articles on *bailliage, lieutenant,* and *présidiaux* in Marcel Marion, *Dictionnaire des institutions de la France aux XVIIe et XVIIIe siècles* (Paris: Picard, 1923); and Roland E. Mousnier, *The Institutions of France Under the Absolute Monarchy, 1598–1789. Vol. II: The Organs of State,* trans. Arthur Goldhammer (Chicago: University of Chicago Press, 1984), pp. 354–57.

36 The crowd was crying: AN X²B 1283, Interrogatoire de Me. François Morin, Mar. 19, 1700, p. 1.

The de facto jurisdiction: The tactic appears not to have worked immediately, however. According to scattered references in interrogations and pleadings compiled in 1698 and 1699, the Luçay seigneurial judge did not undertake an investigation until after the Châtillon magistrates began their own investigation in early Sept. No archival traces of the Luçay investigation remain. This judge ceased his inquiry into the matter in Jan. 1698.

He lost his bid: No papers exist in the ADI for the Châtillon *présidial* prior to 1700. The information presented here comes from Char. fac., p. 4; and Morin fac., pp. 21–22. The latter source claims that when Morin fils began the investigation of the Pivardière murder with Bonnet he had no knowledge of his father's conflict with Charost senior thirty-six years earlier.

37 Furthermore, Morin was a friend: AN X²B 1283, Interrogatoire de Louis Breton, Mar. 23, 1700, pp. 1–2; Morin fac., p. 11.

Morin and Bonnet thus found themselves: On the reasons for Bonnet's hostility to Charost, in addition to the sources in the previous note, see Chauv. fac., p. 4. One should also note that in 1697, the prior's brother, the *lieutenant général* of the Châtillon *présidial*, had filed a suit against the head of the councilors at the *présidial*, the Sieur de Lorme, a close friend of Bonnet and Morin. See ADCL, unnumbered dossiers labeled *Bailliage de Romorantin-Millançay, 1698–99,* Jan. 1698.

39 The criminal ordinance of August 1670: In addition to the works of Marion and Mousnier cited above, Richard Mowery Andrews, *Law, Magistracy, and Crime in Old Regime Paris, 1735–1789. Vol. 1: The System of Criminal Justice* (Cambridge: Cambridge University Press, 1994), esp. pp. 417–514, is an extensive description and evaluation of Old Regime criminal procedure.

"the magistrates were constituted": Quoted in Marc Boulanger, "Justice et absolutisme: la grande ordonnance criminelle d'Août 1670," *Revue d'histoire moderne et contemporaine* 47–1 (Jan.–Mar. 2000): 21.

"Few judges truly make an effort": Quoted in Benoît Garnot, "Le Bon Magistrat et les mauvais juges à la fin du XVIIe siècle," in *Crime et justice aux XVIIe et XVIIIe siècles* (Paris: Imago, 2000): 117.

40 But this decision: François-Alexandre-Pierre de Garsault, *Faits des Causes Célèbres et intéressantes, augmentées de quelques causes* (Amsterdam: Chastelain,

1757), pp. 151–59, summarizes the "Mantes magistrates" case. Two mid-seventeenth-century Burgundian cases of judicial misconduct that involved murder have recently been studied at length: Benoît Garnot, *Intime conviction et erreur judiciaire. Un magistrat assassiné au XVIIe siècle?* (Dijon: Éditions universitaires de Dijon, 2004); and James R. Farr, *A Tale of Two Murders: Passion and Power in Seventeenth-Century France* (Durham, NC: Duke University Press, 2005).

40 Bonnet also authorized the publication: On controversies surrounding the usage of the *monitoire*, see Marion, *Dictionnaire*, p. 383; and Andrews, *Law, Magistracy, and Crime*, pp. 426–27.

42 They hauled the treasure: Lemoyne states she was left behind to watch the animals in her Apr. 18, 1699, interrogation (AN X²B 1283, Interrogatoire de Catherine Lemoyne, Apr. 18, 1699, p. 1). There is some question as to whether the agents of the Châtillon judges seized any goods at Narbonne, and if so which ones. Chauv. fac., pp. 2–3, and d'Aguesseau, p. 407, indicate that the house was stripped of goods, and that the property was sold and the proceeds pocketed by Bonnet. These abusive actions became the justification for Marguerite's appeal filed in Paris on Sept. 20, 1697, claiming that Bonnet was incompetent. But Morin fac., pp. 5–6, 18, asserts that Chauvelin left her most precious possessions with her neighbor Jacquette Doiselle and left the rest of her furniture and belongings with local peasants. These items had been "recovered" by the agents of the Châtillon judges and would be restored to Narbonne when it was once again inhabited.
At Marguerite's request: On Nicholas Mercier's long-standing relations with the seigneurie of Narbonne, and his daughter's employment there, see AN X²B 1283, Interrogatoire de Nicholas Mercier, Apr. 18, 1699, p. 1.

43 Bonnet appears not to have considered: The formal report prepared by Bonnet of the Sept. 28 inspections at Narbonne no longer exists, but firsthand accounts of the incident include Morin int., p. 2; AN X²B 1283, Interrogatoire de Jean Chenu, archer, Mar. 29, 1700, p. 2; AN X²B 1283, Interrogatoire de Jean Gaulin, Apr. 6, 1700, p. 1; and AN X²B 1283, Interrogatoire de Guillaume Crouet, Mar. 30, 1700, pp. 1–2, for the quote about the straw. A contemporary summary of the inspection, based on documents that are now missing, is d'Aguesseau, pp. 407–8. Morin later admitted that he had asked the huissiers who accompanied Bonnet on Sept. 28 if they had noticed the bloodstains when they had been at Narbonne on Sept. 14 to seize Catherine Lemoyne and the livestock and other goods of the estate, and that the huissiers had claimed they had seen nothing because they were intent on arresting witnesses and seizing property.

44 Despite this denial: For details in this paragraph, see AN X²B 1283, Interrogatoire de Marguerite Mercier, Apr. 16–17, 1699, pp. 4–5; AN X²B 1283, Interrogatoire de Guillaume Crouet, Mar. 30, 1700, p. 2; and AN X²B 1283, Interrogatoire de Jean Gaulin, Apr. 6, 1700, p. 1.

45 They were not sites of incarceration: On Old Regime jails, see Marion, *Dictionnaire des institutions*, pp. 456–58; and Andrews, *Law, Magistracy, and Crime*, pp. 374–76.

46 In addition to the jailer: AN X²B 1283, Interrogatoire de Jean Gaulin, Apr. 6, 1700, p. 2, for the prison layout; AN X²B 1283, Continuation de confronta-

tion des accuses, June 19, 1700, p. 4, for the confinement cell. Châtillon jail-house conditions are discussed more fully in chapter 8.
While transcripts of these interrogations: d'Aguesseau, pp. 409–15; Chauv. fac., pp. 3–4; Piv. int., pp. 12–19.
Many neighbors told Bonnet: Morin fac., p. 5.

48 The year before: Char. fac., pp. 7–8; but see Breton's denial at AN X²B 1283, Interrogatoire de Louis Breton, Mar. 23, 1700, p. 1.
The maidservant Lemoyne: AN X²B 1283, Interrogatoire de Catherine Lemoyne, Apr. 18, 1699, p. 4.

50 Miraculously, or so the interrogation transcript implied: d'Aguesseau, pp. 410–11; Char. fac., pp. 2–3; and Chauv. fac., pp. 4–5. Accounts of these in-terrogations by the main participants can be found at AN X²B 1283, Interrogatoire de Me. François Jacquemet, vicegerent, Mar. 18, 1700, pp. 1–2; AN X²B 1283, Interrogatoire de Marguerite Mercier, Apr. 16–17, 1699, p. 5; AN X²B 1283, Interrogatoire de Catherine Lemoyne, Apr. 18, 1699, p 5.
Thus, by the beginning: The following murder narrative derives primarily from Morin fac., pp. 6–9.

52 This group of armed horsemen: For details on Pivardière/Dubouchet's arrival in the Berry in Jan. 1698, and his escort throughout the province, see Piv. int, pp. 47–54; and Info., pp. 9–11.
Several Valençay merchants: For the descriptions of the encounter with the Romorantin magistrate and subsequent confrontations with hundreds of Berrichons, see d'Aguesseau, pp. 417–18; Piv. fac., pp. 8–9; Chauv. fac., 5–6; Piv. int., p. 50; ADCL, unnumbered dossiers labelled *Bailliage de Romorantin-Millançay, 1698–99.*

54 By the end of the day: Information in this paragraph and the next about the events of Jan. 18, 1698, in Jeu-Malloches comes from Piv. int., p. 49; AN X²B 1283, Interrogatoire de Nicholas Mercier, Apr. 18, 1699, p. 2; AN X²B 1283, Interrogatoire de Me. François Jacquemet, vicegerent, Mar. 18, 1700, pp. 6–7; ADCL, unnumbered dossiers labeled *Bailliage de Romorantin-Millançay, 1698–99;* Chauv. fac., p. 6; and Char. fac., pp. 8–9.
For his part, it is possible: AN X²B 1283, Interrogatoire de Me. François Jacquemet, vicegerent, Mar. 18, 1700, pp. 6–7.
The best surviving indication: Piv. int., p. 45, for Pournain at Miséray under the prior; AN X²B 1283, Interrogatoire de Me. François Jacquemet, vicegerent, Mar. 18, 1700, p. 7.

55 The next morning, January 19: For the encounter at the Châtillon prison, I have relied primarily on the accounts given by Louis and Morin in their testi-mony in Paris two to three years later: Piv. int., pp. 47–49; AN X²B 1283, Interrogatoire de Me. François Morin, Mar. 19, 1700, pp. 3–5. I have supple-mented these tellings with the account in d'Aguesseau, pp. 418–19; the latter was privy to the actual transcriptions of the event by the Romorantin scribes, which have subsequently disappeared. Info., pp. 8–12, contains an account of the confrontations by Jean Chenu, one of the archers involved in the case as early as the Sept. 1697 raids on Narbonne. While his account of the confron-tations themselves is suspect, for reasons detailed in d'Aguesseau, pp. 522–24, there is no reason to doubt his evocation of the setting, upon which I have also relied here. The maidservants also gave accounts of the events that day in

which they claimed they had recognized the man in LeComte's charge as their missing master, but their testimony is highly suspect, for reasons I will discuss in more depth in chapter 8, and no one else subsequently claimed they had recognized him that day.

57 The girls may have stuck: In subsequent testimony, both girls claimed that Bonnet and Morin had visited them in jail at six in the morning the day of their confrontation with the alleged Louis; the point of the visit, they alleged, had been to threaten them with torture and death if they recognized their master in the Romorantin judge's entourage. But no other witness confirmed this visit, and the fact that Bonnet and Morin had been in Jeu-Malloches until late the day before makes it less likely that they would have returned to Châtillon by six the next morning to intimidate the maidservants.

58 Others claimed: Morin fac., pp. 9, 24–26; AN X²B 1283, Continuation d'information, May 18, 1699, pp. 1–2, for testimony of the Châtillon monk Chauvin.

59 The initiative of Marguerite: d'Aguesseau, pp. 417–19; BnF 4 Fm 34389, *Arrest de la cour de Parlement, intervenue sur les contestations d'entre la Dame de la Pivardiere et les Officiers de Chastillon sur Indre, du 23 juillet 1698*, pp. 4–5.
To complete the humiliation: On Charost's capture and imprisonment, see Char. int., pp. 1–2; Char. fac., p. 12.

60 "I ask nothing else": The transcripts of the confrontations have not survived. The fragments quoted here, as well as other excerpts, are reproduced in Piv. fac., 16–18; I have converted the third-person testimony to first person.
Only fragments of the transcripts: d'Aguesseau, pp. 412–14, offers a summary of the transcripts by a contemporary judge who read them carefully; see especially his remarkable analysis of the sessions on p. 413.

61 Both servants were told: Char. fac., pp. 10–12; AN X²B 1283, Interrogatoire de Catherine Lemoyne, Apr. 18, 1699, pp. 5–6; AN X²B 1283, Interrogatoire de Marguerite Mercier, Jan. 20, 1700, pp. 6–7; AN X²B 1283, Interrogatoire de Catherine Lemoyne, Jan. 21, 1700, pp. 5–6; AN X²B 1283, Interrogatoire de Me. François Morin, Mar. 19, 1700, p. 6.
Even worse, the various parties: The various motions are catalogued in BnF 4 Fm 34389, *Arrest de la cour . . . du 23 juillet 1698*, pp. 7–13.

3. Preliminary Judgment

65 The potential for corruption: On caseloads, see Colin Kaiser, "The Deflation of the Volume of Litigation at Paris in the Eighteenth Century and the Waning of the Old Judicial Order," *European Studies Review* 10 (1980): 309–60. On the number of magistrates, see Roland E. Mousnier, *The Institutions of France Under the Absolute Monarchy, 1598–1789. Vol. II: The Organs of State and Society*, trans. Arthur Goldhammer (Chicago: University of Chicago Press, 1984), p. 308, who gives a figure of 267 magistrates in 1685. On the price of office, see Marcel Marion, *Dictionnaire des institutions de la France aux XVIIe et XVIIIe siècles* (Paris: Picard, 1923), pp. 431–32; and Mousnier, *The Institutions*, vol. II, pp. 341–43. The most senior magistrates, and the most important cases, found their way to the Grande Chambre, the main courtroom in which the

judges heard oral pleading. Five courts of inquest handled written appeals from lower courts throughout the Parlement's vast jurisdiction, while two courts of request reviewed demands from aristocrats and other elites to have their causes heard initially in the high court. Finally, the Tournelle handled all criminal matters (the Pivardière case was judged here), the Marée handled maritime questions for the court, and the Vacations responded to all legal matters from Sept. 9 to Oct. 27 every year, while the other chambers were closed for business.

66 A Venetian ambassador: On the history of the Palais de Justice and its commercial and social aspects by the late seventeenth century, see François Bluche, *Les Magistrats du Parlement de Paris au XVIIIe siècle* (Paris: Economica, 1986), pp. 205–24; and J. H. Shennan, *The Parlement of Paris* (Ithaca, NY: Cornell University Press, 1968), pp. 86–109.

67 Bookshop browsers in the Palais: On the complex relations of print, manuscript, and orality in the centuries after the introduction of the printing press in Europe, see David McKitterick, *Print, Manuscript, and the Search for Order, 1450–1830* (Cambridge: Cambridge University Press, 2003); Asa Briggs and Peter Burke, "The Print Revolution in Context," in *A Social History of the Media: From Gutenberg to the Internet* (Cambridge: Polity Press, 2005), pp. 13–60; and for France in particular, Robert Darnton, "Communication Networks," in *The Forbidden Best-Sellers of Pre-Revolutionary France* (New York: W. W. Norton and Company, 1996), pp. 181–97.

69 By then, a publication: Howard M. Solomon, *Public Welfare, Science, and Propaganda in Seventeenth-Century France: The Innovations of Théophraste Renaudot* (Princeton, NJ: Princeton University Press, 1972); Nicolas Blegny, *Le Livre commode des addresses de Paris*, ed. E. Fournier (Paris: Daffis, 1878), pp. v–lx.

70 "It is called the Tournelle": Claude-Joseph de Ferrière, *Dictionnaire de droit et de pratique* (Paris, 1769), vol. II, p. 289; cited in Richard Mowery Andrews, *Law, Magistracy, and Crime in Old Regime Paris, 1735–1789. Vol. 1: The System of Criminal Justice* (Cambridge: Cambridge University Press, 1994), p. 89.

71 A majority of at least two votes: Andrews, *Law, Magistracy, and Crime*, p. 475. The second hearing: AN X²B 1135, *Audiences de la Tournelle, 1696–1698. Chemise 1698*, lists the cases on the docket for each day the criminal court was in session, but gives minimal details of the proceedings.

By the beginning of July: These journals, whose French circulation the Crown tried to prevent, differed significantly in content, production, and means of distribution. Some of them were four- or eight-page pamphlets that appeared twice a week, while others, dozens of pages long, were published monthly. For an introduction see Hans Bots, "Les Provinces-unies: Centre de l'information européenne au XVIIe siècle," in *L'Informazione in Francia nel seicento*, ed. J-P Seguin (Bari: Adriatica, 1963), pp. 283–306; and Ibid., *"La Gazette d'Amsterdam* entre 1688 et 1699: Titres, éditeurs, privileges et interdictions," in *Les Gazettes européennes de langue française (XVIIe–XVIIIe siècles)*, eds. Henri Duranton, Claude Labrosse, and Pierre Rétat (St. Etienne: Publications de l'Université de St. Etienne, 1992), pp. 31–39. Information on individual titles can be found in Jean Sgard, ed. *Dictionnaire des journaux* (Paris: Universitas, 1991). Bots notes the irony that the most complete collection of these journals today is not in the Netherlands, but in Paris, at the Bibliothèque nationale de

France, because Louis XIV and his ministers collected them assiduously to study what the Huguenot press was writing.

71 "There is a trial": BnF G 4286, *Gazette d'Amsterdam*, Thursday, July 17, 1698. Article de Paris, July 11, 1698.

72 "curiosity attracts a large crowd": Ibid., July 28, 1698. Article de Paris, July 21, 1698. Other Dutch news gatherers also reported on the trial's beginnings; see BA 4 H9847, *Histoire journalière*, July 24, 1698; and BnF G4466, *Supplément à l'Histoire journalière*, July 24, 1698. The latter article speculates on the risk involved in Marguerite Chauvelin's decision to incarcerate herself before the trial began.

By the 1770s: Sarah Maza, *Private Lives and Public Affairs: The Causes Célèbres of Prerevolutionary France* (Berkeley and Los Angeles: University of California Press, 1993), provides analysis of the highly politicized content of these briefs in the decades before the Revolution. See Maza, *Private Lives and Public Affairs*, pp. 36–38, for a discussion of the circulation of the briefs in the 1770s and 1780s.

73 "all one hears": Mme. du Noyer, *Lettres Historiques et Galantes, de Deux Dames de condition, dont l'une est à Paris, & l'autre en province. Ouvrage Curieux. Nouvelle édition, revue, corrigée, augmentée et enrichie des figures.* (Amsterdam: Pierre Brunel, 1720), vol. I, p. 189.

The four briefs: Each brief lists the date on which its printer received permission to publish it; these dates range from June 30 to July 11, 1698. The *Histoire journalière* report on the case dated July 18, 1698, mentions the appearance of the *factum* written on behalf of Louis, while the *Gazette d'Amsterdam* article for July 21, 1698, states that the four works had appeared "a few days previously." The first verdict in the case was issued on July 23, 1698. It seems reasonable to assume that the briefs appeared in bookshops in mid-July a week or two prior to the court's initial verdict. In addition to the briefs, lawyers for Louis, Marguerite, and the prior also published brief, two- to-four page *Conclusions* in mid-July, in an effort to sway the magistrates and the reading public; see BnF 4 Fm 17548 (2 & 6) and BnF 4 Fm 3517.

"A priest-prior and a married woman": Morin fac., p. 1.

74 The exigencies of courtroom pleadings: One also finds tales of adulteresses and female murderers on the French tragic stage of the day, and in other causes célèbres; see, for example, the character of Roxane in Racine's *Bajazet*, or the cases in François Gayot de Pitaval, *Causes célèbres et intéressantes avec les jugemens qui les ont décidées* (The Hague: J. Neaulme, 1734–1743), vol. III, pp. 179–284; vol. V, pp. 336–52.

"there suddenly arose": Piv. fac., p. 8.

75 "the shadow of the Sieur de la Pivardière": Ibid., pp. 9–10.

"effort to embellish the novel": Morin fac., p. 32.

77 For the next several months: The following narrative of events from Louis' disappearance from the Berry in Aug. 1697 until his alleged reappearance in Jan. 1698 is based on accounts in the briefs published in the summer of 1698 on behalf of Louis, Marguerite, and the prior, as well as their interrogation transcripts from Mar. and Apr. 1699.

The high court: d'Aguesseau, p. 416; Chauv. fac., pp. 2–3; ADLC, Bailliage de Romorantin-Millançay, 1698–1699, group of unpaginated, uncatalogued documents from 1697–1699 recording correspondence between the Parlement of Paris and the lieutenant general of Romorantin regarding the Pivardière affair.

78 Later that day: There is no direct testimony from either Pillard or her mother that would allow us to learn the precise moment when they became aware of Dubouchet's deceptions, but Marguerite in her 1699 interrogation notes that Joseph Charost spoke with Pillard on Oct. 6, 1697, at which point he must have recounted the facts of Louis' Berrichon existence; Chauv. int., p. 9. In his interrogation, Louis claims not to remember the precise moment when he informed Pillard of his first marriage, but vaguely recollects admitting to her that he was a bigamist in Oct. 1697; Piv. int., p. 41.

This text, described as: ADCO 4^{E}112 / 135, "Declaration, ratiffication, et authorisation du Sr Louis de la Pivardière," Oct. 22, 1697. The encounter at the Flavigny notaries' bureau is briefly recounted at Chauv. int., pp. 9–10. Piv. int., p. 39, affirms that the text prepared by the notaries was based on one brought with him by Sousmain.

79 He had in his possession: Piv. int., p. 37, for the four copies and the cover letters.

A notarial act would not do: d'Aguesseau, pp. 416–17, notes that Marguerite appeared before the Romorantin Lieutenant General LeComte on Nov. 12, 1697, to obtain permission to seize her husband and bring him back to the Berry.

Sometime in late November: Char. int., p. 6, names those who gathered in Dijon. There is some confusion in the prior's account as to whether he, his brother, and Sousmain went to Etalante first before their rendezvous with the two valets in Dijon. AN X^{2}B 1283, Interrogatoire de Claude Regnault [a valet of the prior], Apr. 18, 1699, pp. 3–4, indicates that Charost and Sousmain may have also obtained the services of a huissier in Dijon to assist them in Etalante. "saw the Sieur de la Pivardière": Char. int., pp. 6–11, for this quote and the details on which I base this account of the expedition to Etalante.

80 He had been married: "A Double Life—Two Families Twenty Miles Apart," *St. Petersburg Times*, June 4, 2003.

82 Only two years after: Beatrice Gottlieb, "The Meaning of Clandestine Marriage," in *Family and Sexuality in French History*, eds. Robert Wheaton and Tamara K. Hareven (Philadelphia: University of Pennsylvania Press, 1980), pp. 49–53; Philippe Ariès, "The Indissoluble Marriage," in *Western Sexuality: Practice and Precept in Past and Present Times*, eds. Philippe Ariès and André Béjin (Oxford: Basil Blackwell, 1985), pp. 140–57; Charles Donoghue, Jr., "The Canon Law on the Formation of Marriage and Social Practice in the Later Middle Ages," *Journal of Family History* 8 (summer 1983): 144–58; Sarah Hanley, "Engendering the State: Family Formation and State Building in Early Modern France," *French Historical Studies* 16 (spring 1989): 9–11; *Edit du Roi concernant les formalités qui doivent être observées dans les mariages, registré en Parlement le 11 mars 1697*, reprinted in *Journal du Palais* (Paris: David Jeune, 1755), vol. II, pp. 912–13.

At the extreme end: On alternatives to divorce, see Roderick Phillips, *Putting Asunder: A History of Divorce in Western Society* (Cambridge: Cambridge University Press, 1988), esp. pp. 279–313; on *lettres de cachet*, Michel Foucault and Arlette Farge, *Le Désordre des familles. Lettres de cachet des Archives de la Bas-*

tille (Paris: Gallimard, 1982); on English wife sale, E. P. Thompson, "The Sale of Wives," in *Customs in Common* (New York: The New Press, 1991), pp. 404–66.

82 Statistics in England: Henry Kamen, *Inquisition and Society in Spain in the Sixteenth and Seventeenth Centuries* (Bloomington: Indiana University Press, 1985), p. 183, has counted 2,790 cases of bigamy tried by the Inquisition in Castile and Aragon between 1540 and 1700, while Richard Boyer, *Lives of the Bigamists: Marriage, Family, and Community in Colonial Mexico* (Albuquerque: University of New Mexico Press, 1995), p. 8, has noted 2,305 cases brought before the Inquisition in colonial Mexico from 1535 to 1789. On Spain and its colonies see also Mary Elizabeth Perry, *Gender and Disorder in Early Modern Seville* (Princeton, NJ: Princeton University Press, 1990), pp. 69–72; André Fernandez, "The Repression of Sexual Behavior by the Aragonese Inquisition Between 1560 and 1700," *Journal of the History of Sexuality* 7 (1997): 469–501; José Cobos Ruíz de Adana, "Matrimonio, Amancebamiento y Bigamia en el Reino de Córdoba durante el Siglo XVII," *Hispania Sacra* 37 (1985): 693–716; Richard Boyer, "Juan Vázquez, Muleteer of Seventeenth-Century Mexico," *The Americas* 37 (1981): 421–43; Alexandra Parma Cook and Noble David Cook, *Good Faith and Truthful Ignorance: A Case of Transatlantic Bigamy* (Durham, NC: Duke University Press, 1991). For England, see Mary Jo Kietzman, *The Self-Fashioning of an Early Modern Englishwoman: Mary Carleton's Lives* (Aldershot: Ashgate, 2004); Lawrence Stone, *Uncertain Unions: Marriage in England, 1660–1753* (Oxford: Oxford University Press, 1992), pp. 237–74; Ibid., *Broken Lives: Separation and Divorce in England, 1660–1857* (Oxford: Oxford University Press, 1993), pp. 49–78; Larry Gragg, "Bigamy on Barbados: The Case of Nicholas Foster," *The Journal of Caribbean History* 29 (1995): 1–10; David Lemmings, "Marriage and the Law in the Eighteenth Century: Hardwicke's Marriage Act of 1753" *The Historical Journal* 39 (1996): 339–60. *The Proceedings of the Old Bailey London, 1674 to 1832*, www.oldbaileyonline.org, consulted Nov. 12, 2003, show that 263 bigamy cases came before that London court in the 1714–1799 period. Although not all these trials resulted in conviction, their frequency in the British capital at least hints that the rate of bigamy nationwide may have been comparable to that in Spain and its colonies. (My thanks to Julie Hardwick for this last reference.)

83 "while bigamy is a very great crime": Jean-Baptiste Denisart, *Collection de décisions nouvelles et de notions relatives à la jurisprudence actuelle* (Paris: Chez Savoye, 1763), p. 282.
Convicted female bigamists: Jean Imbert and Georges Levasseur, *Le Pouvoir, les juges, et les bourreaux* (Paris: Hachette, 1972), p. 121; Denisart, *Collection de décisions nouvelles*, vol. I, pp. 282–83; Claude Henrys, *Œuvres de M. Claude Henrys, Conseiller du Roi et son premier Avocat au Bailliage & Siège Présidial de Forez* (Paris: Chez les Libraires Associés, 1771), vol. II, p. 588; Pierre le Ridant, *Code matrimonial ou Recueil des édits, ordonnances & Declarations sur le mariage avec un dictionnaire des Décisions les plus importantes sur cette matière* (Paris: Hérissant fils, 1766), p. 62. On Delorme, see Harvard Law Library, Loménie de Brienne Collection, *Arrest de la Cour de Parlement*, May 16, 1727; on bigamists sent to the galleys, Paul W. Bamford, "The Procurement of Oarsmen for French Galleys, 1660–1748," *American Historical Review* 65 (Oct. 1959): 37–38.

The story of Jean Capé: Gayot, *Causes célèbres et intéressantes*, vol. VIIII, pp. 128–63, recounts the Capé case.

87 "full of tenderness": Chauv. fac., pp. 8–9.

88 Her shoulders and most of her chest: For examples of more provocative female portraits in the period, see *Visages du grand siècle: Le Portrait français sous le règne de Louis XIV* (Paris: Somogy, 1997), pp. 51, 54, 60, 64, and 68–69.

90 These impressions are strengthened: Chauv. int., p. 25 (for the mark on his cheek and his legs); Info., pp. 24–25 (for his teeth). AN X²B 1283, Interrogatoire de Claude Regnault, Apr. 18, 1699, p. 2, provides another firsthand account of Louis' ragged appearance in the late 1690s.

91 These images invoked unknown: On seventeenth-century French portraiture, see Linda C. Hults, *The Print in the Western World: An Introductory History* (Madison: University of Wisconsin Press, 1996), pp. 282–90; Erica Harth, "Of Portraits," in *Ideology and Culture in Seventeenth-Century France* (Ithaca, NY: Cornell University Press, 1983), pp. 68–128; and Lianne McTavish, "Looking the Part: Men-midwives on Display," in *Childbirth and the Display of Authority in Early Modern France* (Aldershot: Ashgate, 2005), pp. 113–42.

The criminal court rendered: BnF 4 Fm 34389 *Arrest de la Cour de Parlement, intervenue sur les contestations d'entre la Dame de la Pivardiere & les Officiers de Chastillon sur Indre. Du 23 juillet 1698.* (Paris: Pierre Ballard, 1698). A partial version of this printed text was recorded in the court registers at AN X²B 1135, July 23, 1698.

In their conclusions: BnF 4 Fm 17548 (2), *Conclusions pour la Dame de la Pivardière* . . . (Paris: Claude Mazuel, 1698); BnF 4 Fm 3517, *Conclusions pour Me. Silvain Francois Charost* . . . (Paris: Claude Mazuel, 1698). Their lawyers also asked that Marguerite and the prior be awarded six thousand livres in damages from the Bourges ecclesiastical judges.

4. Nobleman, Commoner, or Impostor?

94 "Believe me, this decision" BnF G4286, *Gazette d'Amsterdam*, July 31, 1698, report from Paris dated July 25, 1698; BnF G16201, *Lettres historiques, contenant ce qui se passe de plus important en Europe, et les reflexions necessaires sur ce sujet*, Aug. 1698, pp. 211–15.

A key component: BnF 4 Fm 17548 (6), *Conclusions du Sieur de la Pivardière demandeur contre les Sieurs Bonnet et Morin deffendeurs* (Paris: Claude Mazuel, 1698), published prior to the July 23, 1698, verdict, requested a safe-conduct for the man in hiding.

The document issued: BnF 4 Fm 17548 (12), *Sauf-conduit du Roy, accordé à Louis de la Pivardière, Escuyer, Sieur du Bouchet, cy-devant Lieutenant au Regiment de Saint Hermines. Donné à Versailles le vingt–sixième Aoust 1698* (Paris: Claude Mazuel, 1698).

He arrived in Paris: Piv. int., p. 61; Info., pp. 15–16, for the details of his first days in Paris. Other Berrichon natives mentioned in these sources who met with Pivardière during his stay at the Baudran residence include the Abbot Boisgard, the Sieur Lenoir de Jouy, the Oratorian priest Joseph David, Dame Marie-Anne de St. Ciran, and Claude de la Chastres, seigneur du Pled.

252 · *Notes to Pages 95–104*

95 On September 1: BnF 4 Fm 17548, *Emprisonnement volontaire du Sieur de la Pivardière du Bouchet, à l'effet de justifier qu'il est véritablement Louis de la Pivardière Escuyer Sieur du Bouchet, mary de Dame Marguerite Chauvelin. Extrait des registres des prisons royalles du Fort l'Evesque à Paris, du premier septembre 1698.*

96 In 1674, however: For the history of the Fort l'Evêque prison, see Frantz Funck-Brentano, *La Bastille des comédiens: Le Fort l'Evêque* (Paris: A. Fontemoing, 1903).
     A counterfeiter named Chevallier: Funck-Brentano, *La Bastille des comédiens*, pp. 135–37, for these examples.

97 Even people who had not: Info., pp. 1–2, 20, 22–24.
     Perhaps the most interesting evidence: Archambault's account of his encounter with Pivardière can be found in Info., pp. 17–19.

99 A week later, the *Histoire journalière:* BnF G4286, *Gazette d'Amsterdam*, editions of Sept. 11 and 15, 1698; quote in Sept. 11 edition (the report from Paris is dated Sept. 5); BA 4 H9487, *Histoire journalière . . .* and Sept. 8 and 15, 1698. The newcomer's arrival in the capital, and the interest it generated, is also recorded in BnF G16201, *Lettres historiques*, Sept. 1698, pp. 322–23, and Oct. 1698, pp. 424–25.
     Early that month: In the 1699 interrogation, Louis claimed that he left Narbonne in Jan. 1695 and did not arrive in Auxerre until Mar. (Piv. int., p. 26). If his memory was accurate, he must have traveled at an exceedingly slow rate, with some lengthy layovers along the way.
     The town was approximately: On Auxerre during the Old Regime, see Jean-Pierre Rocher, et al., *Histoire d'Auxerre des origines à nos jours* (Roanne-Le Coteau: Horvath, 1984), pp. 191–252; Daniel Ligou, ed., *L'Intendance de Bourgogne à la fin du XVIIe siècle. Edition critique du Mémoire pour l'instruction du Duc de Bourgogne* (Paris: Editions du CTHS, 1988), pp. 395–411; and Thomas Brennan, *Burgundy to Champagne: The Wine Trade in Early Modern France* (Baltimore: Johns Hopkins University Press, 1997), esp. pp. 114–40, which describe how Parisian wine merchants "colonized" Auxerre and its surrounding areas for commercial wine production.

101 "having arrived in Auxerre": Piv. int., p. 25. The written account of the prisoner's firsthand testimony was transcribed in the third person; I have placed it in the first person in my translation. See chapter 7, pp. 175–83, and accompanying notes for a discussion of interrogation practices and transcription methods at this time in France.

102 The marriage contract: ADY 3E14/418, Apr. 29, 1695; the parish register recording their wedding ceremony is at ADY 5Mi99, Apr. 30, 1695.

104 At the same time: On venality of office, see Roland E. Mousnier, *La Vénalité des offices sous Henri IV et Louis XIII* (Rouen: Editions Maugard, 1945); and William Doyle, *Venality: The Sale of Offices in Eighteenth-Century France* (Oxford: Clarendon Press, 1996). There is no kingdom-wide study of the inquests of the 1660s and early 1670s, although Monique Cubells, "A propos des usurpations de noblesse en Provence, sous l'Ancien Régime," *Provence historique* 20 (July–Sept. 1970), pp. 224–301, offers useful remarks on the complex, often contradictory meanings of nobility throughout the realm in the second half of the seventeenth century, in addition to a detailed study of the inquest in Provence. Other regional studies of the inquests include Edmond Esmonin, *La*

Taille en Normandie au temps de Colbert (1661–1683) (Paris: Hachette, 1913), pp. 195–231; Jean Mayer, *La Noblesse Bretonne au XVIIIe siècle* (Paris: S.E.V.P.E.N., 1966), pp. 29–73; Jean-Marie Constant, "L'Enquête de noblesse de 1667 et les Seigneurs de Beauce," *Revue d'histoire moderne et contemporaine* 21 (Oct.–Dec. 1974), pp. 548–66; James B. Wood, *The Nobility of the Election of Bayeux, 1463–1666: Continuity Through Change* (Princeton, NJ: Princeton University Press, 1980), pp. 20–42; Arlette Jouanna, "Qualité noble et réputation: les enquêtes de noblesse aux états de Languedoc (de 1670 à la fin de l'Ancien Régime)," in *Société, politique, culture en méditerranée occidentale, XVIe–XVIIIe siècles. Mélanges en l'honneur du Professeur Anne Blanchard.* (Montpellier: Imprimerie Université Paul-Valéry-Montpellier III, 1993), pp. 11–26; and Ibid., "Mémoire nobiliaire. Le Rôle de la réputation dans les preuves de noblesse: l'exemple des barons des Etats de Languedoc," in *Le Second Ordre: L'Idéal nobiliaire. Hommage à Ellery Schalk.* (Paris: Presses de l'Université de Paris-Sorbonne, 1999), pp. 197–206.

It proclaimed a new direct tax: François Bluche and Jean-François Solnon, *La Véritable hiérarchie sociale de l'ancienne France. Le Tarif de la première capitation* (Geneva: Droz, 1983), reproduces the classifications and offers suggestive quantitative and qualitative analysis. But see the summary of reservations expressed by subsequent historians about these classifications as a guide to Old Regime social structure in Michael Kwass, *Privilege and the Politics of Taxation in Eighteenth-Century France: Liberté, Égalité, Fiscalité* (Cambridge: Cambridge University Press, 2000), pp. 69–70.

105 Another records the example: Esmonin, *La Taille en Normandie*, p. 215; Pierre de Vaisserie, *Gentilshommes campagnards de l'Ancienne France* (Paris: Perrin, 1904), pp. 381–83; Marcel Marion, *Dictionnaire des institutions de la France aux XVIIe et XVIIIe siècles* (Paris: Picard, 1923), p. 398.

107 Did she maintain her honor: It is of course possible that they had sexual intercourse before the marriage, but did not conceive until after the wedding. ADY 5 Mi 99, the register for the St. Eusèbe parish where the couple resided, records the following baptisms and burials for their three children: Marie-Elizabeth Dubouchet, baptized Jan. 15, 1696, no recorded burial; Jacques Dubouchet, baptized Oct. 8, 1696, buried Oct. 15, 1696; Louis Dubouchet, baptized and buried Jan. 14, 1699.

109 Lacunae in the Auxerre archives: Piv. int., pp. 28–29; ADY 3E7/90, June 13, 1696.

The loan documents: On his children with Pillard, Piv. int., p. 40, and ADY 5 Mi 99; on his transactions with Edme de La Curne, ADY 3E7/91, May 13, 1697, and attached papers, and Aug. 26, 1697.

110 In April or early May: His letters to Marguerite from this period formed part of the evidence at his trial in 1699, but unfortunately they have not survived. In her trial brief in the summer of 1698, Chauvelin claimed she had received fifteen letters from Pivardière between 1692 and 1697, and that he had visited her at Narbonne three times in that period, once in the winter of 1694–1695, and then twice in 1697 (Chauv. fac., pp. 11–12). For the rumors of the war's impending conclusion, see John A. Lynn, *The Wars of Louis XIV, 1667–1714* (London: Longman, 1999), p. 257.

Marie and her mother: Piv. int., pp. 56–58; Chauv. int., pp. 20–21.

111 French law since the 1530s: *Ordonnance criminelle*, Saint-Germain-en-Laye, Aug. 1670, reprinted in François André Isambert, et al., eds., *Recueil général des anciennes lois françaises* (Paris: Berlin-Le-Prieur, 1829), vol. 18, pp. 386–88; *Edit contre les faussaires*, Saint-Germain-en-Laye, Mar. 1680, reprinted in Pierre Néron and Etienne Girard, *Recueil d'édits et d'ordonnances royaux* (Paris: Montalant, 1720), vol. II, pp. 161–62; *Dictionnaire de l'Académie française*, 1st ed. (Paris, 1694), p. 441; Denis Diderot et Jean le Rond d'Alembert, eds., *Encyclopédie, ou dictionnaire raisonné des sciences, des arts, et des métiers* (Paris: 1751–1777) vol. VI, pp. 440–41.

The best known of these trials: When François Gayot de Pitaval published his path-breaking twenty-volume collection of Old Regime cause célèbres in 1734, the false Martin Guerre affair was the lead case in the first volume. Renewed attention to the case in our day is due to the 1982 Daniel Vigne film *Le Retour de Martin Guerre*, and the superb study by Natalie Zemon Davis, *The Return of Martin Guerre* (Cambridge, MA: Harvard University Press, 1983).

113 The hundreds of people: Morin fac., pp. 29–31; Piv. fac., pp. 21–24.

114 In 1638, Claude de Veré: Curiously, the Veré case is not related in Gayot, but it is told twice in François Richer, *Causes célèbres et intéressantes, avec les jugements qui les ont décidées* (Amsterdam: Michel Rey, 1772–1788), vol. VII, pp. 462–81 (1774), *"enfants adultérins d'un imposteur, déclarés légitimes,"* and vol. XVIII, pp. 1–89 (1781), *"imposteur bigame."* The version provided here is drawn primarily from the latter, more complete, account. For an earlier summary, see Claude Poquet de Livonnière, *Coustumes du pays et duché d'Anjou . . .* (Paris: Coignard, 1725) vol. II, pp. 1155–57.

119 Nevertheless, she cooperated: For debate on this point, see the critique of Davis by Robert Finlay, "The Refashioning of Martin Guerre," *American Historical Review* 93 (June 1988): 553–71; and Davis' response, "On the Lame," *op. cit.*, pp. 572–603.

In a brief from the late 1650s: BnF 4 Fm 8708, *Plaidoyé pour les enfants de Guy de Veré*, esp. pp. 156–57.

120 Did these decisions: After the Martin Guerre case, perhaps the best-known instance of alleged imposture prior to the Pivardière affair was that of Jean Maillard, a soldier of fortune, tailor, and watchmaker who left his Parisian wife, Marie de la Tour, ultimately settling in a convent in Reinselstein, in the German state of Hesse; like Claude de Veré, he disappeared in 1638, in the midst of the Thirty Years War. Marie de la Tour remarried, and when her second husband died in the early 1670s, his family challenged the succession by sending for Maillard in Germany, whose continued existence would render Marie a bigamist and nullify the second marriage. A man who claimed to be Maillard appeared in Paris and confronted his wife, who alleged he was an impostor. Extensive judicial investigation into the man's identity followed, during the course of which he passed away. The court ultimately ruled, posthumously, that the man who had returned from Germany was the true Jean Maillard and deprived his wife of the inheritance she received from her second husband. The Maillard case is summarized in Garsault, *Faits des causes célèbres et intéressantes, augmentés de quelques causes* (Amsterdam: Chastelain, 1757), pp. 85–91. An important eighteenth-century assessment of the legal issues and findings in the case is Claude Blondeau and Gabriel Gueret, *Journal du Palais*

. . . (Paris: Durand, 1755), pp. 494–520. Ibid., p. 504, lists several other intriguing Old Regime imposture cases that made it to court. "Ultimately, the judges understood nothing": Mme. du Noyer, *Lettres Historiques et Galantes, De Deux Dames de condition, dont l'une est à Paris, & l'autre en province. Ouvrage Curieux. Nouvelle édition, revue, corrigée, augmentée et enrichie des figures.* (Amsterdam: Pierre Brunel, 1720), vol. I, pp. 189–90.
On September 3: BnF 4 Fm 17553, *Requeste civile du Sieur de la Pivardière, entherinée par Arrest contradictoire de Nosseigneurs de Parlement* (Paris: Claude Mazuel, 1699), p. 3.

5. Stage Plays

122 "Never has an affair": BnF 4 Fm 17548 (9), Maître de Merville, *Reflexions sur l'accusation de la Dame de la Pivardière au sujet du prétendu assassinat du Sieur de la Pivardière son mary* (Paris: Fournot, 1699). Although the work was signed "Maître de Merville, avocat," contemporaries questioned this attribution. A satirical, handwritten note, bound with a copy of the brief in a volume now conserved in the BnF (BnF Thoisy 379, folio 36, *Sur les reflexions faites au sujet de l'affaire de la Pivardière par Me Merville, qui n'étoit avocat d'aucune des parties interessées dans cette affaire*) poked fun at the supposed author of the pamphlet. Its verses suggested that the publication was a "tragicomedy" in which Merville was "the least important actor," and it claimed that the publication was a "bizarre adventure" in which a writer hiding behind a pen name set out to refute the charge of imposture made against the Fort l'Evêque prisoner. This stealth attack did not propose an alternative author, but the content of the pamphlet makes it probable that it was penned by someone in the Chauvelin camp, because the writer argues at great length for the need to investigate the prisoner's identity before trying the murder case. On the strong undercurrent of satire and farce in Parisian legal culture, see Sara Beam, *Laughing Matters: Farce and the Making of Absolutism in France* (Ithaca, NY: Cornell University Press, 2007), pp. 44–110.
123 The playwright who adapted: On Dancourt's biography, see the exhaustive André Blanc, *Le Théâtre de Dancourt* (Lille: Atelier, reproduction des thèses, Université de Lille III, 1977), vol. I, pp. 23–268, which intersperses biographical details with brief analyses of all his plays in chronological order; for a reliable summary of his life, see the entry for Dancourt in Anthony Levi, ed., *Guide to French Literature: Beginnings to 1789* (Detroit: St. James Press, 1994), pp. 197–201. For documents related to several of the more picaresque incidents in his career, see Emile Campardon, *Les Comédiens du roi de la troupe française* (Paris: H. Champion, 1879), pp. 1–10; and Alex A. Sokalski, "Dancourt injurié: épisode inconnu," *Revue de la société d'histoire du théâtre* (1976): 220–28. Interestingly, Blanc notes that Dancourt was relieved of his responsibilities as an orator in February 1698, eight months before the premiere of *The Husband Returned*, following an address he made to the audience that caused "disorder" in the theater; the content of the address is unknown. The next day, while the troupe closed the playhouse, its representatives traveled to Versailles to answer to the Crown. Blanc, *Le Théâtre*, vol. I, p. 182.

125 The mid-eighteenth-century governmental minister: René Louis de Voyer de Paulmy, Marquis d'Argenson, *Notices sur les Oeuvres de Théâtre*, ed. Henri Lagrave, *Studies on Voltaire and the Eighteenth Century* 42 (1966), p. 171 (see also his comment on *Le Galant jardinier* on p. 178); Voltaire to the Marquise de Bernières, August 20, 1725, in Voltaire, *Correspondence and Related Documents*, ed. T. Bestermann (Oxford: Voltaire Foundation, 1968–1977), 51 vols., letter D246.

This joint exercise in interpretation: Jeffrey S. Ravel, *The Contested Parterre: Public Theater and French Political Culture, 1680–1791* (Ithaca, NY: Cornell University Press, 1999), pp. 13–66, evokes the experience of Parisian theater-going before the Revolution.

127 "The style today": L'Abbé Pierre de Villiers, *Entretiens sur les contes de fées et sur quelques autres ouvrages du temps, pour servir de preservative contre le mauvais goût. . . .* (Paris: J. Collombat, 1699), pp. 259–60. (My thanks to Nicholas Paige for this reference.)

Of particular interest: Contemporary accounts of the Compiègne war games include Louis de Rouvray, Duc de St. Simon, *Mémoires de Saint-Simon*, ed. A. de Boislisle (Paris: Hachette, 1886), vol. V, pp. 348–75, 584–91; *Mémoires de Saint-Hilaire*, ed. Léon Lecestre (Paris: Renouard, 1909), vol. III, pp. 7–9; *Mémoires du Joseph Sevin, Chevalier de Quincy*, ed. Léon Lecestre (Paris: Renouard, 1898):, pp. 79–100; *Mémoires du Marquis de Sourches*, eds. Le Comte de Cosnac and Edouard Pontal (Paris: Hachette, 1886), vol. VI, pp. 58–73; and *Journal du Marquis de Dangeau*, ed. Feuillet de Conches (Paris: Firmin Didot, 1856), vol. VI, pp. 405–26.

"These are the games": *Gazette d'Amsterdam*, September 1698, reproduced in St. Simon, *Mémoires de Saint-Simon*, vol. V, p. 586.

129 "It is impossible to imagine anything": St. Simon, *Mémoires de Saint-Simon*, vol. V, pp. 351–52.

131 At the outset: For summaries of the play, see Henry Carrington Lancaster, *A History of French Dramatic Literature in the Seventeenth Century* (Baltimore: Johns Hopkins University Press, 1940), part IV, vol. 2, pp. 804–6; and Blanc, *Le Théâtre de Dancourt*, vol. I, pp. 141–45. One might also compare Dancourt's one-act with a novel, *La Rivale travestie, ou Les Avantures galantes arrivées au camp de Compiègne, avec tous les mouvemens de l'armée* (Paris: Michel Brunet, 1699), published by a minor military official and man of letters named François Nodot. Nodot alternates detailed descriptions of the military maneuvers with a fictional plot in which a noblewoman assumes the disguise of a nobleman to thwart her lover's overtures to the wife of a bourgeois merchant. Like Dancourt's play, the plot transpires on the outskirts of the games, incorporates acts of imposture and deception, and ultimately foils the schemes of nobles and commoners who wish to transgress class distinctions. In the preface to the novel, Nodot claims that his narrative is a faithful account of events that actually transpired during the course of the war games.

"fine clothes, with big swords": Dancourt, *Les Curieux de Compiègne*, in *Il Teatro "à la mode" di Florent Carton Dancourt*, ed. Nivea Melani (Naples: Istituto Universitario Orientale, 1972), p. 180.

132 Monsieur Valentin, the other bourgeois protagonist: Ibid., p. 181.

133 But the implied mockery: See Guy Spielman, *Le Jeu de l'ordre et du chaos*:

comédie et pouvoirs à la fin du règne, 1673–1715 (Paris: Honoré Champion, 2002); and Christian Biet, *Droit et littérature sous l'Ancien Régime: le jeu de la valeur et de la loi* (Paris: Honoré Champion, 2002), pp. 285–338, for important reappraisals of post-Molière, *fin-de-siècle* comedy.

134 The average figures: It should be noted, however, that *The Husband Returned* ranks in the second half of Dancourt's 1694–1698 one-acts in terms of number of performances during its initial run. It was performed only twenty-two times in the fall of 1698, versus fifty-one performances for the leader, 1695's *Vendanges de Suresnes*. It is somewhat of a mystery why the run of *The Husband Returned* ended with the twenty-second performance on December 7, 1698, because box office receipts continued to be strong through that date. It is possible that the troupe was discouraged from continuing performance because the Parlement was preparing to resume hearings in the case, but I have not found any evidence to support this hypothesis. Attendance and box office statistics are from Henry Carrington Lancaster, *The Comédie-Française 1680–1701: Plays, Actors, Spectators, Finances* (Baltimore: Johns Hopkins University Press, 1941).

135 "fair and precise allegory": *Mercure de France*, October 1725, pp. 2487–88. For another contextualized reading of the play, see Blanc, *Le Théâtre de Dancourt*, vol. I, pp. 145–47, and 380.

"[o]ne always likes to see": D'Argenson, *Notices*, pp. 185–86, in a comment on Dancourt's 1694 one-act comedy *Les Vendanges*.

137 The choice of occupation: Steven L. Kaplan, *Provisioning Paris: Merchants and Millers in the Grain and Flour Trade During the Eighteenth Century* (Ithaca, NY: Cornell University Press, 1984), pp. 264–97.

140 But spectators in November 1698: This was the case two decades later, when the playwright Marc-Antoine Legrand visited the thief Cartouche in prison in preparation for writing a play based on his experiences. See Christian Biet, "Cartouche et le mythe de l'ennemi public no 1, en France et en Europe," in Marc-Antoine Legrand, *Cartouche ou les voleurs*, eds. Christian Biet, Martial Poirson, and Romain Jobez (Paris: Lampsaque, 2003), pp. 10–92.

144 "Mlle Lolotte: Having two lovers": Florent Carton Dancourt, *Le Mari retrouvé*, in *Chefs-d'œuvre des auteurs comiques* (Paris: Firmin-Didot frères, 1860), vol. II, p. 132. For Touvenelle's contract, see Blanc, *Le Théâtre de Dancourt*, vol. I, p. 458, n. 1.

6. Judicial Doubt

146 On December 7: BnF 4 Fm 17553, *Requeste civile du Sieur de la Pivardière, entherinée par Arrest contradictoire de Nosseigneurs de Parlement* (Paris: Claude Mazuel, 1699). For unknown reasons, the lieutenant general of police, Marc-René de Voyer d'Argenson, did not give permission to publish this document until the end of July 1699, by which time the case had been decided definitively. The transfer of the prior and the maidservants to Parisian prisons (the prior to the Châtelet, the maidservants to the Conciergerie, where Marguerite was already incarcerated) is noted at BnF G 4466, *Histoire journalière* ..., Dec. 18, 1698.

147 They claimed that it was not necessary: D'Aguesseau, pp. 431–47, summarizes these arguments.

148 "masterpieces of eloquence": Pierre-Jacques Brillon, *Dictionnaire des Arrêts: ou, Jurisprudence universelle des parlemens de France . . .* (Paris: G. Cavelier, 1727), vol. 3, p. 712 (for Nivelle's threatened *mémoire*) and p. 715 (for the desire to publish the courtroom pleadings).
"vigorous male eloquence": D'Aguesseau, pp. 421–22.
"This most unusual case": BnF G 4287, *Nouvelles extraordinaires de divers endroits,* Jan. 29, 1699. See also mention of the continuing interest in the case in BnF G 4290, *Gazette d'Amsterdam,* Jan. 22, 1699; and BnF G4287, *Gazette de Rotterdam,* Feb. 5, 1699.

149 Henri-François d'Aguesseau was the most: The most recent survey of his life and thought is Isabelle Storez, *Le Chancelier Henri François D'Aguesseau, 1668–1751. Monarchiste et libéral* (Paris: Editions Publisud, 1996), which gives equal play to his career as a jurist and political figure, and to his thought as expressed in his voluminous, posthumously published writings. Georges Frêche, *Un Chancelier Gallican: D'Aguesseau* (Paris: Presses Universitaires de France, 1969) is a serious consideration of d'Aguesseau's Gallican leanings and his political legacy. Jean-Luc Chartier, *De Colbert à l'Encyclopédie. Tome II, Henri-François d'Aguesseau, Chancelier de France, 1668–1751* (Montpellier: Presses du Langue-doc, 1988) is an exhaustive, but largely uncritical, account of his career by a practicing attorney. (The first volume of this work is a biographical treatment of d'Aguesseau's father, who was councilor of state under Louis XIV.) For an evaluation of the d'Aguesseau administrative dynasty, see Richard Mowery Andrews, *Law, Magistracy, and Crime in Old Regime Paris, 1735–1789. Vol. I: The System of Criminal Justice* (Cambridge: Cambridge University Press), pp. 241–78, esp. pp. 265–68 on the d'Aguesseau clan.
D'Aguesseau published little: *Œuvres de Monsieur le Chancelier d'Aguesseau* (Paris: Libraires Associés, 1759–1789), 13 vols. These volumes contain addresses he made to assemblies of Parisian barristers and Parlementary magistrates from 1691 to 1717, print versions of his oral pleadings before the Parlement in those same years, and his reflections on education, religion, politics, and other matters written during periods of exile while serving as lord chancellor after 1717.

150 He was celebrated: Subsequent observers have placed him in the company of some of the Old Regime's most distinguished civil servants, including Michel d'Hopital and Maximilien de Béthune, Duc de Sully; see, for example, Storez, *Le Chancelier,* pp. 19–21. One might also situate d'Aguesseau as a thinker in relation to some of his contemporaries. While also a Gallican and fervent supporter of the principles of absolute monarchy, he differed from Jacques Bénigne Bossuet in his greater tolerance for Protestants and for those subjected to hardships by the nature of absolutist rule. Yet he never overtly criticized the monarchy in the same way as François de Salignac la Mothe de Fénélon, preferring to work from within for reform. The practical nature of the day-to-day work he assumed, in which decisions had to be made and actions taken, prevented him from approaching the same levels of uncertainty and despair as Pierre Bayle, although it is worth noting that in his final year in office he signed the approval for the first volume of Denis Diderot and Jean-

Baptiste le Rond d'Alembert's *Encyclopédie*, the great *summa* of the French Enlightenment that was heavily indebted to Bayle. On d'Aguesseau's thought, see Frêche, *Un Chancelier*, pp. 7–13, 55–69; and Storez, *Le Chancelier*, pp. 357–565.

151 "and the Public that sees them": On d'Aguesseau's education, see Storez, *Le Chancelier*, pp. 75–96; on his early dislike for the stage, Frêche, *Un Chancelier*, p. 7. The passage on judges in the theaters is from the *mercuriale* "L'Amour de son Etat," *Œuvres*, vol. I, pp. 45–46.

152 D'Aguesseau was only thirty years old: "Mr. d'Aguesseau qui est encore fort jeune, & cependant le plus anciens des trois Avocats Généraux du Parlement de Paris, doit parler aujourd'hui dans la Chambre de la Tournelle sur l'affaire de Mr. de la Pivardière. . . ." BnF G 4287, *Gazette de Rotterdam*, Feb. 19, 1699, report from Paris dated Feb. 13.

153 He urged magistrates: Both orations can be found in d'Aguesseau, *Œuvres* vol. II, pp. 1–28. "The Independence of the Barrister" is discussed in a different context by David A. Bell, *Lawyers and Citizens: The Making of a Political Elite in Old Regime France* (Oxford: Oxford University Press, 1994), pp. 63–66.

154 The clarity and analytic quality: On the 1696 Duc de Luxembourg case, see Chartier, *De Colbert à l'Encyclopédie* vol. II, pp. 49–71; on the 1700 Duc de Guise case, see Aimé-Auguste Boullée, *De la Vie et des ouvrages du Chancelier d'Aguesseau* (Paris: Desenne, 1835), vol. I, pp. 129–30; and on the 1695–1698 Conti/Nemours affair, see Boullée, *De la Vie*, vol. I, pp. 130–34, and Chartier, *De Colbert*, vol. II, pp. 43–48. D'Aguesseau's pleadings in these affairs can be consulted in the *Œuvres*.

155 "to entertain the vain curiosity": D'Aguesseau, *Œuvres*, vol. III, p. 154. His first pleading in the *Conti v. Nemours* case begins with similar sentiments.
in spite of the wife's inconsistent story: D'Aguesseau, *Œuvres*, vol. III, pp. 154–95.
"No matter how heavy": D'Aguesseau, *Œuvres*, vol. III, p. 171.

156 D'Aguesseau, no doubt aware: How closely do the printed texts resemble the two discourses d'Aguesseau delivered before the Tournelle on Feb. 13 and July 22, 1699? In *Œuvres* vol. II, pp. xi–xii, the preface to the first of several volumes of the collected works that contains his *plaidoyers*, the editor writes that at times d'Aguesseau would only make sketchy written notes prior to a pleading, but that "every year in some cases he would write out the majority of his discourse." Even in these cases, however, when it came time to deliver the report, his editor notes that d'Aguesseau would sometimes vary from the written text in order to embellish his argument. Taken together, the 143 pages of print occupied by the two Pivardière *plaidoyers* are the longest text in the fourth volume where they appear, and among the longest *plaidoyers* in the *Œuvres*. Even if d'Aguesseau followed his standard procedure of improvising for rhetorical effect in the courtroom, he must have put a great deal of time and thought into the written versions that appeared in print after his death. Absent any further information on the editorial procedure followed in the compilation of the *Œuvres*, it seems reasonable to assume that they offer an accurate view of his thoughts on the affair in 1699.
The singularity of the facts: D'Aguesseau, p. 399. [Emphasis mine.]
Dancourt and the Comédie-Française: At two points in the *plaidoyers*, D'Aguesseau distinguishes the actions of Marguerite and Louis, which he

views as genuine, from the falsity of the stage: "ce n'est point un de ces dénouements de théâtre, qu'on ne fait paroître qu'à la fin du spectacle, & qu'on y amène par des machines," D'Aguesseau, p. 480, and repeated almost word for word in the second *plaidoyer* at Ibid., p. 513.

157 "Louis de la Pivardière, if he still breathes": Ibid., p. 401.

158 "of doubt, of cloudiness": Ibid., p. 419. This passage in d'Aguesseau's *plaidoyer* apparently inspired the title of Maurice Soulié's 1926 treatment of the Pivardière case, *La Mort et la résurrection de M. de la Pivardière* (Paris: Perrin, 1926).
"I dare say that": Ibid., pp. 447–48.

159 In each instance: Ibid., pp. 448–52.
The best proofs: Ibid., pp. 460–72.
At the same time: Ibid., pp. 473–82.

160 "When we consider": Ibid., pp. 482–83.
"We doubt everything": Ibid., pp. 482–83. [Emphasis mine.] Storez, *Le Chancelier*, pp. 441–44, identifies Cartesian doubt as the lifelong centerpiece of d'Aguesseau's judicial sensibility.

161 But Voltaire had his own ax: Voltaire, "Prix de la justice et de l'humanité," in *Œuvres completes de Voltaire* (Kehl, 1785), vol. XXIX, p. 333. Voltaire, *Treatise on Tolerance, and Other Writings*, ed. Simon Harvey (Cambridge: Cambridge University Press, 2000), provides an introduction to some of Voltaire's judicial crusades in the 1760s.

7. Interrogation

164 Third, they ordered Bochart: The Feb. 1699 sentence, with these details, is reprinted in d'Aguesseau, pp. 490–92.

166 Their task was to determine: AN X²B 1283, *Pièces de comparaison*, Apr. 28, 1699; and AN X²B 1283, *Vérification des dix letters missives escriptes par la Pivardière depuis sa prétendu mort*, May 8, 1699.
Claiming that calligraphy: Roger Chartier, *The Cultural Origins of the French Revolution*, trans. Lydia Cochrane (Durham, NC: Duke University Press, 1991), p. 69 for adult literacy rates ca. 1700; Christine Métayer, "De l'école au Palais de Justice: L'Itinéraire singulier des Maîtres Ecrivains de Paris (XVIe–XVIIIe siècles)," *Annales ESC* (Sept.–Oct. 1990): 1217–37, for the view that the master scriveners "policed" the handwritten page. For more on the history and struggles of the Master Scriveners Guild, see Jean Hébrard, "Des Écritures exemplaires: l'art de maître écrivain en France entre XVIe et XVIIIe siècle," *Mélanges de l'École Française de Rome: Italie et Méditerranée* 107–2 (1995): 473–523; and Métayer, "Normes Graphiques et pratiques de l'écriture: Maîtres écrivains et écrivains publics à Paris aux XVIIe et XVIIIe siècles," *Annales HSS* (July–Oct. 2001): 881–901.

167 The scriveners themselves: For a defense of the scriveners' claims to expertise in handwriting comparison, see Jacques Raveneau, *Traité des inscriptions en faux et reconnoissances d'Escritures & Signatures par comparaison et autrement* (Paris: Thomas Jolly, 1666); but note as well the equivocations in the chapter titled "Discours touchant l'aire de l'escriture," pp. 48–55. For a critical response, see

Roland le Vayer de Boutigny, *Traité de la Preuve par Comparaison d'Ecritures* (Paris: Henry Charpentier, 1666), which became the standard work denying the scriveners' claims to scientific accuracy. Vayer, a Parisian barrister, had lost the Jean Maillard case in the 1660s in large part due to the testimony of handwriting experts from the Scriveners Guild. Ultimately, he found it ludicrous that a handwriting expert would conclude that two similar samples had necessarily come from the same hand: "[O]f all possible arguments," he noted, "is there a single one as weak as that of resemblance? Who has ever learned to reason this way: something is similar, therefore it is equivalent?" For more on Vayer and the Maillard case, see Jacques Bonzon, *La Corporation des Maîtres-Écrivains et l'expertise en écritures sous l'Ancien Régime* (Paris: V. Giard and E. Brière, 1899), pp. 41–55; and the references in the note to p. 120.

These debates were damaging: *Ordonnance criminelle*, issued at Saint-Germain-en-Laye, Aug. 1670; reprinted in François André Isambert, et al., *Recueil général des anciens lois françaises* (Paris: Belin-Leprieur, 1829), vol. 16, pp. 385–86.

168 One of them: Etienne de Blegny, *Traité concernant la maniere de proceder a toutes verifications d'ecritures contestees en justice* (Paris: Guillaume Cavalier, 1698; reprinted in 1699, 1700, and 1706). The goal of his work, he claimed in the preface, was to provide master scriveners in Paris and the provinces with the exact procedure mandated by the courts for handwriting verification, including suggested wording for acts of authentification. Nicholas Lesgret, *Livre d'exemplaires composé de toutes sortes de lettres de finance et italienne bastarde, avec des instructions familières touchant les préceptes généraux qu'il faut observer, pour bien imiter les exemples qui y sont compris* (Paris: Chez l'auteur, 1694).

Their use of words: AN X²B 1283, *Vérification des dix letters missives escriptes par la Pivardière depuis sa prétendu mort*, May 8, 1699, p. 4 (*aura*), and p. 7 (*spirit*).

"Handwriting is nothing more": Le Chevalier de Jaucourt, *Comparaison d'écritures (jurisprudence)*, in Denis Diderot and Jean-Baptiste le Rond d'Alembert, eds. *L'Encyclopédie, ou Dictionnaire raisonnée des arts, des sciences, et des métiers* (Paris, 1751–1777), vol. V, pp. 369–70.

169 Then, if the witness appeared: *Ordonnance criminelle* in Isambert, et al., *Recueil général*, vol. XVI, pp. 400–3.

Bochart was given a list: Info., and AN X²B 1283, *Continuation d'information de l'existence de Louis de la Pivardière, Sieur du Bouchet*, May 18–19, 1699, contain the transcripts of the twenty-seven depositions. AN X²B 1283, *Procès-verbal & reconnoissance de Louis Dubouchet, Sieur de la Pivardière*, May 6–21, 1699, contains the transcripts of the nineteen confrontations. D'Aguesseau, p. 526, notes that Bochart was given a list of sixty potential witnesses.

170 The man she saw: Info., pp. 1–2, for du Gripon's deposition; and AN X²B 1283, *Procès-verbal & reconnoissance de Louis Dubouchet, Sieur de la Pivardière*, pp. 5–6, for her confrontation with the prisoner.

In the deposition: Info., p. 20, for Carré's deposition; and AN X²B 1283, *Procès-verbal & reconnoissance de Louis Dubouchet, Sieur de la Pivardière*, p. 3, for his confrontation with the prisoner.

171 Mothe's verification was echoed by: Info., p. 23–24, for Coquard de la Mothe; Info., p. 2, and AN X²B 1283, *Procès-verbal & reconnoissance . . .* , p. 6, for Elie de

Saint-Hermine; Info., p. 5, and AN X²B 1283, *Procès-verbal & reconnoissance*
. . . , pp. 2–3, for Louis François de Villefort, the major in the dragoon regiment; and Info., pp. 24–25, and AN X²B 1283, *Procès-verbal & reconnoissance*
. . . , pp. 7–8, for Louis Gobinet, the regiment's supply master.

172 The Lady of St. Ciran: Info., pp. 13–14, for St. Ciran's deposition; and AN
X²B 1283, *Procès-verbal & reconnaissance* . . . , p. 10, for her confrontation with
the prisoner.

Unlike the Lady of St. Ciran: For Douault, see Info., pp. 20–21, and *Procès-
verbal & reconnoissance* . . . , 8; for David, Info., pp. 3–4, and AN X²B 1283,
Procès-verbal & reconnoissance . . . , pp. 3–4.

173 Given these facts: For Chenu's deposition, see Info., pp. 8–12; for the dismissal
of his testimony, see d'Aguesseau, pp. 522–24.

174 Among other charges: AN X²B 1283, *Continuation d'information de l'existence de
Louis de la Pivardière, Sieur du Bouchet*, May 18–19, 1699, pp. 1–2, for Chauvin's
deposition; d'Aguesseau, p. 524, for the letter from Chauvin's ecclesiastical superior to Bochart. It appears that the Châtillon rift between the Charost clan
and their opponents reached even as far as the town's Augustinian monastery;
Chauvin's superior was most likely a Charost partisan.

175 "Although the witness claims": AN X²B 1283, *Procès-verbal & reconnaissance*
. . . , pp. 11–12.

176 "a speaking portrait": BnF 4 Fm 17458 (9), Merville, *Reflexions sur l'accusation
de la Dame de la Pivardière au sujet du prétendu assassinat du Sieur de la Pivardière*,
pp. 6–9.

Bochart questioned the suspect: Frantz Funck-Brentano, *La Bastille des
comédiens: Le Fort l'Evêque* (Paris: A. Fontemoing, 1903), image between
pp. 48–49, which is a reproduction of a 1774 floor plan drawn by the prison's
concierge.

178 While he never entirely abandoned: Piv. int., pp. 11–12, 19.

And in the next-to-last session: Piv. int., pp. 2, 20, 26, 28, 62.

180 The prisoner replied: Piv. int., pp. 21, 34.

In the face-to-face confrontation: Piv. int., pp. 31–32.

181 In each of these instances: Piv. int., pp. 41, 48, 53, 67.

Is it not true: Piv. int., pp. 24–25. The transcript of the interrogation is written
in the third person, but my translation rewrites this exchange in the first person, to provide the reader with a better feel for the interrogation.

182 At one point: Piv. int., p. 65.

This was why: The pattern occurred again in the interrogations of Marguerite
Chauvelin and Sylvain François Charost, where both responded repeatedly to
questions about the assassination they supposedly committed the night of Aug.
15, 1697, by saying that Louis de la Pivardière was alive and well in Fort
l'Evêque prison.

183 "assembles within himself": d'Aguesseau, p. 401.

The prisoner answered: Piv. int., pp. 27–28. Bochart also asked Marguerite,
during her interrogation, if she had any insight into Louis' mysterious abdication of military rank and social position; she replied that she assumed it was to
hide his dishonorable second marriage. (Chauv. int., p. 21.)

184 Marguerite told Bochart: Chauv. int., p. 5.

185 This work, Louis hoped: John A. Lynn, *The Wars of Louis XIV, 1667–1714*

(London: Longman, 1999), pp. 259–61, on the Spanish front in 1697; Geoffrey Symcox, *The Crisis of French Sea Power, 1688–1697: From the* Guerre d'escadre *to the* Guerre de course (The Hague: M. Nijhoff, 1974), pp. 43–55, for the place of Bayonne in French naval strategy and planning; Piv. int., pp. 31–32, for Planque and his Bayonne adventure.

186 When questioned about this distant: Piv. int., p. 55, on the trip to Blaye.

188 "It won't be long": BnF G 4287, *Histoire journalière* . . . , Apr. 9, 1699.

8. Verdicts

189 "[O]ne might almost say": Mme. du Noyer, *Lettres Historiques et Galantes, De Deux Dames de condition, dont l'une est à Paris, & l'autre en province. Ouvrage Curieux. Nouvelle édition, revue, corrigée, augmentée et enrichie des figures* (Amsterdam: Pierre Brunel, 1720), vol. I, p. 246.

190 The central character: Noyer, *Lettres Historiques*, vol. I, p. 248. Contemporary narratives of the Tiquet affair include BnF G 4287, *Histoire journalière*, Apr. 20 to July 9, 1699; BnF G 4287, *Nouvelles extraordinaires*, June 23 to July 14, 1699; BnF G 1623, *L'Esprit des cours d'Europe*, July 1699, pp. 155–67; Louis de Rouvray, Duc de St. Simon, *Mémoires de Saint-Simon*, ed. A. de Boislisle (Paris: Hachette, 1886), vol. VI, pp. 433–37; *Journal du Marquis de Dangeau*, ed. Feuillet de Conches (Paris: Firmin Didot, 1856), vol. VII, pp. 61–62, 71, 93–94, 99–100; *Mémoires du Marquis de Sourches*, eds. Le Comte de Cosnac and Edouard Pontal (Paris: Hachette, 1886), vol. VI, pp. 144–45, 150, 155, 162, 164–66; *Mémoires du Chevalier Joseph Sevin, Comte de Quincy*, ed. Léon Lecestre (Paris: Renouard, 1898), pp. 115–17.

191 On July 20: BnF G 4287, *Histoire journalière* . . . , May 7, June 22, July 20, 1699.

192 "It's a sad thing": BnF ms. Fr. 12643, f. 25. On the elite compilers and audiences for these songs, see Claude Grasland and Annette Keilhauer, "La Rage de collection: Conditions, enjeux et significations de la formation des grands chansonniers satiriques et historiques à Paris au début du XVIIIe siècle," *Revue d'histoire moderne et contemporaine* 47, 3 (July–Sept. 2000), pp. 458–86. Picking up on this unease: Noyer, *Lettres Historiques*, vol. I, p. 243.

In addition, no matter how heinous: On executions, and the crowds that watched them, see Paul Friedland, "Beyond Deterence: Cadavres, Effigies, Animals and the Logic of Deterrence in Premodern France," *Historical Reflections/Réflexions historiques* 29 (summer 2003), pp. 259–317; and Thomas Laqueur, "Crowds, Carnival, and the State in English Executions, 1604–1868," in Lee Beier, David Cannadine, and James Rosenheim, eds., *The First Modern Society: Essays in Honor of Lawrence Stone* (Cambridge: Cambridge University Press, 1989), pp. 305–55.

193 Furthermore, according to the Dutch reporter: The delays are noted at BnF G 4290, *Gazette d'Amsterdam*, July 9, 1699; and BnF G 4287, *Histoire journalière* . . . , July 16 1699.

194 Furthermore, he argued that: I take these summaries of the lawyers' arguments from d'Aguesseau, pp. 501–9.

"or perhaps the fable": Ibid., p. 494.

194 "Today the veil is lifted": Ibid., p. 503.
195 D'Aguesseau listed a set: Elaborated in detail at Ibid., pp. 513–17.
"On each man": Ibid., p. 503.
It was not uncommon: Ibid., pp. 520, 529.
196 As with the handwriting evidence: Ibid., pp. 521–25, 529.
197 "Absolutely speaking": Ibid., pp. 518–19, 528–29.
198 "We know," he said: Ibid., p. 528.
199 "What is left to us then": Ibid., p. 531.
200 A Dutch journal hinted: BnF G 4290, *Gazette d'Amsterdam,* July 30, 1699. This, of course, was the theory the barrister Nivelle had set forth the previous Jan.; see chapter 6 above, as well as BnF G 4290, *Gazette d'Amsterdam,* June 29, 1699.
The embers were stirred: For these passages, see BnF G 4287 *Histoire journalière,* July 30, Aug. 6, and Sept. 3, 1699.
201 "Justice manages to pierce": BnF G 16545, Nicholas Gueudeville, *L'Esprit des cours de l'Europe,* Apr. 1700, p. 399. See also BnF G 16204, *Lettres historiques . . . ,* Apr. 1700, p. 443.
202 She knew that: This paragraph summarizes details found in AN X²B 1283, Interrogatoire de Marguerite Mercier, Apr. 16–17, 1699; AN X²B 1283, Interrogatoire de Marguerite Mercier, Jan. 20, 1700; and her confrontations with Morin, Jacquemet, and the lesser Châtillon policing officials from Mar. through June 1700, transcripts available at AN X²B 1283. The quote comparing the Narbonne bedchamber and the courtroom is at AN X²B 1283, Interrogatoire de Marguerite Mercier, Apr. 16–17, 1699, p. 9. The "black as the chimney" quote is at AN X²B 1283, Confrontation d'accusés l'un à l'autre, Apr. 26, 1700, p. 3.
203 Although he denied it: BnF 4 Fm 34387, *Second Memoire pour Me François Morin substitut de Monsieur le Procureur Général au Siège Présidial de Chastillon sur Indre, et pour Louis Breton cy-devant Greffier au meme Siège;* AN X²B 1283, Interrogatoire de Me François Morin, substitut du Procureur Général du Roy au Chastillon sur Indre, Mar. 19, 1700; AN X²B 1283, Confrontation d'accusés l'un à l'autre, Apr. 26, 1700, pp. 12–13 (confrontation between Marguerite Mercier and François Morin).
204 "Pray to God for me": AN X²B 1283, Interrogatoire de Guillaume Crouet, Mar. 30, 1700, pp. 2–4; AN X²B 1283, Interrogatoire de Jean Gaulin, Apr. 6, 1700, pp. 2–3; AN X²B 1283, Confrontation d'accusés l'un à l'autre, Apr. 26, 1700, p. 6. The question of these purchases came up in the 1700 interrogations and confrontations because Mercier was asked if the goods she had received were bribes from the Prior Charost and his family.
205 Others reported that: AN X²B 1283, Interrogatoire de Me François Morin, substitut du Procureur Général du Roy au Chastillon sur Indre, Mar. 19, 1700, p. 2.
While it is plausible: The transcripts recording this testimony, taken by Bonnet, the Luçay seigneurial judge in the fall of 1697, and the lieutenant general of Issoudun in Sept. and Nov. 1699, no longer exist, but references in BnF 4 Fm 34387, *Second Memoire pour Me François Morin . . . ,* p. 10, and the confrontations recorded in Apr. and June 1700 in Paris (transcripts at AN X²B 1283), provide enough information to make this claim.

206 During the investigation: BnF 4 Fm 34387, *Second Memoire pour Me François Morin* . . . , p. 3; AN X²B 1283, Confrontation d'accusés l'un à l'autre, Apr. 26, 1700, p. 14; AN X²B 1283, Continuation de confrontation d'accusés, June 19, 1700, p. 3.

207 But the high court: The 1701 verdict is reprinted, with brief commentary, in d'Aguesseau, pp. 537–38, 540–41. ADI 2B 43, "Minutes de l'audience de la prévôté d'Issoudun, Rapport des laboureurs," unpaginated f. 31, refers to an *arrest de Parlement* dated Aug. 19, 1699, ordering Morin to pay for repairs to Narbonne.

208 In November 1699: The visit is recorded at ADI 2B 43, "Minutes de l'audience de la prévôté d'Issoudun, Rapport des laboureurs."

209 "When one has had": François Gayot de Pitaval, *Causes célèbres et intéressantes, avec les jugements qui les ont décidés* . . . (The Hague: Jean Neaulme, 1735), vol. III, p. 83.

210 But it is an unverifiable tale: Gayot de Pitaval, *Causes célèbres et intéressantes*, vol. III, p. 82. Gayot's source for this information was untrustworthy, as we shall see in the epilogue. There are no records of his service in the skirmishes with smugglers in the Old Regime military archives.

211 "Monsieur, most people ": Molière, *Le Bourgeois gentilhomme*, act III, scene xii, ll. 8–23.

Epilogue: Rewriting a Cause Célèbre

214 Voltaire's *Letters on England:* See Colin Jones, *The Great Nation: France from Louis XV to Napoleon* (New York: Columbia University Press, 2002), for a recent synthetic overview of eighteenth-century French history.

215 Only once do we have: For these details of her life subsequent to her marriage to Louis, see ADY 5Mi99; ADY 3 E6/124; and ADY 3 E7/257. G. Ficatier, "Histoire rocambolesque et tragi-comique de Messire Louis de la Pivardière, Sieur du Bouchet et châtelain de Nerbonne," *L'Echo d'Auxerre* (1968), p. 38, n. 2, claims she was Jean Pillard's godmother. Although not otherwise especially trustworthy, Ficatier provides the correct birth and death dates for Marie's three children by Louis, as well as the proper names of her final two husbands. The author states that these details were provided by a M. Paul Richard, who extracted them from the ADY. Although I have not verified the accuracy of the 1715 parish signature, the accuracy of Richard's other details makes this claim seem probable.

216 One literary historian: Jean Sgard, "La Littérature des Causes Célèbres," in *Approches des lumières: Mélanges offerts à Jean Fabre* (Paris: Klincksieck, 1974), pp. 459–70.
The Marquise de Brinvilliers: On the publishing history of the *Causes célèbres*, in addition to Sgard, "La Littérature," see Hans-Jürgen Lüsebrink, *Kriminalität und Literatur im Frankreich des 18. Jahrhunderts* (Munich: Oldenbourg, 1983), pp. 104–72, esp. pp. 168–72 for the reception of the genre in France and Germany. According to Lüsebrink, the success of the *Causes célèbres* genre continued in France and elsewhere in the nineteenth century and beyond; in Germany the term *Pitaval* became synonymous with crime literature, as in the

1888 *Lustiger Berliner Pitaval*, or the 1953 *Pitaval der Weimarer Republik*. In addition to editing a German version of the Pivardière affair, Hermann Hesse also wrote a review titled "Der alte Pitaval" in the journal *März. Halbmonatsschrift für deutsche Kultur* 5, i (1911): 382–83. On the case of the Marquise de Gange in particular, see Marquis de Sade, *La Marquise de Gange, précédée des Opuscules politiques d'Oxteirn, ou les malheurs du libertinage* (Paris: Cercle du livre précieux, 1964); and the discussion in Lüsebrink, *Kriminalität und Literatur*, pp. 134–52.

217 Gayot's *Causes célèbres:* For one introduction to the literary concerns of the period, see Jay Caplan, *In the King's Wake: Post-Absolutist Culture in France* (Chicago: University of Chicago Press, 1999).

218 "[W]ith respect to the second wife": Quotes in this paragraph in François Gayot de Pitaval, *Causes célèbres et intéressantes, avec les jugements qui les ont décidés*... (The Hague: Jean Neaulme, 1735), vol. III, pp. v, 2–3, and 83. In addition to Pillard, it is likely that Gayot spoke with the jurist Pierre-Jacques Brillon, who had attended the Paris courtroom hearings in 1698–1699, and written about them in his *Dictionnaire des Arrêts: ou, Jurisprudence universelle des parlemens de France*... (Paris: G. Cavelier, 1727), vol. 3, pp. 709–15, which Gayot would have consulted; and Brillon was still alive in the early 1730s. D'Aguesseau was also still alive, but would Gayot have been able to obtain an audience with the lord chancellor to discuss a case that was over thirty years old?
"and he felt himself": Gayot de Pitaval, *Causes célèbres*, vol. III, p. 5.
Nowhere in any of the sources: In Pivardière's *factum* from summer 1698, he had claimed that when he left the military in the mid-1690s, he had purchased the post of huissier from Pillard's mother as a source of income; he then also agreed to marry Pillard to seal the deal; Piv. fac., p. 3. BnF 4 Fm 17548 (9), Maître de Merville, *Reflexions sur l'accusation de la Dame de la Pivardière au sujet du prétendu assassinat du Sieur de la Pivardière son mary* (Paris: Fournot, 1699), p. 11, made a similar claim.

219 "His second wife": Gayot de Pitaval, *Causes célèbres*, vol. III, pp. 15–16.

220 "A girl as beautiful as you": The account of Pillard at Versailles, including the quotes in this paragraph, is at Ibid., pp. 51–52.
A little more than a month later: BnF G 4286, *Gazette d'Amsterdam*, July 31 and Sept. 8, 1698.

221 Louis XIV refused to grant: For accounts of the Tiquet family at Versailles, see Louis de Rouvray, Duc de St. Simon, *Mémoires de Saint-Simon*, ed. A. de Boislisle (Paris: Hachette, 1886), vol. VI, p. 436; and BnF G 4287, *Histoire journalière*, June 15, 1699.
Caillant, of course, was inspired: Chauvelin's meetings with Caillant and Pillard are recounted at Chauv. int., p. 20; details on the payment to Caillant are at Piv. int. pp. 55–57.

222 In his version of the Martin Guerre case: Natalie Zemon Davis, *The Return of Martin Guerre* (Cambridge, MA: Harvard University Press, 1983), p. 130, notes that Gayot's version of the Martin Guerre case "is the only one to speculate freely on the possibility that Bertrande was the accomplice of Arnaud du Tilh." For representations of women in causes célèbres during the second half of the eighteenth century, see Tracey Rizzo, *A Certain Emancipation of Women:*

Gender, Citizenship, and the Causes Célèbres of Eighteenth-Century France (Selins-grove, PA: Susquehanna University Press, 2004).

223 "Do men who are unfaithful": Gayot de Pitaval, *Causes célèbres*, vol. III, pp. 7–8. By the early twentieth century: Maurice Soulié, *La Mort et la résurrection de M. de la Pivardière* (Paris: Perrin, 1926), pp. 165–74.

224 The moment of the heroic: For a generic view of the nobility, see Pierre Serna, "The Noble," in Michel Vovelle, ed., *Enlightenment Portraits*, trans. Lydia G. Cochrane (Chicago: University of Chicago Press, 1997), pp. 30–84.

225 She triumphed over individual misfortune: See the work of Sarah Hanley cited in the note for p. 20.
"Although there was no physical evidence": Gayot de Pitaval, *Causes célèbres*, vol. III, p. 2.

226 "The prejudice of the people": Ibid., pp. 83–84.

227 Gayot's account of the Pivardière affair: One example of such "ignorance and superstition" at the time were the activities of the convulsionnaries in the St. Médard cemetery in the 1730s; see B. Robert Kreiser, *Miracles, Convul-sions, and Ecclesiastical Politics in Early Eighteenth-Century Paris* (Princeton, NJ: Princeton University Press, 1978).
According to the most recent: Emmet Kennedy, et al., *Theatre, Opera, and Au-diences in Revolutionary Paris: Analysis and Repertory* (Westport, CT: Green-wood Press, 1996), pp. 133–34. See also CESAR, www.cesar.org.uk. Only 40 of the 107 revolutionary performances of *Le Mari retrouvé* were staged at the Théâtre de la Nation or the Théâtre de la rue Richelieu, the two groups into which the Comédie-Française splintered in the 1790s; thirteen other troupes also staged the work at various points during the decade.

229 This version was subsequently published: See the selected bibliography for references to the works mentioned in this paragraph; and *L'Humanité*, Apr. 10, 1972, for the criticism of the TV show.

230 Would Louis, Marguerite, and the prior: Jean Mauzaize, "Une Cause célèbre en Berry: l'affaire La Pivardière," *Académie du centre* (1993): 14–30. Borderioux mentions his archive of the affair, including Louis and Marguerite's marriage contract, in a newspaper clipping dated Nov. 28, 1972, that can be consulted at ADI 48 J SC 1138, Fonds Joseph Thibault, dossier La Pivardière.
These modern-day gossips: "La Légende admet le meurtre de M. de la Pivardière. L'Histoire n'en veut plus entendre parler," *La Nouvelle république*, Apr. 9, 1955; see also ADI 48 J SC 1138, Fonds Joseph Thibault, dossier La Pivardière, "L'Enigme La Pivardière," a nine-part version of the affair serial-ized in an unidentified 1953 Berrichon newspaper.

Selected Bibliography

This bibliography includes, in chronological order, all nonfiction works on the Pivardière affair I have found, and one I have published, as well as three novels and a made-for-TV movie. Some of these authors have consulted the *mémoires judiciaires*, d'Aguesseau's *plaidoyers*, or Gayot de Pitaval's version of the case. None, with the possible exception of Soulié who does not cite any sources, have worked with the manuscripts in Parisian and provincial archives. None mention the Dancourt play. Most sensationalize the case, making serious factual errors along the way. Duliège (1877) is the most accurate post-1800 account of the affair, although he is primarily concerned with using the case as a demonstration of the flaws in Old Regime criminal procedure. Soulié (1926) reproduces many excerpts from the briefs and d'Aguesseau, but interjects too many flights of fancy and makes fundamental chronological errors.

Gayot de Pitaval, François. *Causes célèbres et intéressantes, avec les jugements qui les ont décidées.* . . . Paris, 1734. vol. III, pp. 1–118. First, and most important, retelling of the story. Reprinted frequently throughout the eighteenth century in France and abroad. Key eighteenth-century translations and revisions of Gayot's version of the Pivardière case include:

- François Gayot de Pitaval. *Causes celebres, oder erzahlung sonderbarer rechtshandel, sammt deren gerichtlichen entscheidung. Aus dem franzosischen ubersetzt.* . . . Leipzig: Kiesewetter, 1747–1750, vol. III, pp. 1–108.

• Alexandre de Garsault. *Faits des Causes Célèbres et intéressantes, augmentées de quelques causes.* Amsterdam: Chastelain, 1757, 139–50.
• François Richer. *Causes célèbres et intéressantes, avec les jugements qui les ont décidées. Rédigés de nouveau par M. Richer, ancien avocat au Parlement.* Amsterdam: Michel Rey, 1773, vol. IV, 431–578.
• P-F Besdel. *Abrégé des Causes célèbres et intéressantes, avec les jugements qui les ont décidées.* Pont-à-Mousson: Thiery, 1806 (sixth edition; first Paris edition in 1786), vol. I, 94–105.
• Charlotte Turner Smith. *The Romance of Real Life.* Philadelphia: J. Carey, 1799 (first American edition; first London edition in 1787), 69–83.

Barry, M. A. "Le Procès de la Pivardière et la détention préventive au XVIIe siècle." *Bulletin de la société des sciences historiques et naturelles de l'Yonne* 82 (1928): 181–90.

Bazin, Camille. "Une erreur judiciaire, mêlée de machination: 'l'Affaire la Pivardière.'" *La Bouinotte* 48 (été 1994): 18–22.

Duchesne, Pierre. "L'étrange trépas de M. de la Pivardière," in *Les Évasions célèbres.* Paris: Presses Pocket, 1972, 172–84.

Duliège. *Une Cause célèbre du Berry sous Louis XIV; affaire La Pivardière, mœurs judiciaires du temps. Discours prononcé par Duliège. Cour d'appel de Bourges, audience solenelle de rentrée du samedi 3 novembre 1877.* Bourges: E. Pigelet, 1877, 38 pp.

Ficatier, G. "Histoire rocambolesque et tragi-comique de Messire Louis de la Pivardière." *L'Echo d'Auxerre* 74 (1968): 13–16; 75 (1968): 35–38.

Flor O'Squarr, Ch. M. *Vieilles justices. M. de la Pivardière.* Bruxelles, 1912.

Fornairon, Ernest. "Les Mésaventures de Monsieur de la Pivardière." *Les Œuvres libres* n.s. 180 (1961): 123–150.

Hesse, Hermann. "Louis de la Pivardière" in *Mordprozessen. Herausgegeben von Hermann Hesse.* Bern: Verlag Seldwyla, 1922.

Hoffman, Ernst Theodor Amadeus. *"Die Marquise de la Pivardière, nach Richer's Causes célèbres,"* first published in 1822, reprinted in *Deutsche Criminal-Geschichten.* Frankfurt: Insel Verlag, 1985.

Jouet, Alphonse. "Une grande cause bérrichonne au XVIIe siècle: l'affaire de la Pivardière." *Revue du Berry et du Centre. Revue mensuelle d'archéologie, d'histoire, de science, de littérature et d'art* 42 (1913): 313–18, 339–45, 375–85.

Malbay de Lavigerie. "Une Cause célèbre sous Louis XIV." *Le Bas-Berry*, année 1875, tome 1er.

Mauzaize, Père Jean. "Une Cause célèbre en Berry: l'affaire La Pivardière." *Revue de l'Académie du Centre* (1993): 15–30.

Paladilhe, Dominique. "Heures et malheurs d'un bigame." *Historama* 27 (mai 1986): 32–34.

Ravel, Jeffrey S. "Certitudes comiques et doutes judiciaries. L'Affaire de La Pivardière, 1699." *Actes du colloque, Représentations du procès.* Paris: Collection représentation, 2003, pp. 437–43.

Renault, Amédée. "L'Etrange affaire de Monsieur de la Pivardière," dans *Pellevoisin, Info plus* 9 (janvier-février 1990): 29–31.

Richault, Gabriel. *L'Etrange aventure de la Dame de la Pivardière.* Chinon: Brière, 1924, In-8, 16 pp.

Roth, Jean-Marie. "La Double vie de Louis de la Pivardière" in *Énigmes et ténébreuses affaires au temps des rois.* Paris: Enigma, 1994, 95–105.
Soulié, M. *La Mort et la résurrection de Monsieur de la Pivardière.* Paris: Perrin, 1926.

Novels

Audebrand, Philibert. *La Pivardière le bigame.* Paris: Dentu, 1886, 358 pp. Ends with king pardoning him of bigamy on the scaffold. Narbonne called Vernay, Marguerite is a young beautiful widow with a huge estate and no children from her previous marriage. Suggests in his preface that Charles Dickens was working on a novelized version of the tale at the time of his death, a claim I have been unable to substantiate.
Deschodt, Eric. *Le Roi a fait battre tambour.* Paris: J.Cl. Lattès, 1984. 393 pp. Introspective, psychologizing treatment of the principals in the affair.
Gaillard, Robert. *Le Châtelain de la Pivardière: roman.* Paris: Editions Fleuve noir, 1967, 379 pp. Soft-porn treatment of the case: Louis sleeps with the maidservants, and anyone else he can find; Marguerite is a nymphomaniac; Marie an innocent but willing virgin, etc.

Film

L'Etrange trépas de Monsieur de la Pivardière. One-hour-long French made-for-TV movie, aired the evening of April 15, 1972, on the French National Broadcasting system. One of a series of seven TV movies aired that year under the title *Les Evasions célèbres;* see also the 1972 print version, listed above. (Emphasizes the investigation by Châtillon judges, follows Gayot's lead in making Marie the virtuous heroine of the story. Ends with the king granting Louis a safe-conduct, does not represent the trials before the Parlement of Paris.)

Index